Classical
Guitar Making

Classical Guitar Making

A MODERN APPROACH
TO TRADITIONAL DESIGN

John S. Bogdanovich

Sterling Publishing Co., Inc.
New York

To my parents, Marion and Stanely

Author's Web site: http://www.jsbguitars.com

PHOTOGRAPHY by John S. Bogdanovich, with Mariah Grant, Lacey Haslam, and Franzi Charen *except*:
Photography of Author copyright 2007 and courtesy Berkson Photography, Yasmin Berkson

ART DIRECTOR: Christine Kwasnik
ILLUSTRATIONS: Mario Ferro
BOOK DESIGN: Lori Wendin
COPYEDITOR: Laurel Ornitz
PROOFREADER: Lisa Joanna Smith
EDITOR: Rodman P. Neumann

Library of Congress Cataloging-in-Publication Data
Bogdanovich, John S.
　Classical guitar making : a modern approach to traditional design / John S. Bogdanovich.
　　p. cm.
　Includes bibliographical references and index.
　ISBN-13: 978-1-4027-2060-4
　ISBN-10: 1-4027-2060-2
　1. Guitar—Construction. I. Title.

ML1015.G9B65 2006
787.87'1923—dc22

　　　　　　　　　　　　　　　　　　　　　　2006002554

10　9　8　7　6　5　4　3　2　1

Published by Sterling Publishing Co., Inc.
387 Park Avenue South, New York, NY 10016
©2007 by John S. Bogdanovich

Distributed in Canada by Sterling Publishing
^{c}/o Canadian Manda Group, 165 Dufferin Street
Toronto, Ontario, Canada M6K 3H6
Distributed in the United Kingdom by GMC Distribution Services,
Castle Place, 166 High Street, Lewes, East Sussex, England BN7 1XU
Distributed in Australia by Capricorn Link (Australia) Pty. Ltd.
P.O. Box 704, Windsor, NSW 2756, Australia

Printed in China.

Sterling ISBN-13: 978-1-4027-2060-4
　　　　ISBN-10: 1-4027-2060-2

For information about custom editions, special sales, premium andcorporate purchases, please contact Sterling Special Sales
Department at 800-805-5489 or specialsales@sterlingpub.com.

Contents

ACKNOWLEDGMENTS

L IFE AS A luthier has been made possible for me only with the help of many people. First and foremost, I would like to thank my parents, Marion and Stan, for always supporting me, even when they may not have agreed with me. Without their support, none of this would have been possible. When I was a small boy, I had asked for a carpentry tool set long before it would be appropriate or safe for a child to play with. I was so insistent that my parents finally caved in and bought me one. While I was playing with the tools, set up under a tree in my grandparents' backyard, my grandfather watched from a window. Impressed with how intently I was able to amuse myself for such a long period of time, he told my mother, "That boy is going to do something with his hands."

The time I spent in the Fine Woodworking Program at the College of the Redwoods actually changed my life. I was fortunate to have made some lifelong friends while at the school and will be forever indebted to the outstanding faculty. I would like to thank James Krenov, Jim Budlong, Michael Burns, and David Welter for their guidance, skill, and friendship, and for putting up with me during my time there. I would like to especially acknowledge James Krenov, whose book *A Cabinetmaker's Notebook* inspired me long ago, only to be eclipsed by later studying with

him at the school. As one of his students, I could not help but admire his aesthetic, his approach to the craft, his keen observation of nature around him, and how all of this is evident in his work. I can only hope to follow his example. And thank you, Jim, for your friendship.

There are a few guitar builders who have both inspired and helped me in my journey as a luthier. I would like to thank Jeff Elliott, Cindy Burton, Greg Byers, John Gilbert, and Charles Fox for their generosity in sharing their knowledge of guitar building, and for their friendship. I would also like to thank the many guitarists who have provided feedback, which is invaluable to making a better instrument.

In putting together this book, I called upon a few people to assist in one way or another. I would like to thank Cindy Park for all her help and support. She has helped with this project in more ways than she is probably aware of. I would like to thank Mariah Grant for doing a great job on the bulk of the photography. I would also like to thank Larry White at the University of North Carolina at Asheville for recommending her. In addition, I would like to thank Lacey Haslam and Franzi Charen for their help with the photography. And I would like to thank all the folks at Iris Photo/Graphic for keeping everything straight.

Foreword

H OW ELUSIVE the events that shape our lives!

Many years ago I was a student at a school of cabinetmaking in Sweden. The headmaster there was a man named Georg Bolin. Sometimes Georg would stop at one of the students' workbenches and chat. George was fascinated by sound, pure sound, and how it would be guided, and used, in a musical instrument like a guitar. Georg was not a technician: he wanted to coax the sound rather than to order it. His approach was a unique balance of information, logic—and curiosity. He had an instinct for sound.

Georg built guitars—evenings and weekends. The guitars were wonderful and coveted by many artists.

Georg died a few years ago.

I still remember how—after having finished a guitar, Georg would test it by strumming a few tones from an old tune. It was like an "amen."

Time passes. I became a cabinetmaker of sorts—and later taught at a school in California.

One of my students was Jack Bogdanovich. He was already an advanced cabinetmaker, able to communicate the technically complex—with simple elegance.

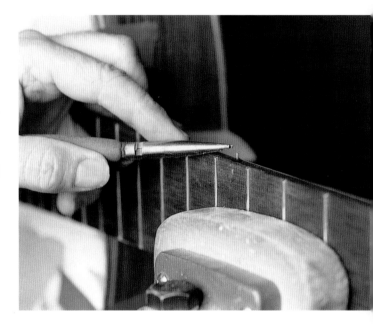

Slowly, I noticed his focus changing; Jack was (and is) a fine guitarist, and he was moving away from cabinetry. "If I stay another year, I would like to try making a guitar," he said. He stayed—and built his first guitar—and it was a good one. And thus began the new life of Jack Bogdanovich. He is a luthier, a builder of exquisite guitars, one at a time—each a challenge, each with its own tone, its own voice.

Jack still plays: Albeniz, Granados, Villa-Lobos.

And who knows? Maybe somewhere Georg Bolin is listening.

—*James Krenov*

Foreword

WHEN I MET John Bogdanovich, he had just begun building guitars. I knew he would succeed as a luthier, because he was passionate about guitars and confident about his work, and had the happy quality of confidence without arrogance, leaving the door to continual growth and discovery wide open. Since that meeting, I have seen his instruments progress from simply good to truly excellent.

The concept of what constitutes an ideal sound, and comfort with the dimensions and response of any guitar are as varied as the people who build and play them. This book fully acknowledges that fact in exploring process and partnership.

In both general and specific terms, John shares his thoughts, knowledge, and experience, and in so doing he offers not just precepts, but a path. And that path is the same for both luthiers and performers: the constant journey toward the goal of excellence in creating a rich musical experience. If this beautiful and engaging book is enjoyed and used by all sorts of pathfinders, it will surely fulfill its author's intent, as he invites his readers to embark on their own journeys with the guitar.

—Jeffrey Van, composer, performer, and head of the guitar department at the University of Minnesota

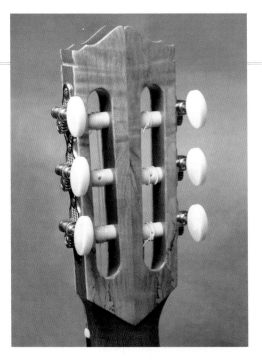

Preface

WHETHER YOU ARE planning to build a guitar for yourself or for someone else, the project can bring a tremendous sense of accomplishment. Hearing music being made on an instrument that you created is an incredible experience. If you are a player, it will bring you closer than ever to your music and you will begin to look at your playing differently than you did before. The process will also make you a better judge of instruments. It will no doubt set you on a course to find the ultimate sound, and when all is said and done, that is what it is all about.

When deciding how to approach this book, I thought back to what kind of reference I would have liked to have had when starting out. The book assumes the readers have some woodworking background and is designed to provide a good base of knowledge for those building their first guitar. The topic of guitar making will be discussed without getting bogged down in an infinite amount of related material, covered elsewhere in far greater detail than would be possible here. Therefore, subjects such as sharpening, milling wood, and some specific woodworking techniques have been purposely omitted in order to give more focus to guitar making.

Building a guitar is a challenging project, regardless of your level of woodworking skills. This book presents one way an average woodworking enthusiast with a minimally equipped shop could approach the project. By saying "minimally equipped shop," I am assuming that the reader either has or has access to a drill press, a band saw, and/or a table saw. There are also a number of hand tools required, which are listed in Chapter 3. The book was written with someone building his or her first instrument in mind, but this does not mean that someone with some guitar-building experience could not also benefit from the topics presented here. Just about everyone building guitars today does things differently, so it is entirely possible that even an experienced guitar builder may find something on these pages that may be of value. There are many ways to do any one of the processes described in this book, so I encourage you to use these instructions merely as a guide.

A key element to successful guitar building is using techniques that not only produce the best results but also are comfortable for the person performing them. If you feel uneasy with any particular method, chances are the results will suffer in some way. Therefore, where space permits, I will suggest alternative tools and techniques you can use.

The design presented here is simple but elegant and can produce a fine-sounding instrument. It is an early design that is a composite of ideas borrowed from several guitars admired for their tonal qualities and aesthetic details. This design should be within the capabilities of the average woodworker and is a good place to start if this is your first guitar.

When I began this book project, guitars were moving out of my shop at a pace like never before. And once again I found myself without an instrument to play. Time for practice is always limited, but I try to maintain some level of proficiency. So, to solve two problems simultaneously, the guitar being made in this book will become my personal instrument. The best motivation for building an instrument is to build the one that you are going to play. Building concert guitars for top-level players has been more than a rewarding experience for me, however, and I feel privileged to be a part of something much bigger than myself. Whether this is your first guitar, or you have built a few already and are looking for a new approach to a particular technique, I wish you luck, and to be happy in your work.

For Leila, my love.

Introduction

GUITAR BUILDING USES a combination of many talents and skills, including an eye for aesthetics, an ear for musical tone, woodworking ability, and an organized and methodical approach to the work. With diligence and practice, many of these assets can be developed and honed. Each of us also brings to this endeavor our own set of skills and experience. My own experience prior to building guitars proved to be a valuable asset in the pursuit of building the ultimate guitar.

Initially, it was not my intention to make guitar building a career. Having returned to playing after an extended break, I was in need of a guitar but could not afford to purchase one that suited me, so I decided to try to build one myself. That first guitar turned out well and attracted a couple of local musicians to contract instruments from me. Guitar making felt so right that I put aside all other pursuits and earnestly began to make guitars professionally. A quest for purpose had ended and a new journey had begun.

Before making guitars, there were a number of things that I felt passionate enough about to pursue, yet there would always seem to come a point where I would hit a wall and could go no

further. Music became a big part of my life at the age of ten, and at twelve I took up the guitar. After high school, I majored in music at what is now part of The College of Staten Island. During this time, I was introduced to classical guitar and studied with Julio Prol in New York City. My intent was to become a performer, though I had difficulty performing in front of an audience. After having a few terrible experiences on stage, I realized that I needed to find something else to do, so I decided to follow another passion of mine, woodworking.

As an apprentice cabinetmaker in a New York cabinet shop, I received a great woodworking education at the hands of a small group of old-world European craftsmen. Once my apprenticeship was completed, I decided go back to college rather than continue as a journeyman. I enrolled in the electrical engineering program at Pratt Institute in Brooklyn, New York. AT&T Bell Laboratories recruited me off-campus in my senior year to work in their research and development facility in Holmdel, New Jersey, where I was employed as a hardware designer. Taking part in their one-year on-campus graduate school program, I was able to get my master's degree in electrical engineering at Polytechnic University. Corporate life did not agree with me very much, and luckily just as I decided to change course once again, the company offered a voluntary early-retirement program. Taking advantage of this opportunity enabled me to return to woodworking, this time working for myself designing and building furniture.

Years earlier, I had read James Krenov's book *A Cabinetmaker's Notebook* and its philosophy of life as a craftsman had resonated with me. Shortly after starting my furniture business, I was accepted into the Fine Woodworking Program at the College of the Redwoods, headed by James Krenov, in Fort Bragg, California. My time at the school was invaluable in so many ways. Besides acquiring both technical and aesthetic skills in woodworking, I was able to connect with a community of like-minded people, many of whom have become lifelong friends.

While at the school, I had resumed playing classical guitar. I needed a guitar, so I decided to try to build one myself, becoming the first person to ever build a musical instrument at the school. That experience changed my life.

Traditionally, whenever students finish a project at the school, they are obliged to present it to the class and discuss its design and construction. Presenting my first guitar—to the class, faculty, a number of former students, and local people— was something I will always remember in a very special and personal way. Any insecurities or doubts I had about changing my life's direction once again were removed that day by this very supportive and encouraging group of people. Since then, guitar building has been my only

pursuit. Almost everything I had done with my life up to that point was helping me in some way understand and accomplish what I now set out to do. The amazing thing is that none of this was planned. I had literally stumbled on guitar making out of the need for a guitar and the lack of the funds to buy one, and as I was already designing and making furniture, everything was in place to move forward.

That was merely the beginning of yet another education that continues and will continue far into the future. As with any craft, with guitar building there is an innate desire to always strive for the best and continually improve on what has

come before. In this day and age, a lifestyle as a solitary craftsman of any type is not an easy road, but it has been right for me.

Anyone who has chosen this type of life has done so because of a strong desire to create and an unwillingness to simply live the unexamined life.

Although you may not have a life-altering experience building your first guitar as I did, there is no doubt that building your own instrument will leave you with a tremendous sense of accomplishment and pride. Nor will many people find this to be an easy woodworking project, but usually things worthwhile are far from easy.

CHAPTER ONE

The Guitar

Anatomy
Sound
Choosing to Build
or Buy

THE GUITAR AS WE KNOW IT HAS BEEN AROUND FOR ABOUT TWO HUNDRED YEARS. AND IN THAT TIME, IT HAS UNDERGONE VERY little change. Antonio Torres' innovations with guitar design in the mid–1800s have set the standard for the modern guitar. Torres increased the size of the plantilla (the outline of the top and back), began using a fan-bracing system, and virtually brought the guitar to where it is today.

Innovations in guitar design continue to appear; a few live on, but most do not. The basic design of the instrument has not changed significantly for quite some time. The guitar has been blessed with an abundance of charm that stands the test of time.

The classical guitar must meet the demands of the performer while maintaining its characteristic sound. The fact that the instrument has nylon strings makes this a challenging design problem. A classical guitar is very different from a steel-string acoustic guitar in almost every sense. The nylon strings do not generate anywhere near the tension that the steel strings do, so they produce less sound. Since the steel-string guitar must be able to handle all this tension for the life of the instrument, it must be more sturdily built. In order to pull the maximum sound out of a nylon-stringed instrument, the individual components must be thinner and lighter without becoming structurally unsound. Designing and building a classical guitar is a balancing act between sound production and structural integrity.

The single thing that makes guitar making more of an art than a science is that no part of the instrument is mutually exclusive—there are no isolated components. Everything is connected to everything else, and a small change in any one spot can have immeasurable effects elsewhere by virtue of the mere fact that the guitar is a coupled system. There are so many variables that it is virtually impossible to model and isolate parts to determine their exact relationship to the production of sound. Therefore, most of what has been learned about what makes a good-sounding instrument has been acquired by trial and error.

The guitar must not only have good sound, but it also must be playable. The guitar is a difficult instrument to play well in a physical sense. Extraordinary demands are placed on the left hand. Injuries may result from either aggressively pushing yourself beyond your limits or playing a poorly designed and constructed instrument. Some injuries may be difficult to rehabilitate. When designing and building an instrument, the luthier must never lose sight of the facts that the guitar is a musical instrument whose purpose is to make music, and the music is created by a player with physical limitations.

I try to use natural wood in my details such as purflings, bindings, and rosettes. With proper wood selection all the details blend in a more elegant way.

ANATOMY OF THE GUITAR

Each part of the guitar has its particular function. When designing an instrument, there are many options regarding the different parts as far as dimensions, orientation, and materials go, but their purpose remains the same. Today, many well-constructed yet different-looking guitars are available in the marketplace. Almost every luthier has his or her own design preferences, both visual and acoustic, but all the instruments are composed of the same basic parts (**1-1**).

The Soundboard

Without a doubt, the one part of the guitar that generates more controversy and myth than any other is the top. Usually made of spruce or cedar in classical guitars, the top (also called the soundboard) is primarily responsible for sound production. The top is braced underneath to provide strength while adding little weight.

The large transverse braces on the inside of the top are mainly structural, adding support to the top under the fingerboard and located just above and below the sound hole. The fan braces provide both stiffness and support to the thin wood on the top and provide a limited means of shaping the sound produced. The rosette is merely decorative and consists of either a traditional mosaic made of small pieces of wood or, in this case, natural wood surrounded by a wheat motif.

The Bridge

The bridge anchors the strings to the soundboard and acts as a sort of coupling device, which transfers the energy used in stroking a string to making the top vibrate up and down, moving the air and

Exploded View of the Guitar

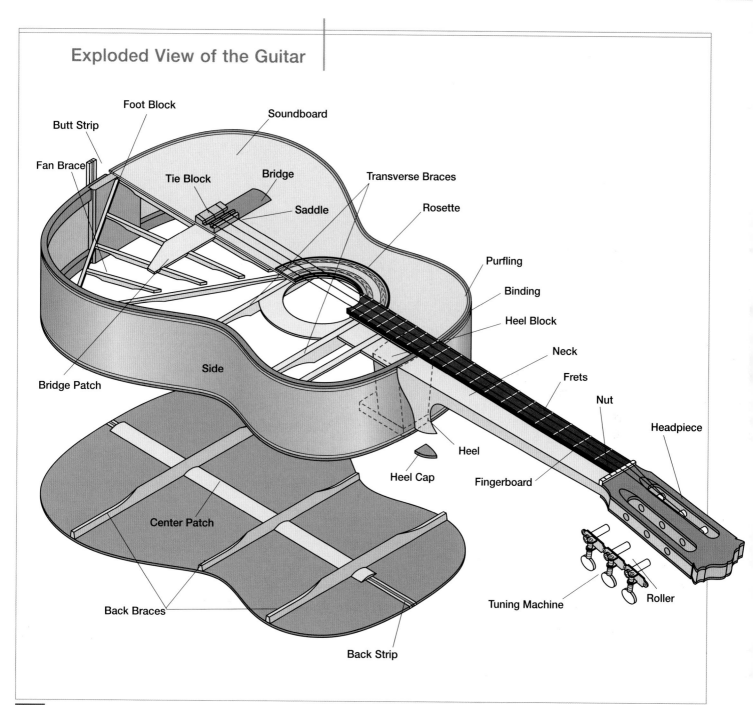

Foot Block

Butt Strip

Fan Brace

Soundboard

Tie Block

Bridge

Saddle

Transverse Braces

Rosette

Purfling

Binding

Heel Block

Neck

Frets

Nut

Headpiece

Side

Bridge Patch

Heel

Heel Cap

Fingerboard

Center Patch

Tuning Machine

Roller

Back Braces

Back Strip

1-1

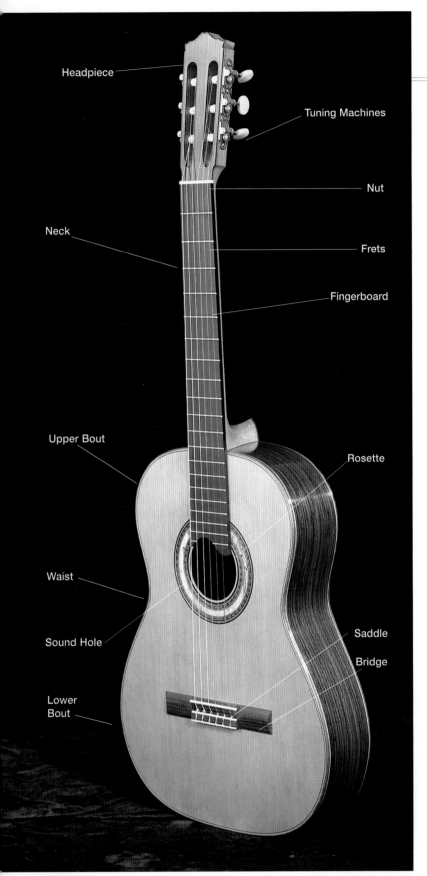

Headpiece

Tuning Machines

Nut

Neck

Frets

Fingerboard

Upper Bout

Rosette

Waist

Saddle

Sound Hole

Bridge

Lower
Bout

1-2

hence producing the sound. There are patches under both the bridge and the rosette. These patches help to stabilize the top in the areas where other wood has been glued to it. It is a general rule in any type of woodworking project that if you glue something to one side, you should glue something similar to the other side. This will prevent problems from occurring down the road from the wood expanding and contracting with changes in humidity (there's more on this in Chapter 2).

The Fingerboard

The fingerboard is glued to the top of the neck, extending partially over the soundboard at the upper bout, and provides a surface on which to play the notes, which are designated by the position of the frets (**1-2**). The headpiece at the top of the neck houses the tuning machines and provides a termination point for the strings. The nut, usually made of bone, is the breakpoint for the strings at the top, and the saddle, also made of bone, is the terminating point for the strings on the bridge. The distance between the breaking edges of the nut and the saddle is known as the scale length. The scale length is simply the length of suspended string.

The Neck

The neck, which is usually made of either mahogany or Spanish cedar on classical guitars, is shaped to give the player access to all the notes on the fingerboard with comfort. The heel, which is visible at the junction of the neck and the body, actually extends inside the instrument. The sides are let into the heel and the remainder of the heel block is inside the body under the neck, providing support and a firm coupling between the neck and the body of the instrument.

The Back and Sides

The purpose of the back and sides has been a subject of debate for quite some time. Torres is said to have made a guitar's back and sides out of papier-maché to prove they added nothing with regard to sound production. The sides along with the linings provide an adequate surface to which to glue the top and back. Linings are made of a large variety of wood such as basswood, poplar, Spanish cedar, mahogany, and even some species of oak. The width of the sides determines the distance between the top and the back, which not only affects the projection of sound but is also an important factor in establishing the resonant pitch of the box. The foot block holds the two sides together at the butt of the instrument.

The back is braced with three large braces, which are usually either mahogany or Spanish cedar. They are largely structural, providing strength and stability to the wide piece of wood used for the back. No one will argue that different species of woods used on the back and sides will produce sounds with slightly different nuances, which would indicate that either the back, or the sides, or both, have some effect on sound.

The Allure of Guitar Building

The way most guitar builders begin is by finding an instrument with a sound they like, and using that design as a starting point, to try to reproduce that sound. It is unlikely that it will be achieved in the first try, and if by accident it is, it is improbable it will be reproduced in subsequent efforts. With more experience your ideal sound will no doubt change over time. The process of finding the ideal sound is never ending. This is the allure of guitar building—the constant challenge of trying to create an instrument with the ultimate sound. If you take a methodical approach, listen and trust your intuition, you will come closer to reaching this goal.

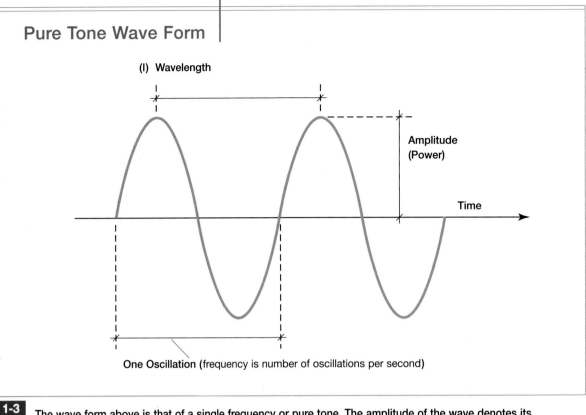

Pure Tone Wave Form

(l) Wavelength

Amplitude (Power)

Time

One Oscillation (frequency is number of oscillations per second)

1-3 The wave form above is that of a single frequency or pure tone. The amplitude of the wave denotes its strength, and the wavelength is the time it takes to complete one oscillation. The frequency is the number of oscillations per second in hertz (Hz). The frequency range for audio is from 20 Hz to 20 kHz.

SOUND

We will be building the guitar with the ultimate purpose of making music. Successful music elicits an emotional response in the listener. The quality of the sound produced by the player on his or her instrument plays an important role in that emotional response. The instrument is the medium the player utilizes to reach the audience. Every player is looking for the ultimate-sounding instrument with which to perform. Most will admit that a great-sounding instrument will actually make them want to practice more. So what is this ultimate sound? This is a very complicated question with many answers. The quality of sound is experienced subjectively and so will be slightly different for everyone. Talking about it does not accomplish much; you have to do a lot of listening.

Sound is a very difficult thing to describe with words. As both the sound and the meanings attached to the words used to describe it are subjective, the same words I would use to describe the quality of the sound I am hearing will have different meaning to almost everyone else. Yet there are some facts about sound that may help you gain a better understanding of the subject.

Pure Tone

Sound is created by air moving in the frequency range of approximately 20 Hz to 20 kHz. A pure tone is a sound made up of a signal with only one frequency. This can be viewed on an oscilloscope as a sine wave (**1-3**). The visual representation of the pure tone provides information regarding its strength (power) and wavelength (frequency). This type of sound is usually produced artificially and rarely occurs in nature.

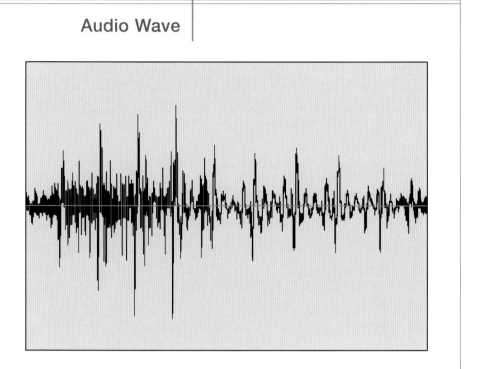

Audio Wave

1-4 This is what an audio signal looks like on an oscilloscope. It is composed of many different frequency components. Following the peaks from left to right, the signal ramps up to maximum, known as the attack, and then decays.

A note played on a guitar will have its strongest component at the frequency of that particular note, with other components at related frequencies with less strength.

An audio tone produced by either the human voice, a musical instrument, or almost any naturally occurring source can be viewed electronically on an oscilloscope (**1-4**). Sound produced from any of these sources is composed of many different frequencies, which give the sound its character.

The Spectrum of a Note

A note played on a musical instrument is actually a summation of many different notes. This summation is known as its spectrum (**1-5**). The spectrum of a note played on a guitar can be viewed as a continuum of an infinite number of points on a graph. One axis on the graph denotes frequency, in hertz, and the other axis designates strength, usually in decibels, which describes what frequencies the particular sound is composed of and their respective strengths. A note played on a guitar will have its strongest component at the frequency of that particular note, with other components at related frequencies with less strength.

The spectrum of a pure tone could be viewed as a spike at one place on the graph, the frequency of the tone. If pure tone were amplified and run through a speaker so that we could hear it, we would hear something similar to the continuous ringing of a doorbell, which is not very interesting nor what we would consider musical.

The sound produced by a musical instrument, however, has many components, which are actually

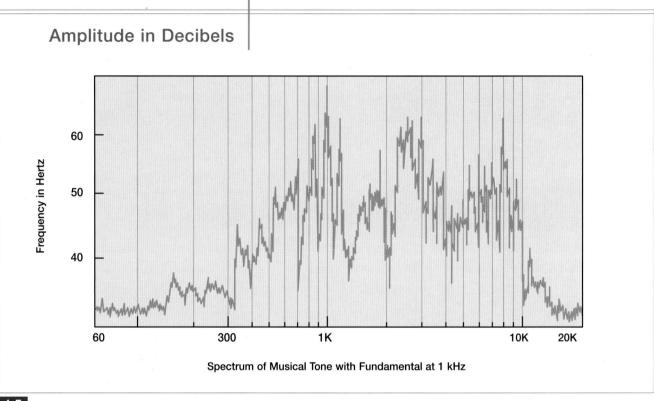

Amplitude in Decibels

Frequency in Hertz

60

50

40

60   300   1K   10K   20K

Spectrum of Musical Tone with Fundamental at 1 kHz

1-5

sounds at other frequencies mixed in at different levels, producing the sound we hear. The mix of these other frequencies and levels actually gives the sound its character, or subjective impression. Each note on a guitar has its own composite pattern, or fingerprint. There are many factors that affect this fingerprint, such as the resonant frequencies of the various individual components, the wood, how it is braced, the scale length, and the size of the body—just about everything has an effect. Owing to the obvious complexity of all the variables and the fact that everything affects everything else, a guitar cannot be designed to produce a particular sound right off the drawing board.

CHOOSING TO BUILD OR BUY

Whether you are a seasoned player or a beginner, you need to find what the ultimate sound is for you. I tell everyone who comes to me without a clear understanding of what a good sound is to go out and play as many guitars as possible. If you do this, eventually you will develop an educated opinion by default.

Buying an instrument can be a very intimidating process. Everyone wants to impart his or her opinion on you whether you want it or not. Neither salespeople, nor teachers, nor even players you respect can provide you with the sound you like—only you can. Others can provide suggestions, but remember it is you who ultimately writes the check, so you owe it to yourself to get what you want. And just because an instrument has a hefty price tag does not guarantee that it will sound great. There are many great-sounding guitars in the middle price range, but you must be able to find them.

Your best assets in learning about guitars are your own powers of observation. As you try different instruments, pay attention to how the sound changes from one instrument to the next, and to different combinations of materials. As a general rule, the little details on the instrument add nothing to the sound, so keep your focus on the larger picture such as the sound, the kinds of wood, and if possible, the design itself.

One thing I have learned by listening to a lot of players and a lot of guitars is that not every guitar will sound good with all players and vice versa. No two players have the same stroke or approach, so it is conceivable that some guitars may not sound that great in the hands of one player as opposed to another. For instance, a player with a very hard nail stroke may sound terrible on a particular guitar, but the same guitar may sound great when played by someone with a softer stroke with more flesh in it.

Finding Your Ideal Instrument

There are many fine instruments out there being produced by many good builders. It is my opinion that there is a guitar out there to suit everyone. But, in order to find your ideal instrument, you first need to have an idea of what it is. If you are either buying an instrument or getting ready to build your own, it is imperative that you find your sound.

As you progress as a player or a builder, your ideal sound will probably evolve and may be quite

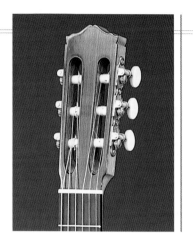

Your intuition as a guitar maker is an important asset. As you experience grows, you are unconsciously storing information that will become the basis for your decisions.

different five years from now than it is today. As a young player, I always liked the older Ramirez guitars, so the first guitar I made was a copy of a Ramirez 1A. As my building experience developed and I matured as a player, my ideal sound changed somewhat and I became very taken with the sound of Segovia's 1937 Hauser. This was a point of departure for me as a builder. My own sense of sound continues to change. There is always some aspect of the sound of a particular guitar that catches my attention. In order to grow, there must be a willingness to embrace the new.

The guitar being built in this book is an early design based on a combination of the '37 Hauser that Segovia played and design aspects borrowed from a number of well-known builders. A complete set of plans for this instrument is included in Chapter 5 (**5-14** through **5-21**). The techniques presented in this book can be used to make any guitar built using the traditional Spanish construction method of letting the sides into the heel. In addition, plans for many historic and well-known guitars such as the '37 Hauser played by Segovia can be purchased from various luthier supply companies (some listed on my Web site given on pages iv and 310).

CHAPTER TWO

The Wood

*Types of Wood
Moisture Content
Cuts, Grain,
    and Selection*

M Y INITIAL ATTRACTION TO WOODWORKING WAS THE WOOD. ITS MANY COLORS, GRAIN PATTERNS, AND TEXTURES make it a wonderfully interesting medium. Having worked as a cabinetmaker, and later as a designer and builder of studio furniture, I had a great deal of experience working with different woods. But it wasn't until I studied woodworking with James Krenov in the Fine Woodworking Program at the College of the Redwoods that I really began to understand the material. Jim taught us all that wood has not only an assortment of physical properties but also a personal effect on both the maker and the client. He would always encourage us to pay attention to the texture, color, and feel of the wood because we relate to things in this way. When it comes to guitars, we can expand on the personal sensory effects with the addition of sound. The wood is basically the reason the instrument sounds the way it does.

Without a doubt, one of the most important aspects of guitar building is wood selection. Even if you have great skills, it will be very difficult if not impossible for you to build a great guitar with mediocre materials. If your desire is to build the best-sounding instrument possible, it is incumbent on you to begin with the best materials you can find. Being able to identify great materials comes with experience, but you can get a good start by just poking around through a number of tops, for instance, at your local luthier supply outlet.

I especially encourage those of you with less woodworking experience to go around and look at as much of the materials as you can. Most suppliers will let you check out the wood in person. Look at the various grades and see for yourself what the differences are in terms of how they look and feel, as well as how they sound as you tap them with your knuckles. Do they make a musical sound or a dull thud? Does the sound sustain and trail off, or does it die out quickly? If you don't have much experience, it may be a good idea to purchase only master-grade material, as it will be difficult at this point to find a real bargain in the lesser grades of wood. It is also probably best to begin building with known entities—that is, sticking with the wood combinations that have proven track records. In this way, you will establish a solid foundation from which you will have a reference for later departures.

Developing a relationship between the wood you are using and the results you want to obtain is paramount to successful guitar building. Your intuition as a guitar maker is an important asset and it needs to be encouraged. Most people already have some ability for accurate observation using their senses—all that is needed is the confidence to acknowledge and be guided by it. As your experience working with the material grows, you are unconsciously creating and storing a collection of information. This information will become the basis for the decisions you make as a guitar builder.

TYPES OF WOOD

Classical guitars tend to be fairly traditional instruments in their design and construction. After all, most of the music played on them is fairly traditional. One thing I have learned is that some things have become established simply because they work. Occasionally, I will try building an instrument using different combinations of materials. Sometimes there are surprises, but generally the traditional combination of rosewood with spruce or cedar works best. And you can't argue with success.

I built my first guitar using western red cedar for the top and grenadillo for the back and sides. Grenadillo is not a wood typically used in guitar making, but it was what was available to me at the time, being low on funds, and as the guitar was for myself, grenadillo was just fine. Besides, it looked a bit like rosewood. But truly the only thing it had in common with rosewood was its density—it was very heavy. The guitar turned out well, although the grenadillo was difficult to work and very hard to bend. Unless using an atypical wood is the only way you can get an instrument built, I recommend using rosewood, even for your first instrument.

A guitar uses an assortment of different woods in its construction. The different types of wood are chosen for particular applications mostly because of their physical properties, but visual considerations cannot be discounted.

For instance, the top, or the soundboard, for a classical guitar is usually made of spruce or cedar. These are both nonporous soft woods that do not dampen sound. Both woods, but spruce in particular, have a high strength-to-weight ratio. This enables them to be made quite thin and maintain adequate strength, while being very light and hence moved easily. Both of these attributes make these very good woods for sound production.

The Back and Sides

The backs and sides of a guitar are usually some type of rosewood. Today, mostly Indian rosewood is used, because Brazilian rosewood is scarce and prohibitively expensive because of an import embargo. These rosewoods are excellent choices for backs and sides, because they are dense, bend easily, and are attractive in both color and grain, as with this

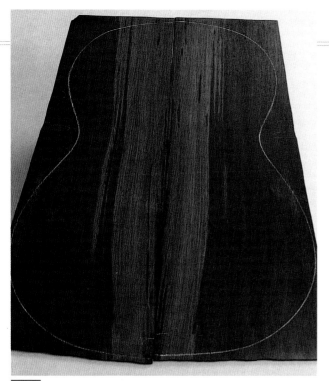

2-1 Brazilian rosewood back

2-2 Indian rosewood back

Brazilian rosewood back (**2-1**) and this Indian rosewood back (**2-2**). In a set of sides, the ideal quality is stiffness. The stiffer and denser the wood, the less dampening it is to sound production. The back acts as a sort of reflector of sound, so again stiffness and density are important.

Both Indian and Brazilian rosewood have natural oil, which is noticeable while you are working it, as it will come off onto your skin and tools. Does this oil have an effect on acoustics? My guess is that it contributes something. Whenever I have used an atypical wood for the back and sides—say, maple, which is not porous and has no oil, or Macassar ebony, which is somewhat porous and has very little oil—I notice a difference in the sound when everything else is the same. It can best be described as a drier, more brittle sound. It is not better or worse, just different. Some woods such as cocobolo and lignum vitae have so much oil they

can be difficult to glue, which can create problems unless handled properly.

Necks are usually made of mahogany. Mahogany is dimensionally stable, has medium density, and is very strong. Spanish cedar is also used for necks. The cedar is lighter and a bit easier to carve. There is also a slight difference acoustically, which most likely can be attributed to the difference in density.

The Fingerboard

Fingerboards are usually made of ebony or rosewood. Higher-end instruments use ebony more often than not. Ebony is very dense and offers excellent resistance to wear. Since the fingers are constantly hammering and sliding around on the fingerboard, ebony seems to be an excellent choice.

What To Know Before Buying Wood

2-3 Stored wood

Always be sure to inquire when purchasing wood if it has been dried or not, and whether it was dried in a kiln or air-dried. If the wood has been air-dried, you will also want to know how long it had been drying.

Wood that has not been dried fully will need to sit until equilibrium is reached. Wood tends to give up moisture much faster through the end grain than the face grain, and that is why you will sometimes notice end checks or cracks. To avoid this, coat the ends of the wood with paraffin wax, or even glue, in a pinch, to retard the loss of moisture through the end grain. In addition, all wood, when not in use, should be stickered. Stickering is placing a small piece of wood under each end of a board—¼ inch square will work just fine—so that air can circulate freely around the entire piece (**2-3**).

The remainder of the components such as the linings, purflings, and bindings are not as critical as far as wood selection goes. For the linings, I use mahogany, but I have seen basswood, tan oak, and Spanish cedar used with success. The wood used for the bindings and purflings mostly has to do with aesthetics. The only necessary characteristics are that the wood can be easily bent and should not be porous, because a porous wood cut very thinly, as for purflings, may appear to have visual defects in the end product.

There are a vast variety of colors available naturally without resorting to dyed wood. Colored dye tends to fade with time and can become quite unattractive. Red is a color that is particularly susceptible to fading. I try to use only natural wood in my details such as purflings, bindings, and rosettes, because I like the natural look and with proper wood selection all the details blend in a more elegant way.

MOISTURE CONTENT

We have briefly touched on some of the properties of wood particular to building guitars in the preceding section, such as density, porousness, natural oils, and ease of bending. This section will address moisture, which affects all species of wood and is the most troublesome to guitars.

When a tree is first cut down, the cells are full of water. Immediately its moisture content begins to decline, and it will continue to decline until equilibrium is reached with the moisture in the air around it. The term for this is equilibrium moisture content (EMC). Without the help of a kiln, the rule of thumb for air-drying wood is one year for every inch of thickness. Kiln drying speeds the process considerably, but may alter the color in some woods. Even with kiln drying, most luthiers will let wood sit in the shop for years before using on a guitar.

Once the wood has reached equilibrium, the moisture exchange with the environment does not stop. As the humidity rises, the wood takes on moisture and grows in dimension. As the air becomes drier, the wood gives up moisture to keep up with its surroundings and shrinks in dimension. This can be witnessed in the shop by placing a freshly milled piece of thin wood flat on the workbench. You will notice that the edges of the wood will curl up, making the wood appear concave, or the piece will bulge up in the middle, creating a domed look. The first scenario indicates that the air is drier than the wood, and the top surface of the wood is giving up moisture and shrinking. The second scenario implies that the air contains more moisture than the wood, and the top surface of the wood is taking on moisture and swelling. In both cases, the dimensions are changing. The introduction of moisture can also cause the wood to warp and twist.

Extreme changes in humidity can have extreme effects on an instrument. Dimensional changes are most pronounced in the largest dimension of a particular piece of wood. For instance, the top or back of a guitar is a piece of wood roughly 2 mm thick but almost 15 inches wide in the lower bout and almost 12 inches wide in the upper bout. The width of the top and the back will move considerably with extreme changes in humidity. Typically in widths fewer than 3 inches, movement is negligible, but 12 to 15 inches is another story. Checks and cracks can develop from drastic changes in humidity toward the dry side; buckling is the result of swelling from humidity. Some components of the guitar have been designed to help with changes in humidity. The finish applied at the end, especially the shellac used in French polish, will also add some barrier to the moisture.

CUTS, GRAIN, AND SELECTION

Knowing the havoc moisture can create in a piece of wood, we can eliminate some of the problems by using the proper cut. The growth rings of a tree are concentric circles centered on the pith. By slicing the log into quarters and then slicing off each face, we have what is known as quartersawn wood (**2-4**). Wood is considered quartersawn when its growth rings are 60 to 90 degrees to the face of the board. By slicing the log from top to bottom, known as flitch cutting, the center slices are the only quartersawn pieces. The growth rings flatten, moving away from the center. Rift-sawn wood is where the growth rings are between 60 and 30 degrees to the face of the board. The pieces near the outer edges are commonly known as flat-sawn and have the familiar grain pattern along the face (**2-5**).

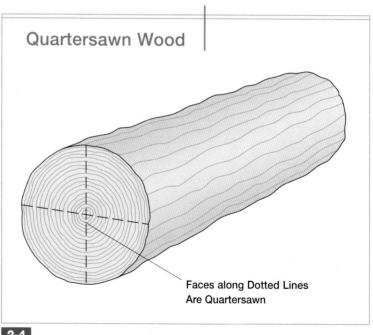

Quartersawn Wood

Faces along Dotted Lines Are Quartersawn

2-4

Plain or Flat-sawn Wood

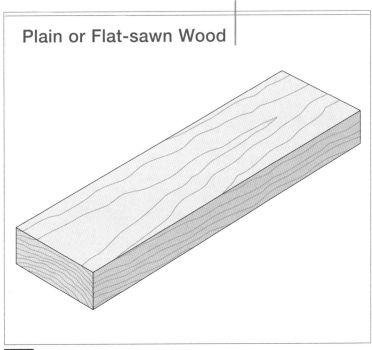

2-5

Different Cuts

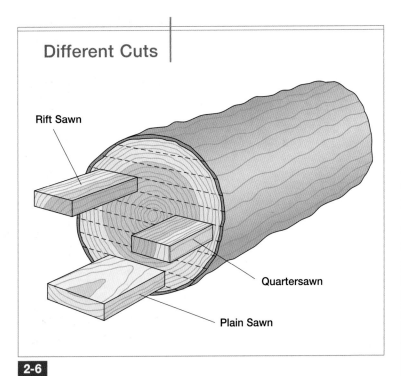

Rift Sawn

Quartersawn

Plain Sawn

2-6

Flat-sawn wood has its growth rings 30 degrees or less with the face. The drawing in **2-6** shows the different sections of the log from which the different cuts are taken.

Dimensional Stability

Quartersawn wood is more dimensionally stable than any other cut of wood. It also has a very calm and pleasing appearance in its straight vertical grain, which runs parallel to the length of the piece and vertical to the front and back faces. A true quartersawn cut will reveal ray flecks, which are intricate little cross-stripes running perpendicular to the vertical grain lines on the face, known as silk, pictured here on spruce and cedar (**2-7** and **2-8**). There is a much better chance, if properly cut, that quartersawn wood will not warp or twist. As the moisture content in the air and wood changes, quartersawn wood will change dimension to a greater degree at right angles to the grain lines. Therefore, the piece will not change dimension in width as much as a flat-sawn piece will. Almost all the wood used to build a guitar is quartersawn.

2-7 Spruce silk

2-8 Cedar silk

We have all seen stunning-looking wood used on guitars—on backs and sides, especially. Highly figured grain patterns create beautiful visual effects, but be careful if selecting some of these because highly figured wood can have inherent instabilities. Some wood that either is or approaches flat-sawn can be quite striking, but it is not recommended for use in guitars. Some striking figure is available in quartersawn cuts, such as quilted maple. Maple is quite stable when quartersawn and should not pose any problems. Crotch (**2-9**) or burl figure (**2-10**) should be avoided, except for small decorative touches, because of their tendency to crack.

In summary, when choosing your wood, select carefully with regard to cut and grain. Almost all the wood used in guitar making should be quarter-sawn, and traditional species should be used whenever possible. Highly figured wood should be avoided, especially in your first instrument. And all the wood should be thoroughly seasoned and properly stored to ensure that it has reached equilibrium with the humidity level in the shop. Controlling the environment in the shop will be discussed further at the end of the next chapter. Now let's move on to working with the tools for building a guitar.

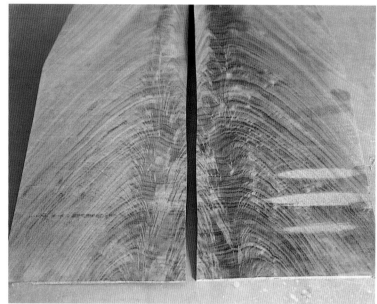

2-9 Crotch figure

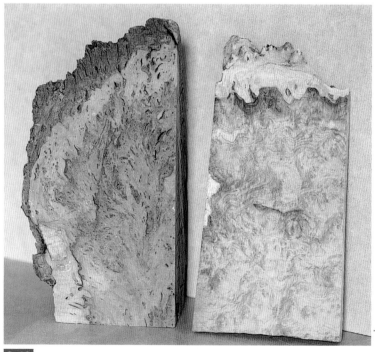

2-10 Burl figure

CHAPTER THREE

The Shop

What You Need
Jigs to Make
Hand Tools
Vises and Clamps
Bench Tools
Specialty Items
Humidity Control

A SHOP CAN BE A DEDICATED BUILDING, YOUR GARAGE, OR A ROOM IN YOUR HOUSE. WHATEVER IT IS SHOULD BE PERMANENT. Setting up and tearing down every time you work can be very draining and will take away from your enjoyment of the project. Because it isn't necessary to have a lot of equipment, and the materials are generally of a compact size, a small space works well. In a small space, it is also easier to control the humidity, which will be discussed later in this chapter.

Most guitar makers work in very tiny shops. My own current shop was built into my home and is only about 440 square feet. Building your guitar, you will probably be spending a good portion of the day in the shop, so it is important to feel good while being in there. Your work environment has an impact on your work. Making your work space comfortable will add immeasurably to your enjoyment of your craft.

There is nothing more frustrating than not being able to do really good work because you can't see well enough. Lighting is an important element of any shop. In guitar making, there are lots of small details that can be seen properly only with adequate lighting. The tiny miter joints where the back and butt strips meet the purflings, for instance, should be attempted only in the best light. Good lighting will also have a huge benefit on the quality of your finishes. I have worked in a space that did not have adequate lighting. After moving into another space, my finishes improved dramatically, and I didn't realize why at first. The moral of the story is not to skimp on lighting. If there aren't enough windows, or you will be working at night, use the best lighting you can afford in your work area. If you have to purchase additional lighting, it will be money well spent.

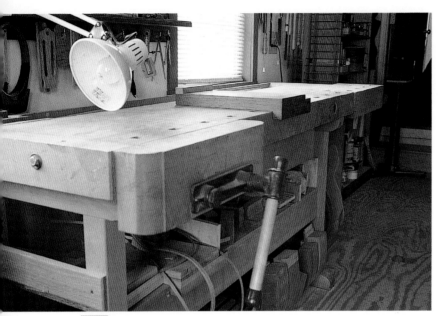

3-1 Cabinetmaker's bench

WHAT YOU NEED IN YOUR SHOP

In addition to having a proper work space, there are some tools and pieces of equipment that are necessary to complete the shop and build a guitar. A complete arsenal of woodworking tools is not necessary to build an instrument, but you may need to purchase a few items that may not be in the shop already. A few woodworking machines, some power tools, a small collection of hand tools, and a few specialty items are required for this project. In this chapter, you will find lists of suggested tools for building the guitar presented in this book. And suggestions will be made regarding the use of alternate tools wherever possible. Because this is a book about guitar making, not tools and equipment, this chapter will not cover the topic of tools comprehensively. For further information about tools, please see the references in the bibliography. In addition, many of the tools and materials mentioned on these pages are available at various supply companies for woodworkers and luthiers. For a listing of some of these companies, please visit my Web site (see pages iv and 310).

Workbenches

Without a good workbench, hand work will be difficult. If you are a woodworker, you may already have a good-quality workbench. Plans are available at woodworking supply companies for many of the popular cabinetmaker workbench designs, if you are so inclined. They also stock a couple of well-known brand names.

Some type of workbench is a necessity. In my shop, I use a number of benches and tables for work surfaces. The main workhorse is the cabinet-

3-2 Built-in wooden vise

3-3 Another wooden vise

Work Surfaces

Whether your shop is well equipped with woodworking machines or you just have the bare minimum, it is usually a good idea to have a work surface near each machine. This will make using the machines safer and less stressful by providing a place to put the workpieces as you perform each task.

maker's bench (**3-1**). This bench has two wooden built-in vises, which are extremely useful (**3-2** and **3-3**). The only additional feature I might consider if I were to buy another bench would be a vise with a swiveling face to clamp stock with angled surfaces.

The cabinetmaker's bench is very versatile and is used in performing almost all the woodworking tasks in building both the instrument and the fixtures used in its construction. Additional work surfaces for performing glue-ups will keep the project moving by keeping the main workbench free. If you are not keen on mounting a pattern maker's vise, a universal vise, or both on your cabinet maker's bench, another table or bench might be a good idea. I don't think there can be too many work surfaces in the shop, and I am always trying to create more. The more work surfaces there are, the more things can be done in parallel **3-4** and **3-5**.

3-4 Additional work surface

3-5 Work surface with vise

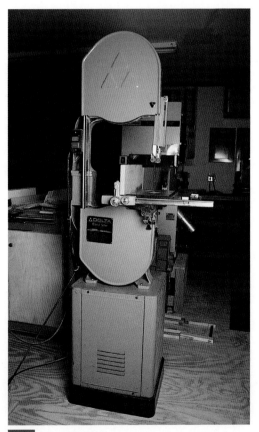

3-6 14" band saw

Equipment

The techniques presented in the construction part of this book were chosen for a shop with a minimum amount of equipment and power tools. It is assumed that the reader either has or has access to a band saw and a drill press. Additional equipment such as a table saw, jointer, portable planer, and drum sander are not essential, but will help reduce the amount of physical labor necessary to perform some of the tasks and will be alluded to when discussing alternative methods of construction. For instance, a table saw is used to make many of the cuts in this book. If a table saw is not available, you can still make all these cuts with a handsaw and square the edges with a hand plane on the bench hook and shooting board.

Band Saw If I had to choose just one piece of equipment to use, it would be a band saw. A band saw is very versatile and will perform any number of tasks, such as cutting out patterns, resawing, and even joinery. Any 14-inch band saw (**3-6**) should be adequate for the tasks here. As the wood we use in guitar making is relatively small, a 36-inch monster would be nice but is not necessary. In the photos, you will notice that I have two band saws. This is a luxury, not a necessity. One band saw is used primarily for resawing and dimension cutting, and the other for cutting patterns and plywood materials. A 14-inch band saw is capable of performing both of these tasks. The resaw band saw is a carryover from my furniture-making days and affords me the luxury of not having to change blades.

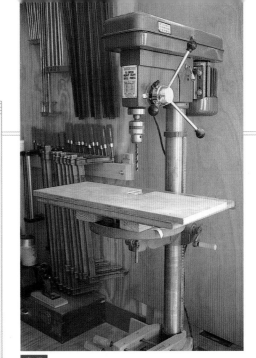

3-7 Standing drill press

Hand Work vs. Power

These days I build guitars using power equipment wherever possible, but I remember all too well the days of doing almost everything by hand. Working without machinery will no doubt develop some hand skills and allow you to work up a sweat every now and again, yet ultimately how you feel about your work and the results are what count. Contrary to the beliefs of some hand-tool purists, I feel there is nothing wrong with using power equipment if it is available. Usually machines are used to perform the labor-intensive tasks, but the final sizing and fitting is almost always done by hand.

Standing Drill Press Another piece of equipment recommended as a requirement is a standing drill press (**3-7**). Although a bench-top model will perform most tasks as well as a standing model, the extra throat depth, stroke length, and height adjustment are indispensable at times. Also, the price difference is minimal when you think of all the benefits you are getting. The drill press is also a versatile tool. It can be used on metal as well as wood, and may also be used as a drum sander.

Other Equipment There are other pieces of equipment that can be very useful if you have access to them. A table saw (**3-8**), jointer (**3-9**), small portable planer (**3-10**), shaper, and drum sander (**3-11**) will save you lots of time, for example. In this book, you will notice that I am using a shaper to perform some tasks, but before I had a shaper in the shop I used the router table shown in **3-12**. This arrangement worked as well as the shaper. The only benefit the shaper affords is easier adjustment. It is basically a standing cabinet with a

3-8 Table saw

3-9 Jointer

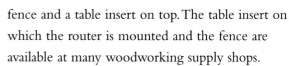

3-10 Small portable planer

3-11 Drum sander

fence and a table insert on top. The table insert on which the router is mounted and the fence are available at many woodworking supply shops.

Notice that I did not say that any of this equipment will improve your accuracy. You can be just as accurate with a band saw and some hand tools with a little practice.

Other Useful Power Tools

Some power tools are a must. A minimum requirement would be a laminate trimming router, a 1½ HP router that accepts both ¼-inch and ½-inch collets, a ⅜-inch drill, and a random orbit sander (**3-13**). The laminate trimmer is used for trimming thin material such as the top and back, cutting the channels for the bindings and purflings, and inlaying the rosette. The 1½ HP router is used for trimming the neck where the stock is thick and may be mounted underneath a router table for trimming stock for the fixtures, as the laminate trimmer's horsepower is inadequate for this and it is safer. This arrangement is also used in the construction of the bridge and the fingerboard.

3-12 Router table

3-13 Routers, drill, and sander

JIGS YOU WILL NEED TO MAKE

Unfortunately, the router accessories required in guitar making cannot be purchased—you have to make them yourself. Fortunately, you only need to make two, one to inlay the rosette and the other to cut the binding channels. The attachment used to inlay the rosette is a circle-cutting device, which is also used to cut out the sound hole and make the doughnut-shaped patch under the rosette. It can be easily fashioned out of almost any thin material. The attachment used in this book is made of Plexiglas (**3-14**), but any clear acrylic can be used. The fact that the attachment is clear allows you to see what is going on as you cut. The device is adjustable and must be capable of a cutting radius from the size of the sound hole on the small end to the outer radius of the rosette on the large end. This means it must be able to cut a radius from approximately 1½ to 2¾ inches (38 to 70 mm). The attachment can be made to fit whatever router you are using.

Router Circle-Cutting Attachment

To begin, cut two pieces of ¼-inch Plexiglas or other dimensionally stable ¼-inch material about 9 inches long and as wide as the router base you plan to use (the attachment shown was built for a Ryobi TRU30 laminate trimming router). Score a center-line the length of both pieces. Next, cut a ¼-inch mortise all the way through one of the pieces, as shown in **3-15**. Then, without changing the setup on the router table, replace the ¼-inch bit with a ½-inch bit and cut the second mortise to a depth that will prevent the bolt head from protruding through the bottom, with the position and length as shown in the drawing. On the other piece, drill

3-14 Plexiglas router attachment

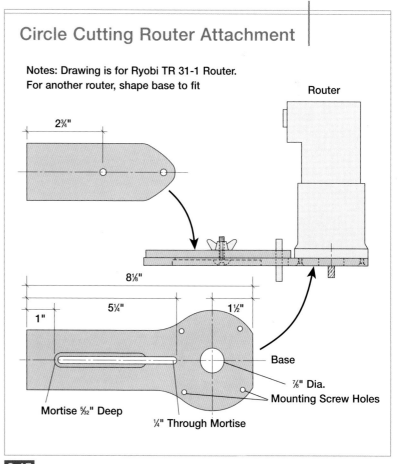

3-15

Binding-Cutter Router Attachment

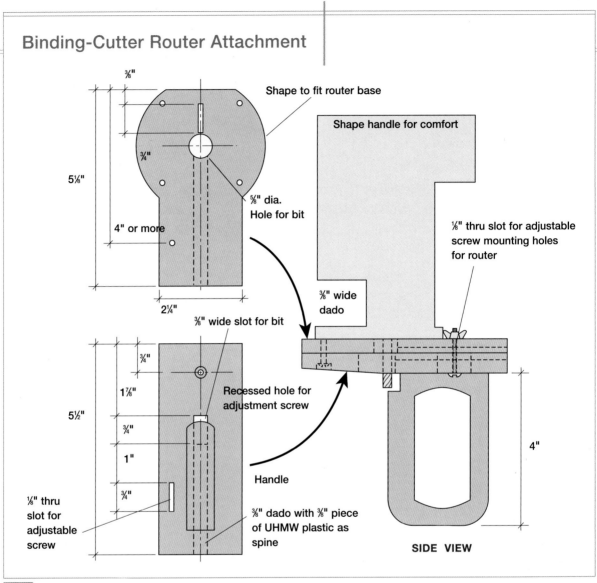

Shape to fit router base

⅜"

5⅛"

4" or more

¾"

2¼"

⅝" dia. Hole for bit

⅜" wide slot for bit

Shape handle for comfort

⅛" thru slot for adjustable screw mounting holes for router

⅜" wide dado

¾"

1⅞"

5½"

¾"

1"

¾"

Recessed hole for adjustment screw

Handle

⅛" thru slot for adjustable screw

⅜" dado with ⅜" piece of UHMW plastic as spine

4"

SIDE VIEW

3-16

3-17 Binding-cutter attachment

the two holes for the pin and the bolt. Lastly, remove the base from the router you are using and place it over the piece with the two holes. Trace the position of the holes, then drill, and countersink the screw holes. It is a good idea to glue strips of fine sandpaper to one of the surfaces that touch to enable fine adjustment without slipping. This can either be left as is or shaped as shown in the drawing. Replace your router base with this device, add a ¼-inch pin to the hole closest to the router, and a ¼-inch bolt, washer, and wing nut to the other hole, and it is ready to use.

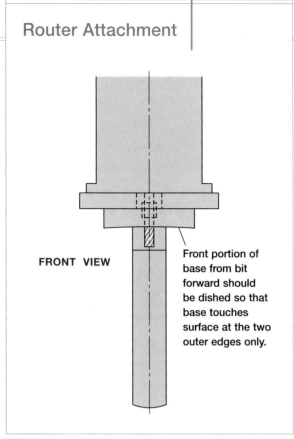

Router Attachment

FRONT VIEW

Front portion of base from bit forward should be dished so that base touches surface at the two outer edges only.

3-18

3-19 Universal binding machine

Binding-Cutter Router Attachment

The binding-cutter router attachment is an adjustable three-point fence that is also mounted to the base of the router (**3-16** through **3-18**). The attachment shown here is made of mahogany, but any stable hardwood will do. The adjustment range on this device is small, because it is used only to cut the channel for the bindings and the purflings. This is a two-part attachment consisting of one part that mounts to the router and the other a platen that rides on the guitar. The two parts are aligned with a ⅜-inch-wide piece of ultra-high molecular weight (UHMW) plastic material that acts as a runner and is glued into one of the dadoes. The platen that rides on the guitar is dished from the bit forward so that only the outside edges

touch the surface of the instrument. The other point of contact is the portion of the handle below the notch for the bit. This edge of the handle is rounded so that the high point is in the middle. This edge rides along the side of the instrument, keeping it perpendicular to the top and back. The results with this machine are worth the effort it takes to make it. Although I use a universal binding machine now, I have built more than sixty instruments with the handheld three-point fence router attachment.

For the very ambitious, there is a universal binding machine (**3-19**). Both the machine itself and the plans for building it are available at various luthier supply companies (some listed on my Web site, given on page iv and 310).

3-20 Measuring and marking tools

HAND TOOLS

A certain number of hand tools are essential in guitar making. When buying tools, it always pays in the long run to buy the best. This doesn't always mean the most expensive. Some older tools such as saws, chisels, and planes are made of better-quality steel than the tools being manufactured today, and really good buys can be had at local flea markets and estate sales. Old saw blades, for instance, are generally too thick for our purposes, but the steel in the blade will make a great scraper or can be used as another type of cutting tool.

Making Your Own Tools

Making some of your own tools can be very rewarding. Not only will you get a genuine feeling of accomplishment, but you can also end up with some very good tools. The first project at the College of the Redwoods' Fine Woodworking Program is making your own hand plane. While at the school, I made a number of planes, which I still use to this day, including a couple of round-bottom planes and a compass plane. (See the bibliography for references on making planes.)

Use the Tools You Prefer

If you are more comfortable with another tool for any particular task, and you are able to get the necessary results, by all means use it. For instance, I prefer Japanese handsaws to western handsaws, because they cut on the pull stroke, and this feels more natural to me, giving me more confidence with every cut. They also make a very narrow saw kerf, allowing for greater accuracy. Everyone must seek his or her own level of comfort and have confidence when using tools. But do not dismiss something without having tried it on a piece of scrap first. You never learn anything if you won't try something new.

Suggested hand tools are listed below.

Measuring and Marking (3-20)
- long flexible ruler at least 700 mm long in millimeters and inches
- 36-inch rigid ruler
- 24-inch straightedge
- 12-inch ruler in millimeters and inches
- small 6-inch ruler
- 3-inch adjustable T square
- 12-inch adjustable T square

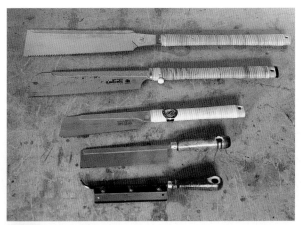

3-21 Hand saws

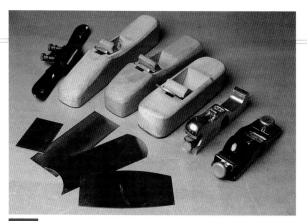

3-22 Planing and scraping tools

3-23 Tools for carving

3-24 Tools for filing

- bevel gauge
- 4-inch or 6-inch calipers in mm and inches
- Xacto knife
- flat-edged Japanese marking knife
- flat chip-carving knife
- silver colored pencil
- compass

Saws (3-21)

- thin-blade dozuki-style saw (blade thickness 0.026 inch)
- Zona saw
- thin-blade Ryobi saw

Planing and Scraping (3-22)

- low-angle block plane
- shoulder plane
- smoothing plane
- shooting plane
- compass plane
- spokeshave
- curved and straight cabinet scrapers

Carving (3-23)

- a good set of chisels, including ⅛ inch, ¼ inch, ½ inch, and ¾ inch
- carving tools, such as large 30-mm No. 1, 3, and 5 gouges; a 12-mm skew; and a 12-mm No. 7 gouge
- small knives for carving

Filing (3-24)

- No. 50 pattern maker's rasp
- 8-inch half-round mill bastard file
- 8-inch rat-tail smoothing file
- 8-inch mill bastard file
- 6-inch mill bastard file
- ⅜-inch round file
- a couple of small rifler files
- a set of needle files

Sanding (3-25)

- foam sanding pads
- formed sanding pads
- 180-, 220-, 320-, 400-, and 600-grit sandpaper sheets
- 120-, 180-, 220-, and 320-grit sandpaper discs
- 80-grit adhesive-backed sandpaper
- Micro-Mesh sanding sheets in 1800, 2400, 3200, and 3600 grits

3-25 Tools for sanding

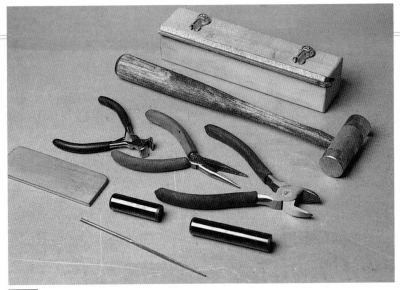

3-26 Tools for fretting

Fretting (3-26)

- fret hammer
- diagonal cutting pliers
- end-cutting pliers
- long-nose pliers
- small triangular file
- small metal straightedge
- fret beveling file
- wooden sanding block with cove in edge for sanding frets

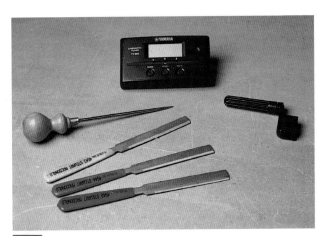

3-27 Tools for setup

Setup (3-27)

- a set of nut files
- awl
- string winder crank
- electronic tuner

Miscellaneous (3-28)

- small roller for applying glue (found in most art supply stores)
- glue brushes
- kitchen timer
- scissors
- artist brush
- double-sided tape
- 3M blue masking tape
- low-adhesive masking tape
- 0000# steel wool
- hygrometer

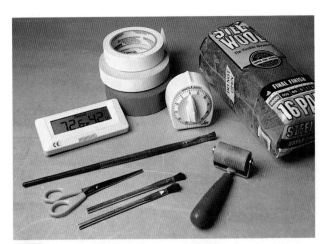

3-28 Additional tools

3-29 Vacuum clamp

3-30 Vises

3-31 Assorted clamps

VISES AND CLAMPS

Holding devices such as vises are indispensable in guitar making. There are many types available, and I have a few different kinds in the shop. Specialized vises make certain tasks easier, while minimizing damage from clamping pressure. The vacuum clamp (**3-29**) works well in holding the body of the guitar, while providing unimpeded access all the way around. Other very useful vises are the universal vise, the pattern maker's vise, and a small portable vise, as shown clockwise in **3-30**. The universal vise in my shop is mounted on a stand and used to hold the solera, providing access all the way around the fixture. The pattern maker's vise will hold anything with a taper very well and can be rotated 360 degrees. It is invaluable when carving the heel, shaping the neck, and setting up the instrument. The small portable vise is extremely useful for cutting small-diameter round stock such as the brass registration pins. It is also used in drilling the string

holes in the bridge and notching the fan braces over the bridge patch.

Clamps are an absolute necessity, and you can never have too many of them. Below is a list of the clamps that are needed for making the guitar in this book.

Clamps (**3-31**)

- sixteen 8-inch clamps with 4-inch throat
- sixteen 4-inch clamps with 2½-inch throat
- eight 8-inch cam clamps with 8-inch throat
- eight 8-inch cam clamps with 4-inch throat
- twelve 2-inch hand clamps
- six 4-inch hand clamps

3-32 Bench hook

BENCH TOOLS TO MAKE

There are a couple of helpful devices that can be easily made that are used on the workbench for a number of operations; they are the bench hook and the shooting board. The bench hook (**3-32** and **3-33**) is used to square an edge (make one edge perpendicular to another) of any material that can be hand-planed. The material to be planed is held perpendicular by the stop fence, and the plane is slid along the ramp. The cleat on the bottom edge keeps everything from sliding around.

The shooting board (**3-34** and **3-35**) is very similar to the bench hook, only it is longer and its purpose is to straighten the edge on a long piece

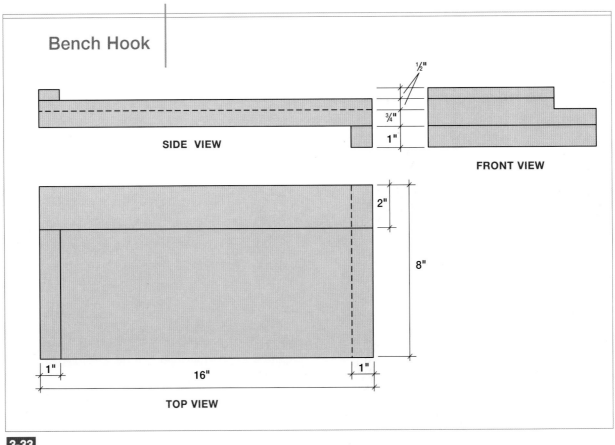

Bench Hook

SIDE VIEW

½"

¾"

1"

FRONT VIEW

2"

8"

1"

16"

1"

TOP VIEW

3-33

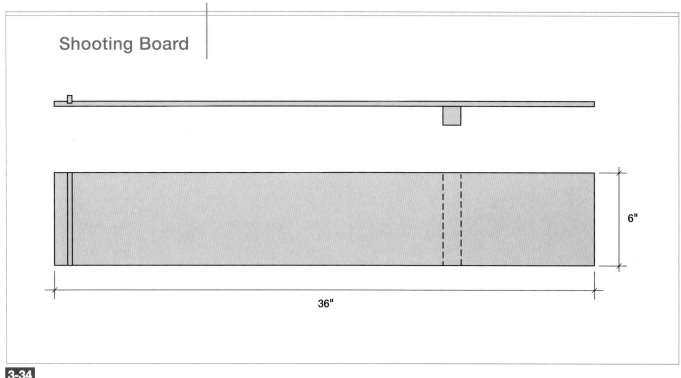

Shooting Board

6"

36"

3-34

of stock. The cleat on the bottom surface of the shooting board fits into the bench vise, and the stop fence keeps the workpiece from moving as it is planed. There is no ramp in this case—the plane slides along the bench. If you don't have access to a jointer, a shooting board will be necessary to joint an edge straight.

Both of these shop aids are easy to make and use. An edge that is planed is much smoother than any edge that is machined. The machine is used to perform most of the heavy work—the rest is done with hand tools. Any cut made is always cleaned up with one or both of these bench tools.

3-35 Shooting board

3-36 Bending iron

SPECIALTY ITEMS

These are tools and accessories that are particular to some aspect of guitar making and have to be either made or purchased at a luthier supply house. Below is a list of suggested specialty items that will make your guitar-building experience easier and more enjoyable.

- bending iron
- calipers for measuring top thickness
- sanding discs dished to a 15-foot and 25-foot
- radius
- bridge clamp

Bending Iron

The first item necessary in construction is a bending iron (**3-36**). It can be purchased anywhere that sells luthier supplies. In the beginning, I used a copper pipe sealed at one end with a tang on the other for mounting in a vise. A propane torch placed inside supplied the heat. This worked well, but it is almost impossible to control the heat, the fumes are unpleasant and may be harmful, and it could be dangerous. I recommend a bending iron with a heat-level control. If you are adventurous, you can build a bending machine (**3-37**). Plans can be purchased along with some of the harder-to-find parts at some luthier supply houses. If you are planning to make many guitars, this may be the way to go, but if you plan on making only one, some form of bending iron will do.

3-37 Bending machine

Calipers

When thicknessing the top and back, it is necessary to have something to accurately measure the thickness across the entire surface. This can be done a few different ways. The easiest is to purchase a dial thickness caliper from a luthier supply house, or you can just buy the dial indicator with a lug mount on the back and make your own calipers. The calipers need to be rigid and can be fashioned out of plywood. The set shown in (**3-38**) was made using two pieces of ½-inch plywood with ¼-inch pieces of wood sandwiched in between every few inches, to allow the tang to be bolted to the frame while keeping the weight down.

3-38 Set of calipers

Sanding Discs

Next, we will need two concave sanding discs, one dished out on one side to a radius of 15 feet and the other similarly dished to a radius of 25 feet, and two convex sanding pads with matching radius (**3-39**). These are used to radius the rim or the sides to accept the domed back and top. They can be purchased at a luthier supply house, or you can make them yourself. The discs sold at luthier supply companies are made of medium-density fiberboard (MDF), and if you decide to make them yourself, I suggest using MDF. The reason is stability. After coating with shellac, they will not change shape or warp. Whether you make the discs yourself or purchase them, a radius stick for each radius will be required (**3-40**). These sticks will be used when making the fixtures in Chapter 4.

3-39 Convex sanding pads

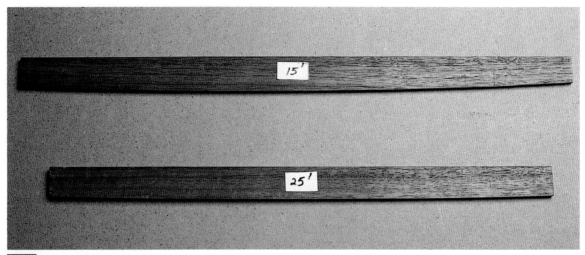

3-40 Radius sticks

To carve the dishes out yourself, cut and shape the applicable radius on one edge of a piece of wood a bit longer than the 2-foot diameter of the disc. Measure the depth at the center, and drill a hole this depth in the middle of the disc. Then, using the drilled hole as a depth gauge, carve out the material, periodically checking the shape with the radius stick until you have a perfectly concave dish. This will take some time, so it may be easier to just purchase them.

The convex sanding pads are easily made using a piece of MDF. Rub the piece on the concave discs covered with 80-grit sandpaper until they conform to the shape exactly, and then cover with adhesive-backed sandpaper. The pads in **3-39** have handles, which will make using them easier and also make it possible to clamp them in a vise.

Bridge Clamps

There are many ways to do almost everything, and gluing on a bridge is no exception, but considering how important it is to locate and adhere the bridge properly, a commercial bridge clamp is highly recommended. Seeing photos of bridges being glued on with wooden cam clamps that wrap around the body of the guitar always makes me uncomfortable, because when applying pressure to the clamp you are actually collapsing the top to some degree and in effect changing its shape. A couple of different kinds of bridge clamps, including a vacuum-type clamp, are available at various luthier supply companies. The bridge clamps used in my shop is shown in **3-41** along with the caul, which is cut to avoid the fan braces under the top.

HUMIDITY CONTROL

Since wood changes dimension with respect to relative humidity (see Chapter 2), in order to build guitars successfully the humidity in the shop must be controlled and maintained. Controlling the humidity will be easier if the work space is both insulated and has a vapor barrier. Also, having fewer windows and entryways will help in this regard. It is advisable to fill in any open spaces to the outside with insulation and seal any leaks wherever possible. Then the humidity level needs to be determined for the particular work area with a reliable humidity gauge. This should be done over a period of time to observe trends and extremes. The ideal range of relative humidity is between 40 and 50 percent.

The humidity level may change from season to season and be influenced by heat and air conditioning. For example, if you are located on the East Coast, in the summer the humidity will no doubt be too high and will need to be dried out a bit with a dehumidifier. Of course, if your work space is air-conditioned, nothing may be needed, as air-conditioning tends to dry out the air. In the winter, if you have forced-air heat, the humidity level will be too low and moisture will have to be added to the air. In this case, you may need a humidifier/dehumidifier to control your environment. Wherever your shop is, it will be necessary to first determine what the humidity level is and then to take the proper course of action to get the levels within range.

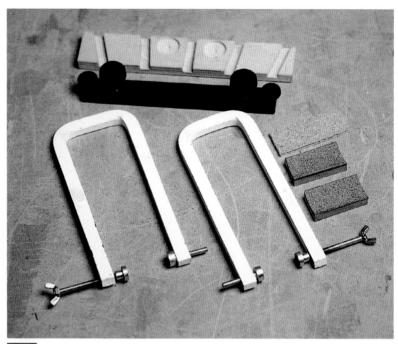

3-41 Bridge clamps and caul

CHAPTER FOUR

Templates and Molds

Plantilla
Transparent Template
Side Mold
Lining Mold
The Solera
Headpiece Template
  and Drilling Jig
Back Workboard

A S WITH ANY CHALLENGING WOODWORKING PROJECT, MUCH PREP
WORK IS NECESSARY BEFORE YOU CAN BEGIN TO BUILD A GUITAR.
There are a number of work boards, molds, and templates required, and the
accuracy of the final product is a direct result of the accuracy of the fixtures, molds, and
templates used in its construction. With this in mind, these things should be approached
as projects in themselves, taking time to make them properly, and if you decide to make
another guitar you will already have everything necessary to do the job.

Every guitar builder uses some combination or another of these things in their work. And
there are probably as many different types of fixtures and molds as there are builders. None
are right and none are wrong—they are just different. We all eventually end up working the
way we feel most comfortable. The techniques used to make the fixtures, molds, and templates in this book have proven reliable over time, but you shouldn't feel compelled to do
everything exactly as presented here. Use whatever means are most comfortable to you that
yield the best results. There are many ways to build an instrument, so don't be afraid to
incorporate some method seen elsewhere that appeals to you. Let the results be the judge.

All the work boards and molds have been made of medium-density fiberboard (MDF),
because it is relatively inexpensive and easy to shape. This material is sold in 4-foot × 8-foot
sheets at any local building supply store. Most building supply stores will cut the material
down for you, which will make it easier to transport and handle once you get it in your
shop. Approximately two sheets of ¾-inch and a half sheet of ½-inch MDF will be necessary
to make all the workboards and molds required in this book.

The templates are made of thin plywood, clear acrylic, or Plexiglas. I prefer a clear material on any template where it is important to see the grain of the wood through the pattern
for grain orientation. These are very stable materials that will not change dimension with

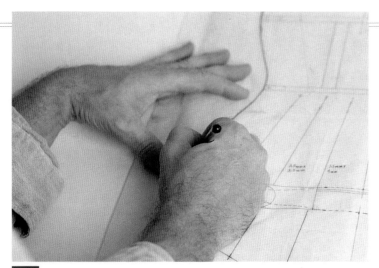

Tracing outline of guitar

4-2 Cutting the outline

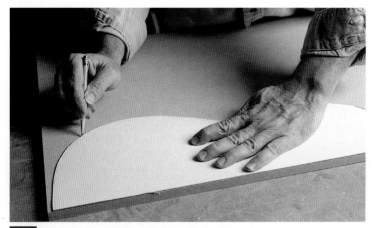

4-3 Tracing onto MDF

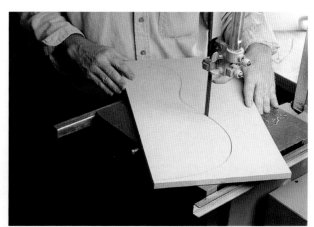

4-4 Cutting just outside the line

changes in humidity and can be easily cut with woodworking tools. The acrylic machines a bit better than the Plexiglas, and it does not chip or crack as easily. We will begin with the templates that are used to make the fixtures and molds.

THE PLANTILLA

The plantilla is the outline template for the top and the back. This template is used in the construction of most of the molds and workboards. The template can be made from the complete set of plans provided in Chapter 5. As with any symmetrical shape, it is best to make a template of half and then use that to make the whole template.

To start, expand the plans to original size as described in Chapter 5. Place a piece of carbon paper underneath half of the guitar's outline and a piece of cardboard poster paper under that. Trace the outline, including a centerline of the copy, pressing hard enough on the pencil for it to transfer to the cardboard (**4-1**). Cut along the outline using a sharp knife (**4-2**). This does not have to be perfect. This becomes your cardboard template used to trace the shape onto a piece of MDF, which will become the master template.

Line up the centerline edge of the cardboard template with the straight edge of the MDF, and trace the shape onto the piece of MDF (**4-3**). Cut the piece of MDF along just outside the line on the band saw (**4-4**). Then using the No. 50 pattern maker's rasp, file the edge of the MDF, while periodically checking it against the original-size drawing until they match (**4-5**). An alternative method to get the half plantilla to final shape would be to use a drill press with sanding drums—it is easier to keep the edge perpendicular this way (**4-6**). Drill the ³⁄₃₂-inch registration holes, which are used to properly position the top on the solera. Drill one hole under the fingerboard on the heel cap

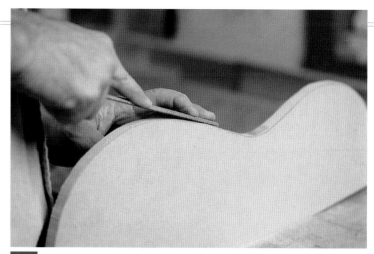

4-5 Filing the edge

4-6 Using drill press with sanding drums

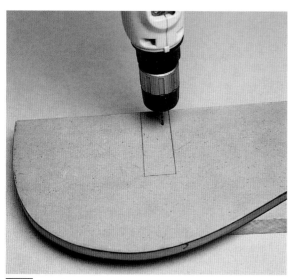

4-7 Drilling registration holes

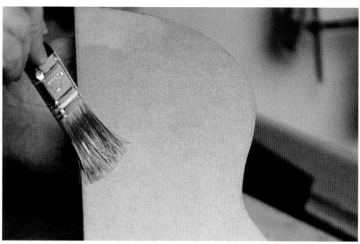

4-8 Finishing template with shellac

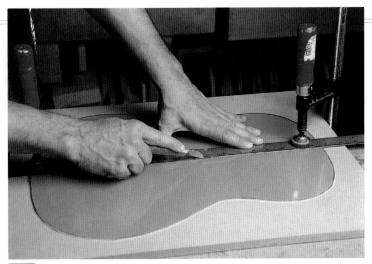

4-9 Scoring a centerline

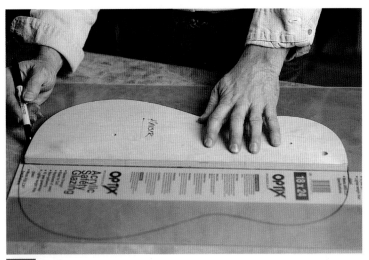

4-10 Tracing outline

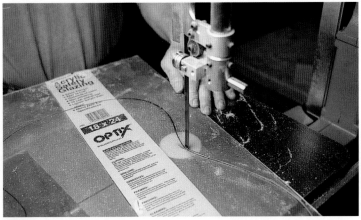

4-11 Cutting with band saw

and the other under the bridge (**4-7**). The exact position of these holes is not important, as long as they are hidden. Finish the template with shellac to seal the MDF to prevent any movement from changes in humidity (**4-8**). Once you have completed this template, you will have a master template from which you can make all the others.

A TRANSPARENT TEMPLATE

A full template can now be made from this out of some clear plastic. Having a transparent template is very useful for lining up grain when laying out the back or top. It enables you to see exactly what you will end up with in the final cut with no surprises.

First, score a centerline on a piece of clear plastic large enough to accommodate both halves of the top (**4-9**). Trace the outline of the plantilla a half at a time, and cut on the band saw to within ⅟₁₆ inch of the line (**4-10** and **4-11**). Drill the ³⁄₃₂-inch registration holes on one side, using the half plantilla to locate them (**4-12**). Using the registration pins, secure the half plantilla to the full template (**4-13**). Then use either a handheld router or a router mounted in a table to trim flush, employing an appropriate trim bit with a bearing (**4-14**). An appropriate bit for ¼-inch Plexiglas would be a ¼-inch shank bit with a ¼-inch cutter diameter. Move the plantilla to the other side, drill the holes, secure with the pins, and trim. Once the template is completed, mark on the Plexiglas template which side corresponds to the top face. This is important in case your registration holes are not exactly symmetrical **4-15**).

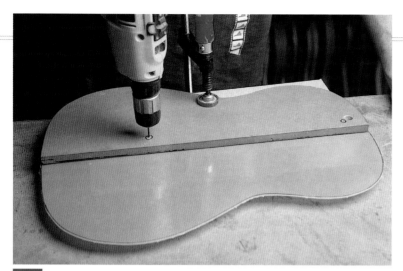

4-12 Drilling registration holes

4-13 Securing with registration pins

4-14 Using router to trim flush

Trim Bit Sizing

A good rule of thumb when trimming material with a trim bit is to try to keep the amount of excess material you are trimming down to about $\frac{1}{16}$ inch and to use a bit with a cutter diameter equal to the thickness of the stock you are cutting. In the case of stock $\frac{1}{2}$ inch to $\frac{3}{4}$ inch thick, a $\frac{1}{2}$-inch cutter diameter will suffice, but the bit should have a $\frac{1}{2}$-inch shank.

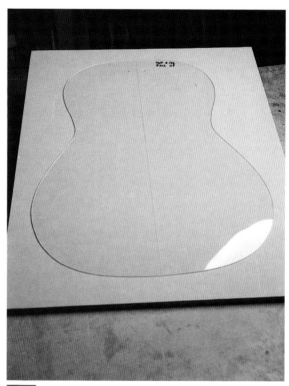

4-15 Completed template

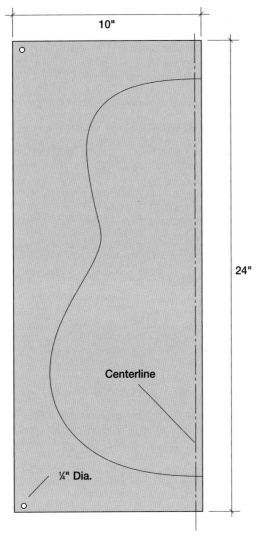

Side Mold Template

10"

24"

Centerline

¼" Dia.

SIDE MOLD

The side mold is used for laminating the sides and gluing on the linings. The mold is constructed from five pieces of MDF cut and stacked to cover the entire width of the sides. The side mold must extend beyond the centerline of the plantilla by about an inch and be approximately 2½ inches thick all the way around.

Template for the Pieces

First, we must make a template that will be used to cut out each of the five pieces for the stack and to position them while gluing (**4-16**). Cut a piece of ½-inch plywood or MDF 24 inches × 10 inches, and draw a line an inch in from the long edge and parallel to it. Center the long straight edge of the plantilla, which is the centerline of the top, on this line so that there is an equal amount sticking out on each edge. Trace the outline of the plantilla, and cut this piece on the band saw close to the line, and shape it the rest of the way with either the drill press/sanding drums or a pattern maker's rasp, until it fits the half plantilla perfectly. Drill a ¼-inch hole in each of

4-17 Tracing the shapes

4-18 Drilling holes

the two back corners of the template. Position the holes so that they will be in a spot that will be trimmed away in the end. These holes are used to align each piece for trimming and gluing.

Cutting the Pieces

To begin, cut five pieces of ¾-inch MDF 10 inches wide and 20 inches long. Using the template, trace the shape onto each piece, and drill the ¼-inch holes in the back corners (**4-17** and **4-18**). Cut to within ¹⁄₁₆ inch of the line on the band saw. Use dowels to attach the template to the piece, and trim flush with either a handheld router or a router mounted in a table, using a trim bit with a bearing (**4-19**). Repeat this on the remainder of the pieces.

Gluing the Pieces

The pieces are now ready to be glued. It is advisable to glue the pieces together one at a time rather than all at once. This way, it will be much easier to maintain a perpendicular face on the mold. Titebond Glue will work well in this application. Spread glue on one surface, trying to avoid

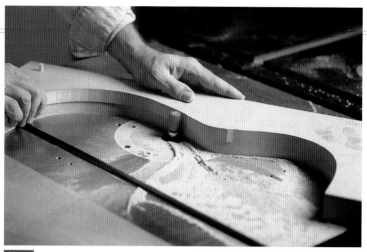
4-19 Trimming Flush

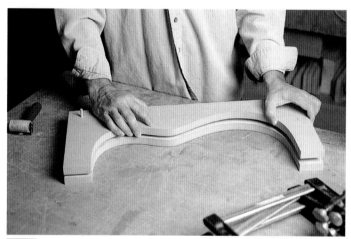
4-21 Using dowels to align pieces

4-20 Spreading glue

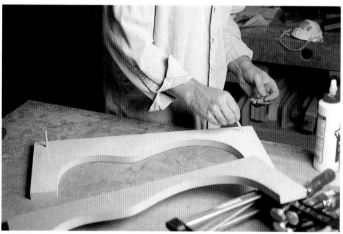
4-22 Aligning the two pieces

4-23 Applying clamps

4-24 Allowing pieces to dry

4-25 Cutting glued pieces

getting glue in the area of the dowels (**4-20**). Use the dowels to align the two pieces and apply clamps (**4-21** through **4-23**). Let these dry for about a half an hour, and repeat until all the pieces are glued (**4-24**). Once you have glued all the pieces, cut to a thickness of approximately 2½ inches all the way around (**4-25**). It is advisable to leave a flat spot at the waist area (see photo) for ease in applying clamps during the lamination of the sides. Check to make sure that the inside face is perpendicular. Careful alignment while gluing only one piece at a time should result in a perpendicular surface, but if there are any irregularities they can be corrected with a pattern maker's rasp (see photo opposite chapter title, page 44).

Finishing the Side Mold

After final shaping, the entire mold should be given a couple of coats of shellac and then a final finish with any water-based clear finish. All fixtures should be finished this way. The shellac shields the fixture from moisture exchange, and the water-

4-26 Applying finish

based finish protects the surface from spills. Water-based finish is used for the final coats because it doesn't really have a solvent, so if you spill something on it you won't mar the surface (**4-26**).

LINING MOLD

The linings, which are glued to the sides to provide a glue surface for the top and back, are fashioned out of four laminations, which are bent and glued in a mold. This mold has two pieces, a male and female component, if you will. Sandwiched in between are the laminations. We will make two of these molds out of MDF or plywood. The final thickness of the mold will be ⅝ inches. You can use ⅝-inch MDF or plywood, or you can use ¾-inch MDF and sand down to ⅝ inches in a drum sander if you have access to one.

Each mold requires eight clamps. Having sixteen will enable you to make two linings simultaneously, speeding up the entire process. To begin, using the half plantilla, lay out the shape on the 12-inch × 26½-inch piece, with the centerline along one of the twenty-six ½-inch edges (**4-27**). Situate the template so that an equal amount of material extends beyond the template in both directions. Both faces of the mold that touch the linings will be covered in ³⁄₃₂-inch gasket material. The additional ³⁄₃₂ inches will compensate nicely for the width of the sides on this piece, so cut on the band saw close to the line and clean up the remainder of the way on the drill press using a sanding drum (**4-28** and **4-29**). Now place the waste piece shaped like the plantilla back where it

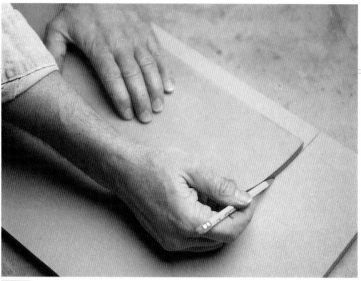

4-27 Laying out shape

4-28 Cutting with band saw

4-29 Using sanding drum

4-30 Tracing the new edge

4-31 Cleaning up

4-32 Shaping back edge

4-33 Trimming with router

4-34 Drilling holes for clamps

was in relation to the piece just cut, and raise the outer piece slightly. Using a small piece of wood approximately 0.270 inches thick (the thickness of the linings) and two pieces of ³⁄₃₂-inches gasket cork as a shim, trace with a pencil the new edge on the inner piece (**4-30**).

Cut on the band saw and clean up to the line on the drill press using a sanding drum (**4-31**). Shape the back edge of the outer piece by cutting on the band saw (**4-32**). The exact shape is not important, but shape to enable easy clamping and be sure to allow a minimum of 2½ inches of material in any one spot.

4-35 Separating the parts

4-36 Slicing gasket material

4-37 Gluing gasket to faces

4-38 Holding with blue tape

Using One Set To Make the Second

There is now a finished piece of each half of the mold with which to make the second mold. Trace the outlines of these pieces onto two pieces of MDF, and cut to within $\frac{1}{16}$ inches on the band saw. Using double-stick tape, tape the finished pieces to their respective rough-cut ones, and trim with a router or on a router table using an appropriate trim bit with a bearing (**4-33**). While they are still together, drill eight 1⅛-inch holes as positioned in the photo for the clamps (**4-34**).

Separate the parts (**4-35**), and slice enough ³⁄₂-inch gasket material the thickness of the mold

4-39 Adding gasket material

Holding with blue tape

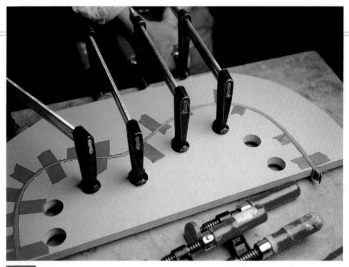

Clamped together

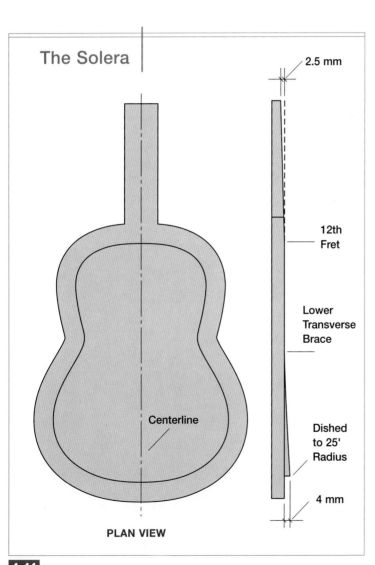

The Solera

2.5 mm

12th Fret

Lower Transverse Brace

Dished to 25' Radius

4 mm

Centerline

PLAN VIEW

4-44

(5/8 inches) to cover the surfaces of the mold that hold the linings (**4-36**). Glue these pieces to the faces, cutting where necessary. Hold them in place with 3M blue masking tape, and clamp them together with some lining material in between (**4-37** through **4-41**). Once the glue is dry, trim any excess gasket material and apply finish to the molds.

THE SOLERA

The solera is where a good part of the guitar is put together, so extra care should be taken in its layout and construction. This is where the top is braced, the neck angle is established, and the top and back are glued on (**4-42**).

The solera is made from two pieces of ¾-inch MDF approximately 39 inches long and 22 inches wide. Mark a centerline on one of these pieces. Position the plantilla on the centerline, making sure there is at least 2½ inches of material outside the plantilla on all sides and there is enough length for the neck beyond the upper bout, to be sure that the ramp ends just short of the place where the nut will be. Draw an outline approxi-

4-43 Tracing plantilla

4-44 Cutting with band saw

4-45 Trimming flush with router

4-46 Tracing outer edge of the rim

mately 2½ inches outside the lines of the plantilla all the way around, and trace the plantilla inside the outline (**4-43**). Mark 2 inches on either side of the centerline and parallel to it where the neck extends. Cut out on the band saw and smooth to final shape (**4-44**). Use this piece as a template for the other piece, trace the outline, and cut on the band saw to within ¹⁄₁₆ inches of the line. These two pieces should be glued together, using the

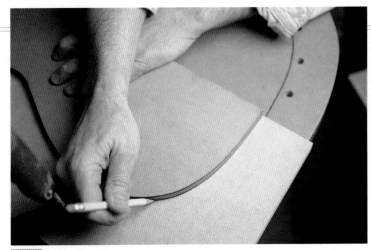

4-47 Using the half plantilla to trace edge

4-48 Marking

piece with the plantilla outline and centerline on it as the top face. The bottom piece can be trimmed flush with a router or router table when dry (**4-45**).

Removable Rims for the Solera

In order to hold the sides and neck in place while doming the top and back edges of the sides to accept the top and back, we will need to make a pair of removable rims for our solera. These rims are made out of MDF much like the side lamination mold, and six pieces 24½ inches x 10½ inches are required. Clamp a piece of MDF with its long edge along the centerline of the solera. Trace the outer edge of the rim underneath up against the solera, and using the half plantilla, trace the inside edge (**4-46** and **4-47**). The rim should extend only to the edge of the ramp at the upper bout. Mark this spot on the piece of MDF (**4-48**).

Remove the clamps and cut to within ⅟₁₆ inches on the band saw. Clean the inside edge to the line with either a file or a sanding drum on the

4-49 Cutting on the bandsaw

4-50 Cleaning the inside

4-51 Trimming flush

4-52 Drilling holes

4-53 Drilling through

4-54 Trimming flush

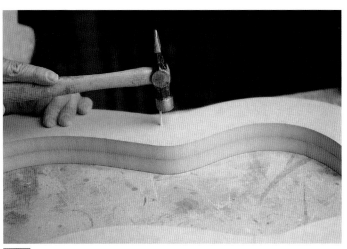

4-55 Securing with dowels

drill press (**4-49** and **4-50**). Shape the outer edge of the rim by clamping back in place on the solera, and trim flush with a router (**4-51**). Repeat this for the other side. These two pieces will now be used as a template to make the remainder of the pieces for their respective sides. Trace and cut the remaining four pieces to within ⅟₁₆ inches on the band saw. Drill three ¼-inch holes in the spot

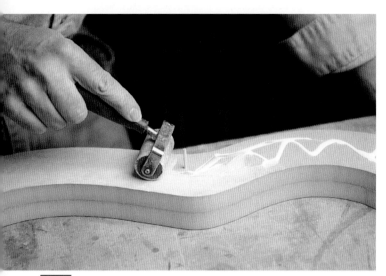

4-56 Applying glue

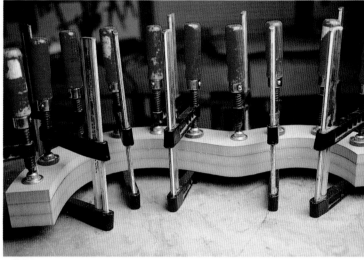

4-57 Clamping in place

4-58 Drilling hole centered on dowel

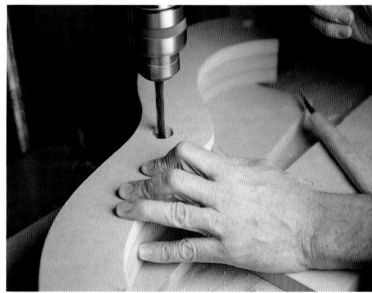

4-59 Drilling holes through the rims

where the ⁵⁄₁₆-inch bolts will go on the template pieces (**4-52**). Clamp the finished piece to the next piece to be shaped, and drill through the ¼-inch holes (**4-53**). Secure with a dowel, and trim flush with a router (**4-54**). Now apply glue and stack the three pieces using the ¼-inch dowels in the registration holes for alignment and clamp (**4-55**, **4-56**, **4-57**).

The rims are removable and will be anchored in place by bolts and T-nuts. Recess the top of the hole to fit the ⁵⁄₁₆-inch bolt and washer by drilling a 1-inch hole with a Forstner bit centered on the dowels deep enough to conceal the bolt and washer (**4-58**). Then drill three ¹¹⁄₃₂-inch holes through the rims at the center of the recess for the bolts (**4-59**). Position the rims as they will be on the solera with the plantilla in place, making any necessary adjustments so that the rims are right up against the plantilla without making it difficult to remove. Clamp the rims in place, and drill a shallow ¹¹⁄₃₂-inch hole in the solera through the holes in the rims (**4-60**).

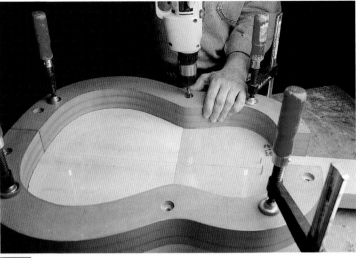
4-60 Drilling shallow hole in the solera

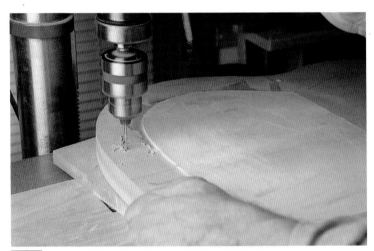
4-61 Drilling pilot holes

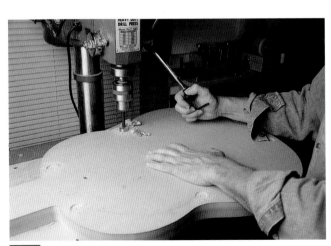
4-62 Drilling on other side

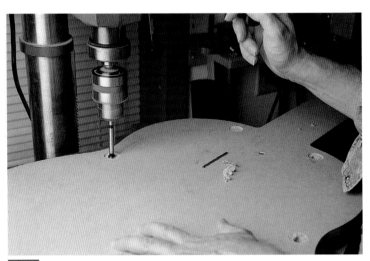
4-63 Drilling hole for shaft of T-nut

4-64 Drilling holes on flip side for bolts

4-65 Banging in T-nuts

4-66 Securing rims with bolts

Why the Top Is Domed and the Lower Bout Is Tilted

The lower bout of the solera is dished to a 25-foot radius that is tilted forward so that the back edge is at least 4 mm higher than the surface of the MDF and the front is level with it. The lower bout of the guitar is domed to avoid problems caused by string tension on the bridge. The tension of the strings acts both to pull the bridge toward the neck and to push it down into the top as it passes over the saddle. If the top is left flat, this tension will in time cause the top to collapse before the bridge and pull up behind it. Doming the top distributes this force more evenly and gives the top a bit more stiffness to handle it. The lower bout of the guitar is lowered and slightly tilted toward the butt to compensate for the additional height in the middle as a result of doming. This translates to the fixture's having to be raised and tilted forward.

The center of this hole will be used to position the T-nuts on the bottom of the solera. Next, drill a small pilot hole through the center of each of the six holes through the solera on the drill press to ensure they are drilled straight down (**4-61**). Flip the solera over, and drill a 1-inch hole with a Forstner bit centered on the small hole drilled just deep enough to conceal the T-nut (**4-62**). Now drill a ½-inch hole centered on the preceding hole deep enough to accept the shaft of the T-nut (**4-63**).

Flip the solera over yet again, and drill ¹¹⁄₃₂-inch holes all the way through for the ⁵⁄₁₆-inch bolts (**4-64**). Apply some glue to the holes on the

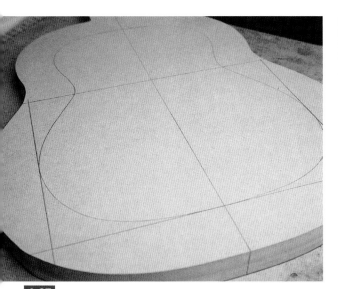

4-67 Box drawn on lower bout

4-68 Alaskan yellow cedar

4-69 Jointed pieces

4-70 Applying glue

bottom of the solera, and bang in the T-nuts
(**4-65**). Turn over the solera, and secure the rims
with the bolts to check fit (**4-66**).

The Lower Bout

The lower bout area now needs to be raised 4 mm
and then dished out to the 25-inch domed radius of
the top while tilted forward. First, this area of the

4-71 Clamping in place

4-72 Tracing plantilla shape

4-73 Trimming to fit the rims

solera needs to be built up in height by 4 mm. Draw a box that extends from the bottom edge of the lower bout to just below the first, or lower, transverse brace and across the full width of the lower bout (**4-67**). This area needs to be covered with a piece of wood that is 4 mm high. Choose a wood that is light in color, soft, and easy to carve. The wood used here is Alaskan yellow cedar (**4-68**). If necessary, joint two pieces to make up the required width. If you are using two pieces of wood, joint them first and then glue them to the fixture. Before gluing to the fixture, clamp a stop just below the position of the lower transverse brace so that the piece being glued will not slide forward. Apply the glue and clamp in place (**4-69, 4-70, 4-71**). Let dry overnight. Remove the clamps and position the plantilla exactly where it should go on the solera. Trace its shape on the wood just glued on (**4-72**). The wood outside the lines must be removed in order to fit the rims on the solera. With a router and a mortising bit, remove the wood to within ¹⁄₁₆ inches of the line. Then, using a chisel, trim to the line (**4-73**). Remove the remainder of the wood down to the MDF.

Creating the Dome

Creating the tilted dome is not as difficult as it sounds, but must be done gradually to be accurate. The 25-foot radius stick (see Chapter 3) will be used to check the radius as material is removed. Drill a hole to a depth of 2 mm with a 1-inch Forstner bit in the center of the lower bout in between the two registration holes to be used as a depth guide (**4-74**). Begin removing material with a large, shallow gouge (**4-75**),

4-74 Drilling a hole as depth guide

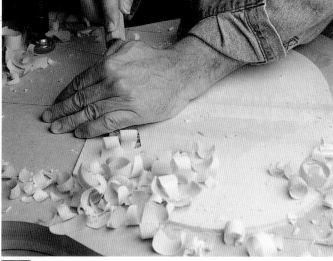

4-75 Gouging

4-76 Shaping solera with plane

4-77 Final shaping with 25'-radius sanding block

starting in the middle and carving across the grain toward the edges, approximating the shape and checking with the 25-foot radius stick as you go.

A compass plane will help shape and smooth the surface as you get close to the final arc (**4-76**). The bottom of the compass plane is curved across both its width and length. This type of plane can be easily fashioned from a round-bottom plane (see the reference for making planes in the

Marking end face of the ramp

4-79 Ramping solera with hand plane

4-80 Adding wood as cleat for vise

bibliography) by adding a curve to the bottom along its length using the large 25-foot radius sanding disc. The solera can be shaped very accurately with this plane. A curved scraper and the 25-foot radius sanding pad will remove the plane marks. Remember, the back edge needs to be a full 4 mm in height and the front edge should be even with the MDF. Take the material down the last bit of the way with the 25-foot radius sanding block (**4-77**).

The Ramp for the Neck

The ramp that the neck will rest on is sloped to create a forward neck angle. This neck angle provides the proper clearance for the strings as they are fretted on the fingerboard to prevent buzzing. To prepare the ramp for the neck, first make sure that when the side and the neck assembly are positioned correctly on the solera, the length of the ramp is just shy of the position of the nut so that the neck will lay flat against the ramp. If necessary, cut the end of the ramp. At the end face of the ramp, mark a line 2.5 mm down from the top face all the way across (**4-78**). The solera must be ramped from the position of the twelfth fret, where the neck meets the body, to the end of the neck ramp. This is done with a hand plane. Starting at the end of the neck ramp where most of the material must be removed, plane across the ramp and work your way back toward the twelfth-fret area (**4-79**). As you do this, always make sure that the surface you are planing remains flat both across the ramp and lengthwise from the twelfth fret to the end of the ramp, checking periodically with a straightedge and a T square.

A piece of stable quartersawn wood such as maple approximately 1½ inches wide and 2 inches

4-81 Finishing the fixture

4-82 Finished fixture

high may be added to the bottom of the solera to act as a cleat for holding in a vise (**4-80**). This piece should run the length of the solera and will add stability to the fixture. Feet can also be added to allow the fixture to be used on a table. The entire fixture should be finished with shellac and a water-based clear finish (**4-81** and **4-82**).

HEADPIECE TEMPLATE AND DRILLING JIG

THE HEADPIECE TEMPLATE can be made using the same technique employed to make the plantilla. Since the headpiece template is symmetrical, first make only half of a template, and then using the half template make a whole one. First, transfer from the drawing to the cardboard, and then use the cardboard template to transfer to plywood (**4-83**). Cut to rough shape on the band saw (**4-84**) and to final shape either by hand or with a drum sander on the drill press to fit the

4-83 Transferring template to plywood

4-84 Cutting to rough shape

4-85 Final shaping with drum sander

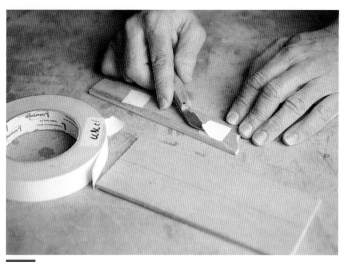

4-86 Applying double-stick tape

4-87 Securing half template

4-88 Rough cutting with band saw

4-89 Rough cutting half template piece

4-90 Trimming flush with router

4-91 Trimming flush

4-92 Half template trimmed

4-93 Trimming other side

4-94 Trimmed template

5-95 Marking openings

5-96 Lowering template to blade

5-97 Repeating on other side

drawing (**4-85**). Use double-stick tape to secure the half template to a piece of ¼-inch plywood or clear acrylic (**4-86** and **4-87**). Rough-cut on the band saw (**4-88** and **4-89**), and then trim flush with a router (**4-90** through **4-92**). Reattach the template to the other side with double-stick tape and repeat the process (**4-93** and **4-94**).

Cutting the Opening for the Tuning Machines

The openings for the tuning machines are cut next. The easiest way to do this accurately is on a router table using a ⅜-inch straight fluted bit. Mark the upper and lower boundaries of the openings on the back of the template, and set the fence so that there will be 8 mm of material left on the outside of the openings. Next, using a piece of wood with a square edge, mark on the fence both sides of the outer reaches of the blade in order to cut within the boundaries of the openings without going beyond them (**4-95**). Carefully lower the template to the blade while against the fence, and slowly push to the marks on both ends (**4-96**). Turn it around and repeat this process on the other side (**4-97**).

Mark the center of the openings with a bevel gauge so that they line up on both sides. These marks will be used to position the drilling jig to drill the holes for the tuning machine rollers.

A Wooden Drilling Jig

The drilling jig for the tuning machine rollers is easily fashioned from any piece of hard, stable wood such as maple. The jig shown in **4-98**, however, is made of steel because of its repeated use.

Tuner Drilling Jig

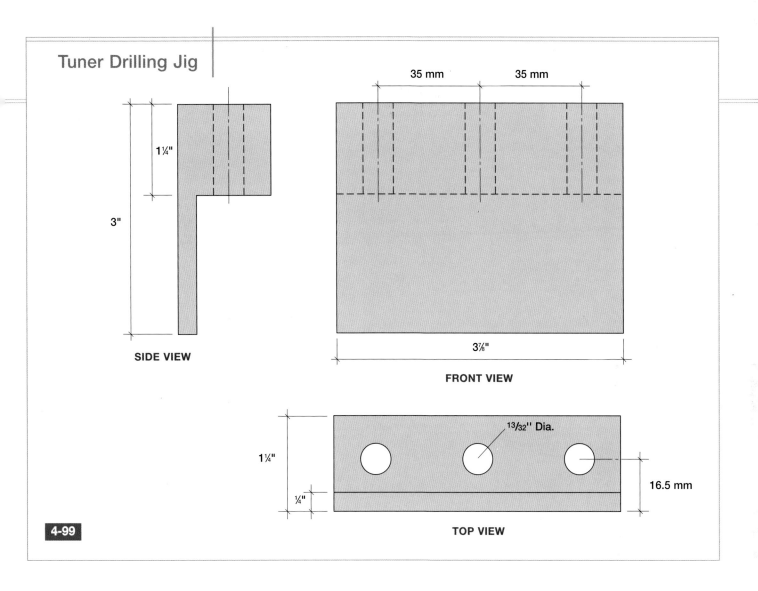

SIDE VIEW

1¼"

3"

35 mm   35 mm

3⅞"

FRONT VIEW

¹³/₃₂" Dia.

1¼"

¼"

16.5 mm

TOP VIEW

4-99

For one instrument, a wooden jig will work adequately and be considerably less expensive. The jig should be about an inch deep and the same thickness as the headpiece, 22 mm (**4-99**). The length is not critical, although you should allow about ½ inch of material beyond the outer holes. The holes for the tuning machine rollers are 35 mm, center to center, and are positioned on the centerline of the 22-mm face. Mark the position of the center hole first and the two outer ones next. Add a piece of ¼-inch plywood to one of the 1-inch faces to register the jig against the top face of the headpiece when drilling.

4-98   Drilling jig for tuning machines

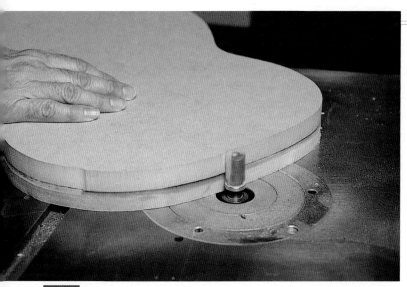

4-100 Trimming with router

4-101 Dishing out with shallow gouge

4-102 Using sanding block

BACK WORKBOARD

Since the back work is dished to a 15-foot radius, it should be thicker than ¾ inches. It is best made by gluing two pieces of ¾-inch MDF together. The extra thickness helps to stiffen the board after it is dished. The two pieces should be about 1½ inches larger than the full plantilla template all the way around. The outer shape is not critical. Cut one piece, final shape, and then glue the two pieces together. The second piece can be trimmed with a router after the glue dries (**4-100**). Begin dishing out the board with a shallow gouge, checking with the 15-foot radius stick as you go (**4-101**). As with the solera, use a compass plane as you approach the final shape (**4-102**). Remove the tool marks with a curved scraper, smooth with the 15-inch radius sanding block, and check for shape using the stick (**4-103** and **4-104**).

Trace the outline of the plantilla in the center of the workboard (**4-105**). Using the acetate of the back, locate and draw the back braces on the dished surface (**4-106** and **4-107**). Finish the board with shellac and a water-based finish (**4-108**).

4-103 Using 15'-radius sanding block

4-104 Checking with radius stick

4-105 Tracing outline of plantilla

4-106 Drawing back braces

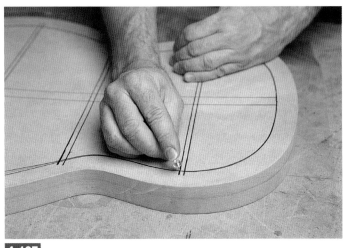

4-107 Locating the back braces

4-108 Finishing with shellac

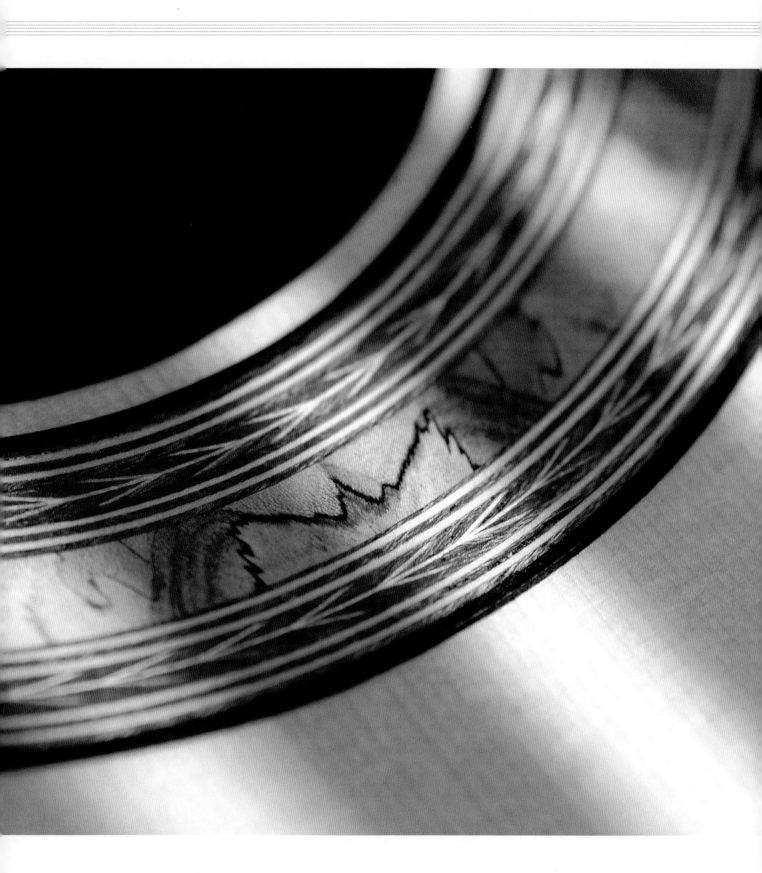

CHAPTER FIVE

Layout and Planning

Color and Design
Materials and Parts
Plans and Layout

THE SUCCESS OF THE ENTIRE PROJECT RELIES ON CAREFUL PLANNING AND PREPARATION. THE TIME SPENT SORTING things out before a piece of wood is cut will pay dividends in the final product. Building a guitar is a large project with many aspects, all of them complex, so it is important to know exactly what it is you are about to do before you do it.

In this chapter, a complete set of plans is provided for the instrument along with complete lists of materials. Study the plans and become familiar with the design. It is not necessary to memorize the sizes of all the parts—just get a feel for how everything will go together. Try to visualize what needs to be done and how you would like to perform each aspect. Athletes have used this technique with astounding success, and so can you. Visualization is a skill that can be developed if practiced. This project offers a unique opportunity to expand many different skills simultaneously.

If you are adding personal touches such as a different rosette, a different color scheme, or additional details, this is the time to decide exactly what they will be. Once construction begins on the top and back, you will be locked into the rosette and purfling scheme, so it is best to have all this figured out before you begin in order to concentrate on the work to be done. It is also advisable to purchase all the materials at this time. If there are any availability issues with the materials selected, this is the time to find out.

5-1 Rosette on a cedar top guitar

CHOOSING THE COLOR AND DESIGN SCHEME

The details of the guitar are what tie everything together aesthetically. Before any work begins on the instrument, the color scheme for things like the rosette and the bindings and purflings must be selected so that there will be cohesiveness in the design. Since certain parts of the guitar containing such details are built almost right away, it is important to have worked out all the details before construction begins. Availability of some of these things may also be a factor, so it is a good idea not to begin until you have all the parts in hand.

The Top Wood

For the classical guitarist, there are basically two choices for tops, either spruce or cedar. These two top woods establish the palette of colored woods used in the details. The challenge when selecting details is to create a striking look without going overboard, because sometimes less is more. The color and design scheme for the instrument presented in this book is one that I have used for a number of years on many western red cedar/Indian rosewood combinations. As mentioned elsewhere, the materials listed here are just suggestions and you can substitute materials for a color and design scheme to suit your own taste. For instance, I have used this rosette on a guitar with a cedar top (**5-1** and **5-2**), but this is not the only color scheme I have used for this combination. I have also used pear and mahogany purflings with a number of different bindings along with thuya and amboyna burl in the rosette. Availability and ease of substitution were the basis for the combinations used here.

On the guitar, highly figured wood does nothing to improve the sound and in fact may adversely affect the structural integrity, as this type of wood has a tendency to behave badly. It is the shape of the guitar that appeals to us on so many levels. Reminiscent of the human form, the shape is the focus of the design. Covering this beautiful shape with wildly figured wood creates a conflict, in my opinion. The wood is competing with the shape for attention. The best wood selection enhances the shape. In the case of a back, this can be achieved with two pieces that have a gentle curve to the grain, inward toward the middle seam.

The Overall Color Scheme

The many species of wood provide us with a large palette of colors as well as textures from which to choose. The texture and grain of some woods, however, may make them unusable for certain details. For instance, purfling is made of wood sliced very thin, which makes open-pored woods such as oak undesirable in this application. For purfling, a smooth, closed-pored wood with even color is a better choice. In selecting the wood for the instrument, you should bear in mind not only the look but also how well the material will work for the methods of construction that will be used.

Dyed wood is available and can add colors not found in nature such as red, yellow, and blue. Dyed wood has a tendency to fade with time, however, and when it does it loses its brilliance and becomes less attractive. I avoid using dyed wood in my instruments for this reason. The only dyed wood I use is black veneer, either pear, castillo, or poplar that has been ebonized, which to my knowledge does not fade. It is also impractical to use ebony for these finely detailed parts because of its scarcity.

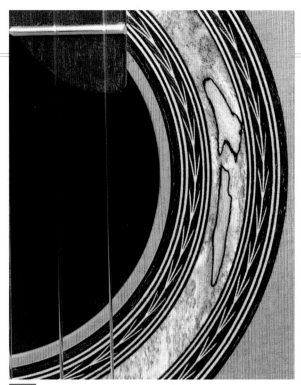

5-2 Rosette detail on a cedar top guitar

Good Design or Great Design?

During my years in the College of the Redwoods' Fine Woodworking Program, it became obvious to me that selecting colors, as well as grain patterns, is always a big part of the process and can make all the difference between a good design and a great one. I began to realize that a subtle grain pattern could be more beautiful than wildly busy wood in certain designs, while also having the advantage of reducing the possibility of problems down the road like warping and cracking. Although a highly figured wood is beautiful in and of itself, an entire piece made of it can be too much, so it is best used sparingly.

5-3 Rosette on a spruce top guitar

- Top—western red cedar
- Back and sides—Indian rosewood
- Headpiece (front and back)—Indian rosewood
- Bridge—Indian rosewood
- Bindings—Louro Preto
- Purflings—Alaskan yellow cedar/mahogany and/or Alaskan yellow cedar/black veneer
- Back/butt strip—Louro Preto center with above purflings on either side
- Rosette—black and maple veneer, ebony/maple wheat motif, with a spalted maple center ring

This combination of woods will produce a rich-looking instrument where all the details are tied to the whole design. If we were to use spruce for the top, the black veneer/maple wheat motif in the rosette could prove to be too much of a contrast for the light-colored soundboard and could look a bit harsh. For a more pleasing effect, the choice of details for a guitar with a spruce top could include a mahogany/maple wheat motif in the rosette and a golden-brown wood such as Louro Preto or koa for the bindings. The spruce will turn a bit golden when finished, especially if Kusmi shellac is used, and the brown details will produce a more cohesive look (**5-3** and **5-4**).

The Back and Butt Strip

Once the purflings and bindings have been selected, the back/butt strip will usually follow suit. In this case, the back/butt strip will have a Louro Preto center and be flanked on either side by the Alaskan yellow cedar/mahogany and/or Alaskan yellow cedar/black veneer purflings. Now construction can begin on various parts of the instrument, and everything will go together nicely.

The natural color of wood will also change with exposure to sunlight and sometimes drastically. It is usually known what color change to expect in a species of wood, and this can be built into the equation. The dark-purplish Indian rosewood will darken further when finish is applied, appearing almost black. However, the color will lighten to a dark brown over time with UV light exposure. This, along with the reddish-brown cedar, will limit the selection of possible colors for the details that will complement the rest of the instrument.

The color scheme chosen for the guitar presented here is as follows:

MATERIALS AND PARTS

In striving for the best possible sound in a guitar, it is advisable to use the best materials. As mentioned in Chapter 2 on wood, the traditional combinations of wood used in making classical guitars, such as Brazilian or Indian rosewood with either spruce or cedar, have been long proven as combinations that work. As Brazilian rosewood is so rare and prohibitively expensive, it probably would not be a wise choice for material on a first guitar. The combination chosen for the purposes of this book is western red cedar with Indian rosewood. Cedar is generally less expensive than European spruce, so I think this is a good choice for a first instrument.

The tendency for most people building their first guitar is to use cheaper materials for fear of ruining something. Although you may agree with this, I urge you to use the best materials you can

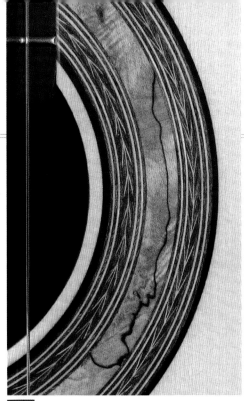

5-4 Rosette detail on a spruce top guitar

afford. Alternatives may prove to be lacking in certain qualities and be more difficult to work with. Building this instrument will be a challenging project for anyone attempting to make a guitar for the first time. To go through all the work only to wish

Purchasing Your Wood

When purchasing these woods, it is best to go to the supply shop yourself and personally hand-select the pieces you will use. The piece of wood used for the top is undoubtedly the most important piece of wood on the guitar as far as sound production goes, so when picking out the cedar for the top, poke through the entire pile until you find a piece that you imagine will make a fine instrument. Granted, if this is your first guitar, you won't have much to base your decision on, except your intuition, but that's okay. Just get familiar with the material, and make the best choice you can. Experience is something you have to acquire yourself, and you have to begin somewhere. Wood selection for any particular part of the instrument is discussed in detail in its respective chapter.

Dyed wood can add colors not found in nature such as red, yellow, and blue. I only use natural wood because dyed wood has a tendency to fade with time, losing its brilliance.

you had made it out of something else in the end would be a real shame.

It is suggested that for your first instrument you use as much precut material as possible rather than cutting and milling material from stock. Unless you have a fully equipped shop complete with a jointer, planer, and drum sander, milling all the wood will be a project in itself, and there will be enough milling to do as it is. With all the decisions having been made regarding wood and details, it is now time to acquire everything necessary to build your instrument. The species of wood commonly used in guitar making are becoming increasingly rare, however. As the old-growth trees disappear, the highest-quality wood is getting harder and harder to find. Sadly, this gets worse every year. Substitute woods are now being offered as alternatives to the

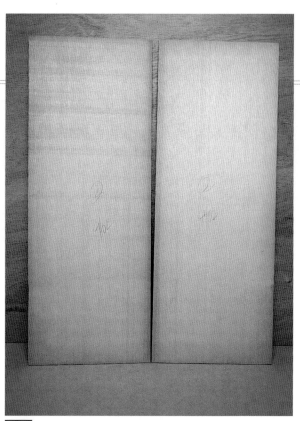

5-6 Western red cedar for top

traditionally used woods. Besides wood, there are only a few additional parts required to make a classical guitar. Suppliers for wood and parts are listed on my Web site (see page iv and 310).

Top, Back, and Sides

It is recommended that most of the wood, especially that for the top, back, and sides, be purchased from a luthier supply house. This wood is always graded. The criteria for grading varies slightly from place to place, but usually entails evenness of color and grain, straightness and tightness of grain, cut (how well quartersawn), and visual defects. The suppliers usually provide a description of their criteria used for grading. The species used here are commonly found in standard sizes used for guitar making (**5-5** and **5-6**). Some suppliers offer to mill the wood to any dimension you like for an

5-5 Indian rosewood for back

additional fee. The wood for these parts is listed below and usually sold in these dimensions:

- Top—western red cedar
  21 inches × 7¼ inches × ³⁄₁₆ inches
- Back—Indian rosewood
  20 inches × 7¼ inches × 0.160 inches
- Sides—Indian rosewood
  32 inches × 4½ inches × 0.120 inches

Side Laminations

The inside wood used to laminate the sides can be cypress, Sitka spruce, or Alaskan yellow cedar. The thickness used is approximately 0.045 inch. This can be either resawn out of rough stock or purchased as veneer. Since it may be difficult to find veneer at this thickness, it may be possible to use two pieces of thinner material. Veneer is sold in many thicknesses, the most common being 0.6 mm. Two pieces at this thickness will be very close to the dimension needed here and may be substituted if necessary (**5-7**).

Neck

Whether you use mahogany or Spanish cedar, you will need two perfectly quartersawn pieces with very little to no run-out. The pieces should be 24 inches long × 3 inches wide × ⅞ inches thick (**5-8**).

Headpiece Veneers

The front and back Indian rosewood veneers can be cut from leftover back material. The veneers should be 2.5 mm and 2 mm thick for the top and back faces, respectively. The black and Alaskan yellow cedar veneers can be cut from the sheets used for the bindings and wheat motif (**5-9**).

5-7 Side laminations

5-8 Perfectly quartersawn pieces for neck

5-9 Front and back headpiece veneers

Veneers for Purflings, Stripping, and Rosette

All veneers (**5-10**) are available at both veneer companies and most of the luthier supply companies listed on my Web site (see page iv or 310). Finding the correct thickness may be difficult, however. The thicknesses and quantities are listed below:

- Black—0.6 mm (~ 0.020 inches), three or four sheets 36 inches × 8 inches
- Alaskan yellow cedar—0.6 mm (~ 0.020 inches), one piece 32 inches × 6 inches
- Maple—0.3 mm (~ 0.010 inches), one sheet 36 inches × 8 inches
- Mahogany—0.6 mm (~ 0.020 inches), one piece 32 inches × 6 inches
- Maple—0.6 mm (~ 0.020 inches), one sheet

The black and maple veneers can be purchased at luthier supply companies. The Alaskan yellow cedar veneer can be cut from a plank and thicknessed on a drum sander, or you can purchase it from a supply company, but it will still most likely

5-10 Veneers for purflings, stripping, and rosette

need to be thicknessed with a drum sander. The amount of veneer depends on how high a wheat stick you choose to make.

Bindings and Back and Butt Strips

The bindings are pieces of hardwood that cover and protect the edges of the top and back of the guitar. The back strip runs down the center of the back, and the butt strip covers the butt seam where the two sides meet. They all have the same purfling pattern so that where they meet they are mitered and have a seamless look like the trim on a fine suit. The bindings can be made of Louro Preto, ebony, Indian rosewood, or any other hardwood you prefer. Bindings can be purchased from a luthier supply company, although the amount of different species available may be limited.

The bindings in this book are made by gluing the already glued purflings to a piece of Louro

Preto 32 inches × 1¼ inches × 0.200 inch and then cutting them off individually. The bindings can also be made by cutting four pieces off the sides before thicknessing. The dimensions of the bindings are 32 inches long × 0.200 inch high × 0.100 inch thick. The back and butt strip requires just one more piece of material approximately 0.090 inch wide, 0.150 inch thick, and 32 inches long. If cutting the bindings from a separate piece of stock for the back and sides, simply cut one more piece for the back and butt strip. All these pieces can also be purchased separately.

Soundboard Bracing

For bracing the top, or the soundboard, use either Sitka or European spruce. One split billet should be enough for the job. For any parts wider than the billet, it may be necessary to joint two pieces to make up the width (**5-11**).

Linings, Foot Block, Center Patch, and Back Bracing

All these parts can be made out of either mahogany or Spanish cedar. Each linings will require four pieces 32 inches long × 3 inches wide × 0.045 inches thick. These pieces can be first cut out of a larger piece of stock and then thicknessed on a drum sander. A slightly larger piece of mahogany will yield the foot block, center patch, and back bracing. The foot block is approximately 12 mm thick and 3 inches wide. The center patch is 0.100 inches thick, ⅞ inch wide, and 18 inches long. This piece is cross-grained and will have to be made up by jointing several pieces to provide the necessary length. For bracing the back, three pieces of quartersawn wood 15 inches long × ¾ inch high

Sound board bracing billets

× ⅜ inch thick are required. All these parts can be cut out of one piece of quartersawn wood 36 inches long, 6 inches wide, and 2 inches thick.

Fingerboard and Bridge Blank

It is recommended that both these parts be purchased at a luthier supply company. It is also recommended that the fingerboard be fretted for a 650 scale length. Both the fingerboard and the bridge blank should be of quartersawn stock. Fingerboards for classical guitars are typically 20-plus inches × 3 inches × ⅜ inch. Classical bridge blanks are typically 7¾ inches × 1¼ inches × ⁵⁄₁₆ inch (**5-12**).

Parts

There are only a few parts necessary for completing the guitar. The nut, saddle, and tie block inlays are typically made of bone, as the use of ivory has put the elephant in danger of extinction. These parts as well as the fret wire and tuning machines are available at various luthier supply companies (some listed on my Web site, one pages iv or 310). Typical sizes used for a classical guitar are listed below (**5-13**):

- Nut—⁵⁄₁₆ inch thick × ¹³⁄₃₂ inch high × 2³⁄₁₆ inches long
- Saddle—⅛ inch thick × ¹⁵⁄₃₂ inch high x 3¼ inches long
- Tie block inlays—2-mm-square profile, with a length at least 80 mm
- Fret wire—18 percent nickel/silver alloy fret wire, with a crown height between 0.037 and 0.043 inches
- Tuning machines—any tuners with rollers on 35-mm centers

PLANS AND LAYOUT

A complete set of plans for the instrument constructed in this book are provided in this section. Drawings **5-14** and **5-15** should be increased to about 305 percent to bring them close to actual size for creating your working plans. The profile of the back edge (**5-21**) should be increased about 455 percent. Check and adjust your plans with the measurements provided:

- Complete drawings of the top and back, respectively (**5-14** and **5-15**); also, a cross-sectional view of both
- Neck detail from headpiece to body (**5-16**)
- Fingerboard detail with fret positions for 650 scale length (**5-17**)
- Detail of headpiece, top view (**5-18**)
- Detail of bridge (**5-19**)
- Detail of side and butt strip (**5-20**)
- Template of side back edge (**5-21**)

5-12 Fingerboard and bridge blank

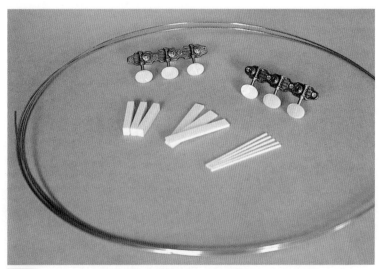

5-13 Nut, saddle, tie block inlays, fret wire, and tuning machines

Sound Board

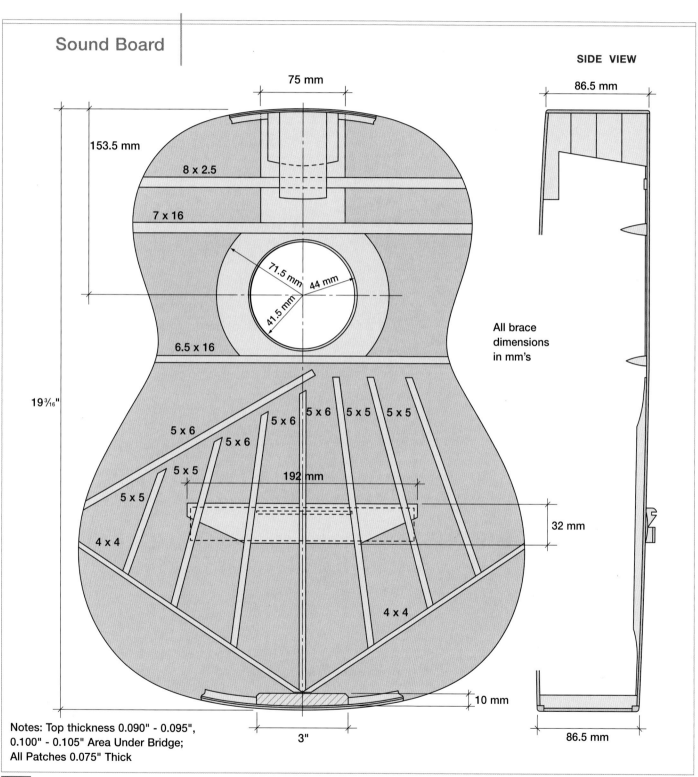

SIDE VIEW

86.5 mm

75 mm

153.5 mm

8 x 2.5

7 x 16

71.5 mm

44 mm

41.5 mm

6.5 x 16

All brace
dimensions
in mm's

19⁹⁄₁₆"

5 x 6

5 x 6

5 x 6

5 x 5

5 x 5

5 x 6

5 x 6

5 x 5

5 x 5

192 mm

32 mm

4 x 4

4 x 4

10 mm

86.5 mm

3"

Notes: Top thickness 0.090" - 0.095",
0.100" - 0.105" Area Under Bridge;
All Patches 0.075" Thick

5-14

Guitar Back Detail

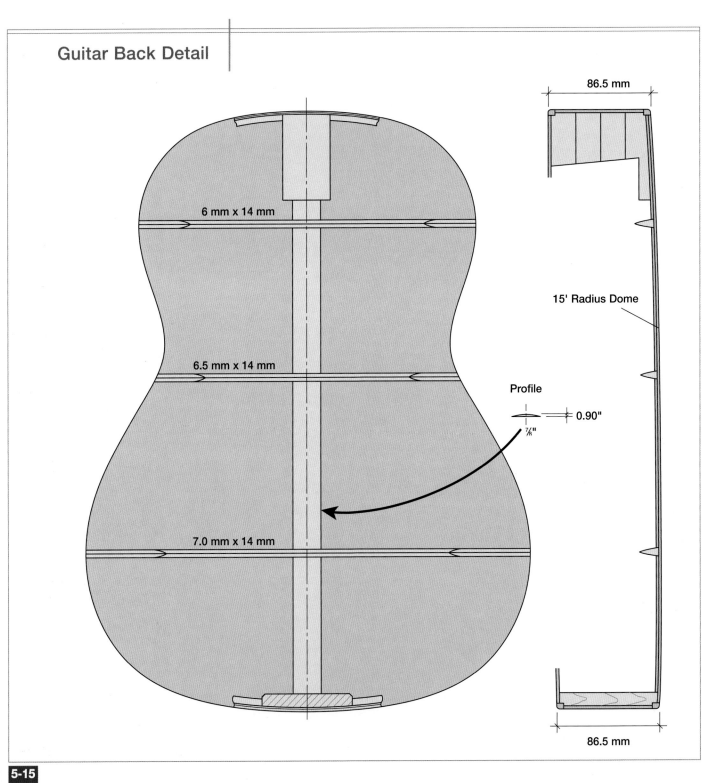

86.5 mm

6 mm x 14 mm

6.5 mm x 14 mm

15' Radius Dome

Profile

0.90"

⅞"

7.0 mm x 14 mm

86.5 mm

5-15

Neck Detail

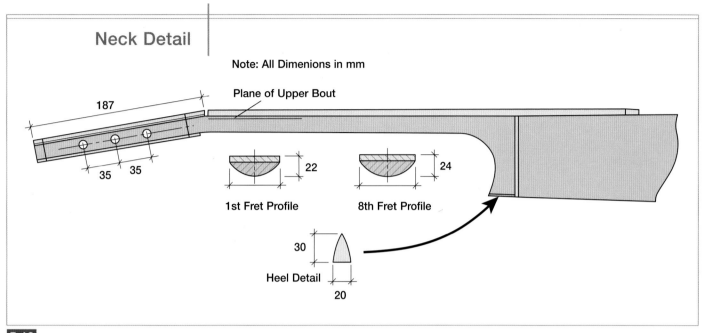

Note: All Dimenions in mm

Plane of Upper Bout

187

35   35

22

1st Fret Profile

24

8th Fret Profile

30

Heel Detail

20

5-16

Neck Detail

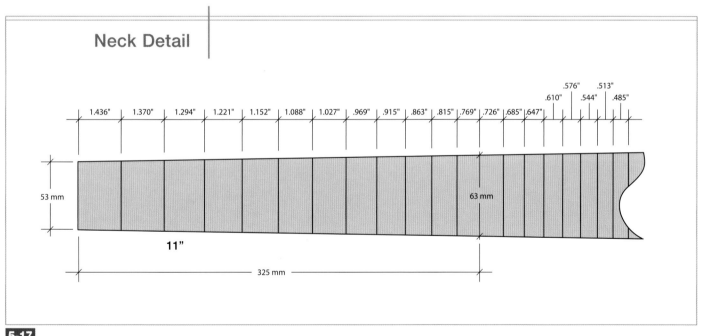

.576"   .513"
.610"   .544"   .485"

1.436"   1.370"   1.294"   1.221"   1.152"   1.088"   1.027"   .969"   .915"   .863"   .815"   .769"   .726" .685" .647"

53 mm

63 mm

11"

325 mm

5-17

Headpiece Detail

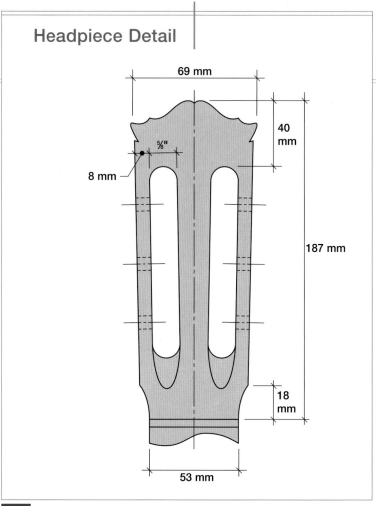

69 mm

40 mm

⅝"

8 mm

187 mm

18 mm

53 mm

5-18

The Bridge

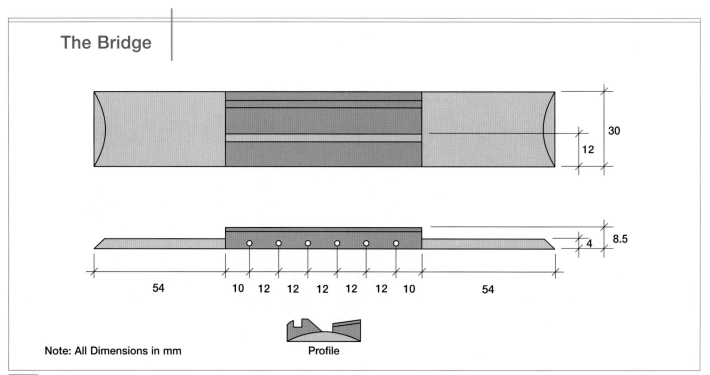

30

12

4   8.5

54   10   12   12   12   12   12   10   54

Note: All Dimensions in mm   Profile

5-19

Side and End Detail

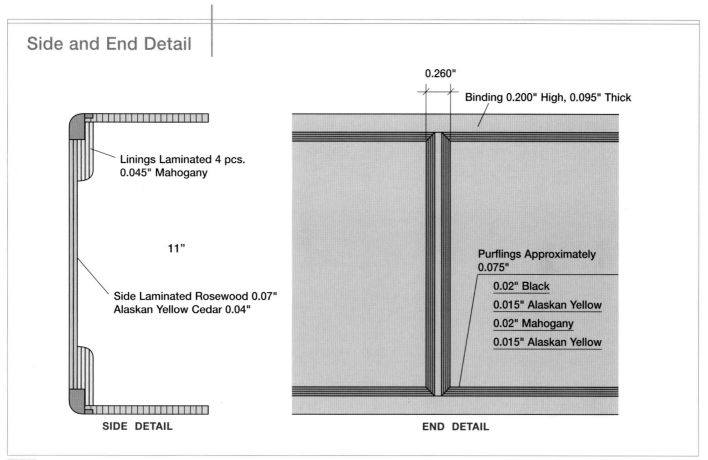

Linings Laminated 4 pcs.
0.045" Mahogany

11"

Side Laminated Rosewood 0.07"
Alaskan Yellow Cedar 0.04"

SIDE DETAIL

0.260"

Binding 0.200" High, 0.095" Thick

Purflings Approximately
0.075"

0.02" Black
0.015" Alaskan Yellow
0.02" Mahogany
0.015" Alaskan Yellow

END DETAIL

5-20

Template for Back Edge

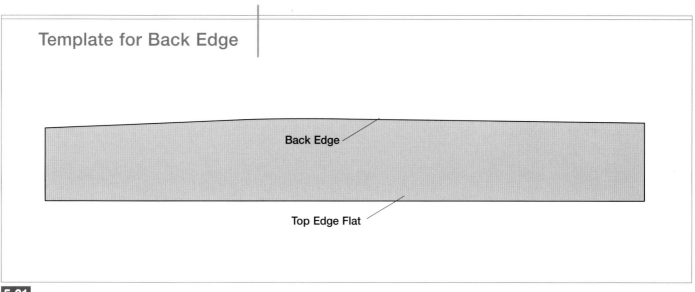

Back Edge

Top Edge Flat

5-21

CHAPTER SIX

The Neck

A T THIS POINT, THE MOLDS AND FIXTURES HAVE BEEN MADE, THE DRAWINGS HAVE BEEN GONE OVER THOROUGHLY TO GET A SOLID understanding of the design and what is involved in its construction, and a good amount of planning has been done as to how all the processes will be handled. Now the building begins.

The sequence of steps presented in this book are identical to those used in my shop, with the exception of a few of the early steps that are constructed in parallel here to save time. If this is your first guitar, it may be advisable to take it slowly to avoid making mistakes and ruining rare and costly wood.

The construction process will begin with the neck. In keeping with the philosophy of using the best materials one can afford, selecting good wood for the neck cannot be stressed enough. The neck must be able to withstand the string tension over the life of the instrument. Only perfectly quartersawn wood should be considered here because of its stability and strength. To have an otherwise perfectly fine instrument become unplayable because of poorly chosen wood for the neck would be a shame and should be avoided at all costs.

Many a fine guitar has been brought into my shop for repair because the player was finding the instrument increasingly difficult to play, only to find out that the neck had warped. Sometimes even the straightest piece of wood will behave badly under tension. The best we can hope to do is reduce the odds of this happening right from the beginning.

After the color and design scheme has been chosen, the neck and the sides are usually where the construction part of the project begins. The neck and sides can be constructed simultaneously to save time. It is all right to skip ahead to the next chapter and begin bending and laminating the sides. The neck is built in stages, so there is a fair amount of time spent waiting for glue to cure.

THE NECK BLANK

Wood for the Neck

The woods most commonly used for the neck on a classical guitar are mahogany and Spanish cedar. These two woods are generally used because they are medium-to-light density and stable and have a good density-to-weight ratio. Will a guitar with a mahogany neck sound different from a guitar with a neck made of Spanish cedar? Yes, although the difference is minimal. Results may vary because, as mentioned earlier, everyone will build an instrument differently, but in general mahogany is a bit denser and may have a slightly richer bass register. The Spanish cedar, on the other hand, is less dense, which has a slight effect on the treble register, sometimes making the sound a little brighter.

TO BEGIN CONSTRUCTION of the neck, straight-grained quartersawn wood with little run-out will give the best possible results here. Run-out can be checked by looking at the grain lines, not at the face of the quartersawn piece, but at the sides (**6-1**). These lines should be as straight as possible along the length of the piece and parallel to the top and bottom faces of the board. They should not intersect the top or bottom face; they should begin and end at the end of the piece. Neck blanks are sold at most luthier supply houses and usually can be purchased either as two separate pieces, in which case you will have to find the best match colorwise, or in one thick blank, which must be resawn.

The Neck Blank

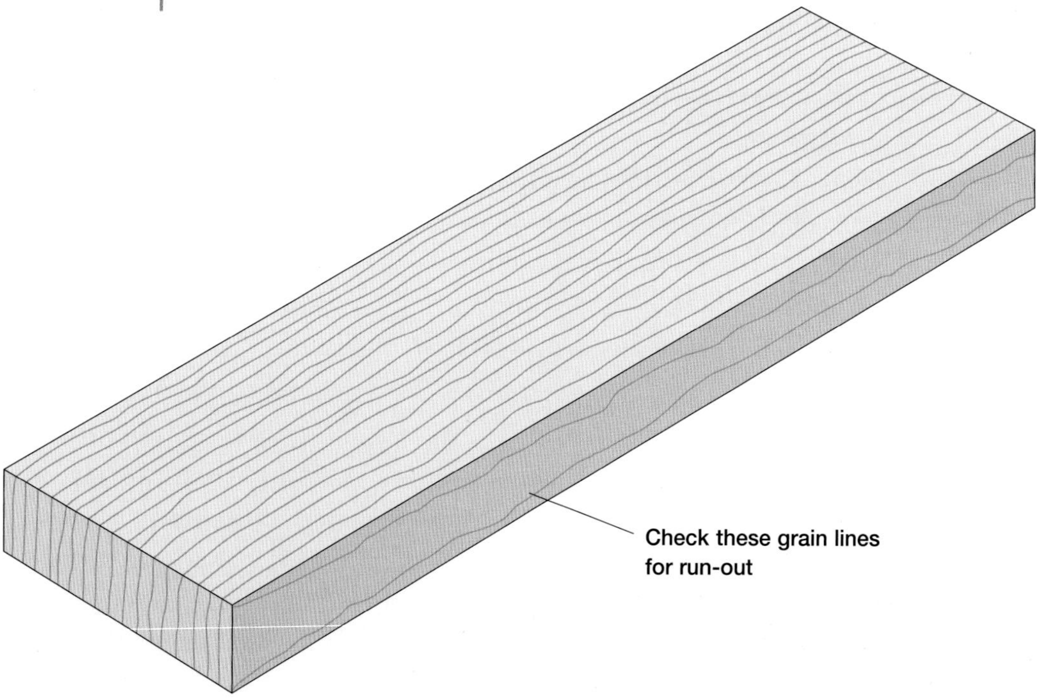

6-1

If the wood is resawn, it is a good practice to cut the wood a bit larger than final dimension and let it sit for a couple of days before milling. This will reveal any tendency for movement. If the movement is slight, it is safe to proceed. If not, it may be best to find another piece. More movement can be tolerated in the piece used to make the heel block, because the pieces will be much shorter in length. Once a suitable piece is found for the neck, mill the piece within ⅟₁₆ inches of the final dimension and let it sit for a few more days. When milling, always be sure to remove wood from both sides of the piece. The wood may move slightly again. Mill the wood flat and to final dimension when it is ready to use.

6-2 Spanish cedar for neck

Determining Which Piece and What Orientation

The neck is constructed from two pieces of wood that are 25 inches long × 3 inches wide × ⅞ inches thick, which in this case have been cut from a single piece of 8/4 Spanish cedar (**6-2**). Determine which piece will be used for the neck blank itself, and decide which surface will be the top that the fingerboard will be glued to, and which end will be the headpiece, and mark accordingly. If the piece you are using has a slight bow from end to end (less than ⅟₆₄ inches would be acceptable), use the concave face as the top surface of the neck and plane flat with a hand plane (**6-3**).

It is a good practice to always mark the orientation of any piece of wood you are working with right from the beginning. It avoids confusion especially when jumping from one thing to another. After marking the orientation, mark a

6-3 Planing neck piece

Headpiece Layout

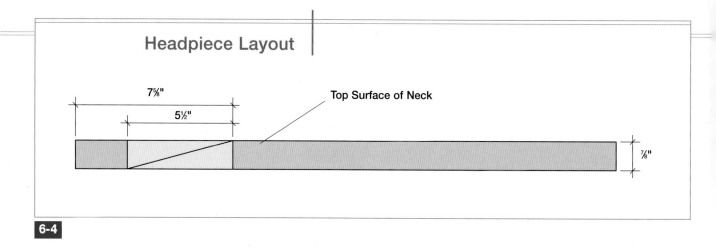

7⅝"

5½"

Top Surface of Neck

⅞"

6-4

6-5 Drawing diagonal for cutting headpiece

6-6 Cutting along line with band saw

line 7⅝ inches and another line 2½ inches down from the headpiece end. With the board on edge, draw a diagonal line from the upper corner of the first line to the lower corner of the second line, as shown in **6-4** and **6-5**. After checking that the blade of your band saw is perpendicular to the table, cut along this line (**6-6**).

Gluing the Neck Blank and Headstock

The longer piece will be the neck blank. The shorter piece is inverted and glued to the back of the neck blank and becomes the headpiece. Before gluing, both pieces should be flattened and smoothed with a hand plane (**6-7** and **6-8**). The glue joint should be checked for a good fit with only slight hand pressure (**6-9**). This may take some time to get right. A good practice is to plane across the grain when flattening in order not to build in irregularities in thickness; then set the plane to a lighter cut and plane with the grain to smooth. Check to see that the top surface remains perpendicular to the side (**6-10**) and adjust if necessary.

Once a good fit is established, put some wax paper on the bench where the glue joint will touch. Butt the upper edge of the headpiece to a

6-7 Planing flat and smooth

6-8 Using plane on second neck piece

6-9 Check glue joint with slight hand pressure

6-10 Top remains perpendicular to side

bench stop. This will prevent it from sliding as you tighten the clamps. Clamp the neck blank in place, making sure it is perpendicular to the bench; then apply glue to the short piece (**6-11**). Yellow PVA glue is used throughout the construction of the instrument, except where otherwise noted. Applying the right amount of glue to any joint is very important. You want enough glue to cause a small bead to appear all the way around after the clamps go on, but not a dripping mess. Use a glue caul on both sides to prevent dents in the neck wood from the clamps—any smooth flat material will work. I usually place a clamp on the

6-11 Applying glue

Selecting Veneer

Veneer is used in guitar making for decorative detail in the headpiece, rosette, purflings, back strip, and butt strip. Veneer is thinly sliced wood and is available in any number of species and also in some colors not found in nature. These colored veneers are dyed and some colors are more prone to fading than others. Black stands up well, and because using ebony veneer is impractical, it becomes a viable substitute. Dyed black veneer is available in a few different woods, such as poplar, pear, and costello. All will retain the color well, although they will not all have the same working properties. The poplar, which is the least expensive and most popular, is soft and may tear out when scrapped or planed. Pear, which is the most expensive, is a bit harder and planes very well, leaving a very good surface for finishing. Costello also planes well and is priced in between the two.

top of both pieces first, in order to keep either of them from sliding up, and then apply the clamps to the face and let dry (**6-12**).

Veneer for the Headpiece

The headpiece veneers in this case will be (from the top down) Indian rosewood, Alaskan yellow cedar, and black veneer (see sidebar). The top veneer of Indian rosewood can be either purchased or made out of the off-cuts of the back. This veneer should be 2.5 mm thick and be large enough to cover the entire headpiece. It is always wise whenever possible to allow excess and to trim later to flush. Make sure there is at least an excess of approximately ⅛ inches over the break in the neck where the nut will go. The Alaskan yellow cedar and the black veneer should be 0.6 mm.

Applying and Trimming the Veneer

Cut the veneers to size and make sure they are clean and free of dust or small particles. Flatten the surface of the headpiece with a small plane (**6-13**), while checking to make sure it remains perpendicular to the sides (**6-14**). Drop a perpendicular line down the side surface of the neck at the exact place the headpiece begins to angle away from the surface of the neck, and continue that line around to the top surface. This will provide a reference for placing the veneers. All veneers must extend slightly beyond this line. The black veneer is on the bottom, so it goes on first, followed by the Alaskan yellow cedar, and then the Indian rosewood. Apply the glue evenly with a roller, trying to apply just the right amount (**6-15** through **6-20**).

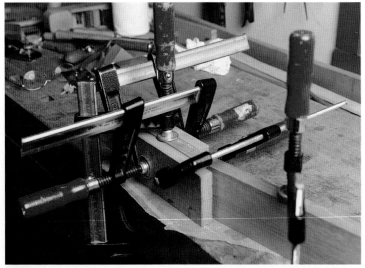

6-12 Clamped pieces

6-13 Flattening headpiece with a plane

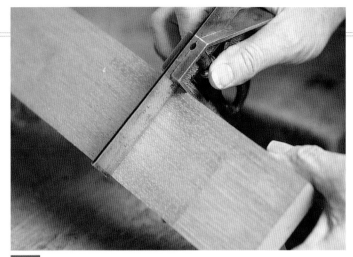

6-14 Check for perpendicular

6-15 Applying glue evenly

6-16 Black veneer

6-17 Applying glue again

6-18 Alaskan yellow cedar

6-19 Applying glue

6-20 Indian rosewood

Tape the veneers in place to avoid sliding (**6-21**). Use a caul on the top and bottom to prevent dents from appearing on the surface from the clamps. Apply pressure to the clamps slowly and only after all are on. This will minimize slipping (**6-22** and **6-23**).

After the glue is dry, remove the clamps and tape, and trim the excess veneer on the sides of the headpiece flush. Drop a perpendicular line exactly where the neck and headpiece surface come to a point. Continue that line around the top of the Indian rosewood veneer perpendicular to the edge of the neck with a silver colored pencil, as the silver will be easier to see against the dark wood (**6-24**). Cut slightly to the neck side of this line with a small handsaw (**6-25**). Cut only down to the black veneer, cut the rest of the way with a knife so as not to mark the surface of the neck, and remove the waste with a chisel (**6-26**). Trim with a rabbet plane to the line (**6-27**), and check to make sure it is perpendicular to the edge of the neck (**6-28**).

6-21 Taping veneers

6-22 Applying pressure slowly

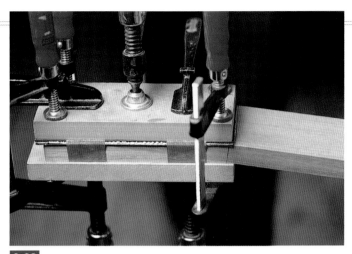

6-23 Clamped pieces

6-24 Drawing line

6-25 Cutting to the neck side

6-26 Removing waste with chisel

6-27 Trimming with rabbet plane

6-28 Checking perpendicular

6-29 Cutting off the back side

On the band saw, cut the headpiece to a thickness of slightly more than 20 mm by cutting off the back side down the perpendicular line at the nut end (**6-29**), and saw across with a handsaw to remove the waste (**6-30**). Plane the back of the headpiece flat to a final thickness of 20 mm (**6-31**). Now glue the Indian rosewood veneer (2 mm thick and approximately 3 inches × 7¾ inches) to the back of the headpiece the same way as the top (**6-32** through **6-35**).

The Heel

The heel is made from the other piece of wood measuring 3 inches × 24 inches × ⅞ inch. Cut four pieces 5¼ inches long (**6-36** and **6-37**). These pieces will make up the stack that will be the heel. Stack the pieces the way they will be in the heel, and draw a line from top to bottom 2¼ inches in from the front edge.

6-30 Sawing across to remove waste

6-31 Planing the back of the headpiece

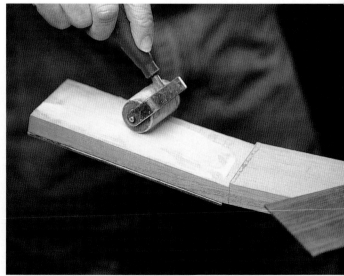

6-32 Applying glue evenly to back

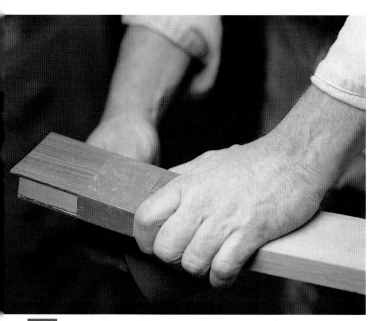

6-33 Gluing Indian rosewood veneer

6-34 Clamping back of headpiece

6-35 Clamped headpiece

6-36 Cutting pieces for heel

6-37 Four pieces to make heel

6-38 Measuring to the twelfth fret

6-39 Scoring side of stack at 12th fret

Place a piece of material equal to the width of the nut (0.225 inches) in the nut slot, and measure down the neck half the scale length (325 mm), or to the twelfth fret (**6-38**). Mark this spot and score a line perpendicularly across the neck at this point and down the side with the heel stack in place (**6-39**). Flatten each face of the pieces of the stack (**6-40**) so that they fit with no gaps, making sure once again that you keep the surface perpendicular to the sides. Cover the bench with wax paper, and apply the glue with a roller, making sure to apply the right amount (**6-41**).

Too much glue in this case will cause the pieces to skid. Use cauls to prevent denting on the surface of the neck. A clamp large enough to span all the laminates, along with the neck, applied on top and clamped to the bench may prevent the stack from skidding. Then apply the rest of the clamps (**6-42**). After the glue is dry, plane the sides of the heel stack, making them perpendicular to the surface of the neck; then cut the height of the stack to 94 mm off the bottom edge of the heel block (**6-43** through **6-45**).

6-40 Flattening each face

6-41 Gluing stack

6-42 Clamped stack

6-43 Planing sides of heel stack

6-44 Heel stack perpendicular to neck

6-45 Cutting the height of the heel stack

6-46 Revealing double-stick tape

6-47 Securing headpiece template

6-48 Trimming excess

THE HEADPIECE

THE HEADPIECE IS WHERE the tuning machines are housed and acts as a termination point for the strings. This is a complicated shape best cut out using the template constructed in Chapter 4. If you are not comfortable using a router for this operation, the entire process can be accomplished by hand with a handsaw, a chisel, and some files. The process will be described here using the router.

Using the Headpiece Template

Secure the headpiece template to its correct position on the headstock using double-sided tape—a piece at both ends and one in the middle will do (**6-46** and **6-47**). Take the neck blank to the band saw, and using a support block underneath to raise the headstock high enough to clear the bend of the neck, trim off the excess on the two sides and top, keeping about 1/16 inches away from the template (**6-48** and **6-49**).

Secure the neck blank in a bench vise at the heel end. Using a router (1 to 1½ HP) equipped with a two-flute ⅜-inch straight trim bit with the bearing above the blade, trim off the excess around the perimeter of the headstock, stopping approximately ¼ inches from the end where the nut will reside (**6-50**). This is best trimmed by hand later after the fingerboard has been installed. Without removing the template, mount the jig constructed for drilling the holes for the machine rollers to the face of the headstock in the correct position with two small clamps (**6-51**).

Using the lower edge of the template as a reference to keep the edge parallel to the table, mount the headstock in a small portable vise and drill the 13/32-inch-diameter holes for the rollers to

6-49 Trimming excess on the sides with band saw

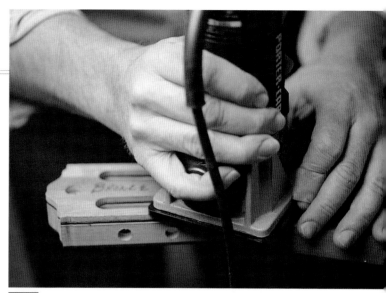

6-50 Trimming excess around headstock with router

6-51 Drilling jig for machine rollers

the correct depth (**6-52**). Drill both sides, then remove the jig, but leave the template, and install a ½-inch Forstner bit in the drill press. Starting at the upper edge of the tuning slots, drill out the material in the center of the slot, working your way down to the lower edge and overlapping the holes by half the diameter of the bit each time (**6-53**). When completed, there will be little peaks along each of the inside walls, which should be removed with a sharp chisel to provide clearance for the router bit, which will be used to trim flush

6-52 Drilling headstock on vise

6-53 Drilling out tuning slots

6-54 Peaks removed with chisel

6-55 Trimming slots with router

to the template (**6-54**). Using the router equipped with the same trim bit used to trim the perimeter, trim the inside of the slots (**6-55**). Before turning on the router, make sure the bit is in the slot and has enough clearance to start up without hitting the sides; if not, trim further with a chisel.

Bringing the Neck Blank to Final Shape

Remove the template carefully with a wide chisel (**6-56**). Clamp the neck blank in the bench vise, and using a ½-inch tapered round file, ramp the bottom of the slots (**6-57**). Care must be taken to make a smooth transition from the routed portion of the slot to the filed ramp. As you approach the final shape, use a finer-cutting file to avoid having to clean up a lot of nasty marks. A half-round rattail smoothing file will work well here.

Since the diameter of the router bit used to trim the perimeter was too large to capture all the detail of the top of the headpiece, the remainder must be done by hand. First, mark a centerline across the top edge, and then take a handsaw and cut a shallow kerf along the line (**6-58** and **6-59**). Using a small triangular file, a chisel, and some sandpaper, shape the top two lobes of the headstock (**6-60** through **6-63**). Next, mark the bottom of the two outer points of the headstock on the sides equally and cut a shallow kerf to a depth of approximately ⅛ inches (**6-64** and **6-65**). Take a chisel and shape the outer lobes to the bottom of this kerf and sand smooth (**6-66** and **6-67**). The shaping of the headstock is completed. It may be easier to sand and prep the headstock for finishing at this point, as the neck is separate. If so, begin with 150 or 180 grit and sand up to 320.

6-56 Removing template with chisel

6-57 Ramping bottom of the slots

6-58 Marking centerline

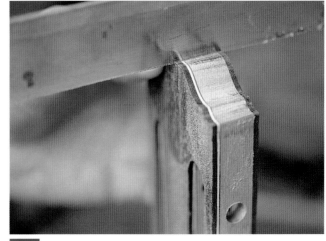

6-59 Cutting a shallow kerf along line

6-60 Shaping with triangular files

6-61 Shaping with chisel

6-62 Shaping with the sandpaper

6-63 Shaping the top two lobes with sandpaper

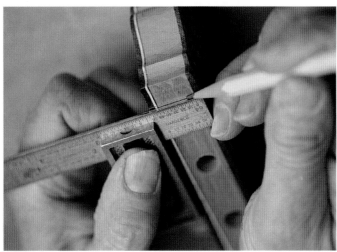

6-64 Marking bottom of two outer points

6-65 Cutting a shallow kerf

6-66 Chiseling and shaping to bottom of kerf

6-67 Sanding smooth

THE HEEL

IN ORDER TO BEGIN carving the heel, the slots for the sides must first be cut. The sides are glued into these slots. The upper edges of the slots are at the twelfth fret, or half the scale length of the instrument. Use a substitute nut as a placeholder to measure down the neck 325 mm, and mark the twelfth fret and the position of the slots (**6-68**). Draw a line perpendicular to the centerline of the neck at this point (**6-69**), and continue that line all the way around the heel block (**6-70**). The lines should all meet. If they don't, that indicates that not all the surfaces of the heel block are square and one or more may need straightening. A small hand plane can be used to correct this.

Once the lines all meet, make a mark 1/16 inches beyond the twelfth-fret line at each edge of the neck blank and draw a line from this point to the centerline on both sides (**6-71**). This line will compensate for the curve of the upper bout where it meets the neck and avoids building in tension or creating a flat spot. Once the lines have been drawn, mark the depth of the slots on both the top and bottom of the heel block. At the top, mark a line 18 mm out from each side of the centerline (**6-72**). At the bottom, mark a line 5 mm out from each side of the centerline.

Cutting the Side Slots

Using a handsaw, begin the cut at the angled line and cut to the depths marked at the top and bottom (**6-73**). The resulting kerf is not wide enough to accept the sides, so it will have to be widened. Insert a scraper blade or a thin piece of sheet metal into the kerf and cut again, always working

6-68 Marking twelfth fret

6-69 Drawing line perpendicular to centerline

6-70 Continuing line around heel block

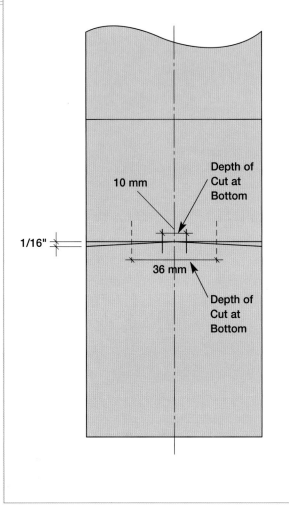

10 mm

Depth of Cut at Bottom

1/16"

36 mm

Depth of Cut at Bottom

6-71

6-72   Making depth mark

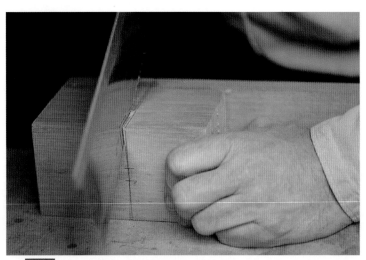

6-73   Cutting at angle to the depth marks

toward the end of the neck blank and away from the twelfth fret (**6-74**). Continue to insert scrapers or sheet metal, recutting until the sides fit into the slots. The fit should be snug, but not forced. If the fit is too loose, a thin wedge the length of the slot can be added to provide the necessary fit.

Shaping the Heel Block

It is usually best to shape the inside heel block first in order to create clearance for the tools when carving the heel. First, the heel block must be cut to length. Measure 72 mm back from the side slots and cut off (**6-75**). Next, make a mark 44 mm in from the inside edge of the slot at the top of the heel block. Then draw a line 18 mm up from the bottom edge of the heel block parallel to it. Along this line, make a mark 32 mm in from the inside edge of the slot. Draw a diagonal between these two points, and make the necessary cuts on the band saw (**6-76, 6-77** and **6-78**).

6-74 Widening the kerf with scraper blade

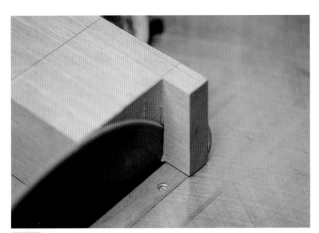

6-75 Cutting heel block to length

6-76 Cutting from the bottom edge

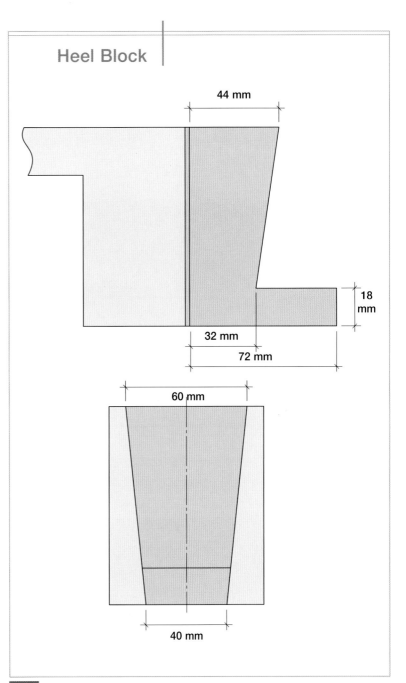

Heel Block

44 mm

18 mm

32 mm

72 mm

60 mm

40 mm

6-77

6-78 Cutting from the inside edge

6-79 Cutting the sides of the heel block

6-80 Shaping with pattern maker's rasp

To cut the cheeks of the heel block, make a mark 20 mm out from each side of the centerline on the bottom of the block and draw two lines parallel to the edges (**6-79**). Make a mark 30 mm out from each side of the centerline at the top edge of the block, and cut along the diagonal formed by connecting these two marks. Use the line along the bottom as a guide for plumb. Be careful not to cut beyond the slots, as any marks on the inside edge of the heel may be visible. Begin shaping by using a No. 49 or 50 pattern maker's rasp to round over the inside face of the block (**6-80**). Repeat this shape on the end of the tang. Switch to finer files to remove the marks left by the rasp (**6-81**). Clean up the cheeks of the block with a small hand plane. Sand the entire heel block, beginning with 150- or 180-grit sandpaper and finishing with 320-grit sandpaper.

6-81 Removing marks with finer file

Preparing to Carve the Heel

Carving a heel can seem intimidating, but if you follow a few simple steps it can actually be accomplished without much difficulty. First, the profile of the neck, including the heel, must be cut on the band saw. Using the side profile template of the heel, trace the outline of the shape onto the wood (**6-82**). Make a mark at approximately the position of the first fret 16 mm down from the fingerboard surface, and draw a line from this mark to the top of the heel profile (**6-83** and **6-84**). Cut to within ⅟₁₆ inches of this line on the band saw (**6-85** and **6-86**). On the bottom surface of the heel, sketch the shape of the heel cap (**6-87**). To avoid making the neck too narrow at the heel area, place the fingerboard template in position on the neck and trace the outline (**6-88**).

Carve with Sharp Tools

Carving is always easier and safer with sharp tools. If the tool is sharp, cutting mahogany or Spanish cedar will not be difficult. If this is your first time carving, it may be wise to mock up a heel block out of scrap wood of the same species as the neck, on which to practice. This way, you will be able to become familiar with the feel of things before carving on a neck that already has a fair amount of time and work invested in it.

6-82 Tracing heel side profile template

6-83 Marking position of the first fret

6-84 Drawing line to top of heel profile

6-85 Cutting heel with band saw

6-86 Continuing cutting on fingerboard

Beginning to Carve

Begin carving by removing as much material as possible while approximating the shape of the heel. It will be difficult if not impossible to trace the contour on the inside surface of the slot, so it must be visualized. With a little practice, it is amazing how accurate your eye can become in seeing complex surfaces in three dimensions. I usually begin carving with a 35-mm No. 1 flat gouge and just remove lots of material while beginning to roughly shape the cheeks of the heel (**6-89** and **6-90**). This is also a good time to roughly shape the neck at the foot of the heel to provide an approximate depth and shape to which to carve the heel, which will prevent carving too deeply. This can be done quickly with a No. 49 or 50 pattern maker's rasp (**6-91**). Also, it is a good idea to leave a margin of safety at the top of the heel where the fingerboard will be installed later. Here, it is important to leave approximately

6-87 Sketching the shape of the heel cap

6-88 Tracing fingerboard template

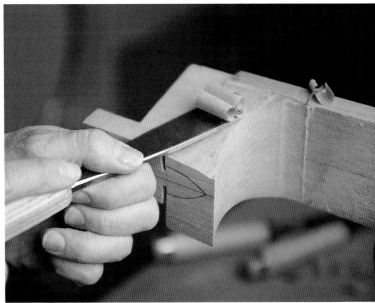

6-89 Carving with flat gouge

⅛-inch excess on each side so that final shaping can be done after the fingerboard is glued on.

Reaching the Final Shape

Once the heel begins to take shape, the cheeks must be rounded in to the centerline of the heel. Here, use whatever tool feels most comfortable. I use a combination of gouges and a knife (**6-92** through **6-95**). As you get closer to the final shape, it may be best to switch to rasps and files to avoid tear-out and going too deep (**6-96** and **6-97**). As further carving will be necessary after the fingerboard is installed, only an approximate shape is required at this time (**6-98**). Gradually progress to a finer-cut file; to remove all file marks, a convex scraper will work well. Sand the heel smooth with 180-grit sandpaper (**6-99**).

6-90 Carving with gouge

6-91 Shaping the neck with rasp

6-92 Shaping with flat gouge

6-93 Rounding cheeks with flat gouge

6-94 Rounding cheeks with gouge

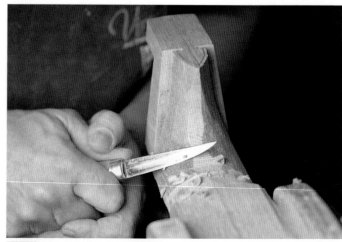

6-95 Rounding cheeks with knife

6-96 Rounding cheeks with file

6-97 Rasps and files avoid tearing too deep

6-98 Only an approximate shape is required

6-99 Sanding the heel smooth

CHAPTER SEVEN

The Sides

Bending and
* Laminating the Sides*
Linings
Assembling the Neck
* and Sides*

A S A YOUNG PLAYER, I COULDN'T WAIT FOR MY GUITAR LESSON
EACH WEEK. THE PROSPECT OF LEARNING A NEW PIECE WAS VERY
exciting. Even more exciting to me was that, because I traveled into
Manhattan on the Staten Island Ferry and subway for my lessons, my teacher let me play
his guitar at the lesson so that I wouldn't have to carry mine. He had a 1960s vintage
Ramirez 1A. It sounded so much better than my guitar that it was hard to play mine
afterwards. Everything about it was different than mine—better trebles, and booming
basses; the only negative was that it was harder to play. But I never forgot that sound.

Needless to say, my first guitar was built from a set of Ramirez 1A plans. The plans
called for the sides to be laminated. The French luthier Daniel Fredrich also laminates the
sides on his guitars. As I admired both of these builders and had a fair amount of experience laminating shapes making furniture, I felt I must also do the sides this way. As I
gained more experience building guitars, I began to understand that there are many
advantages to laminating the sides. First, a lamination is stiffer than a solid piece of wood,
and with sides, stiffness is important. Secondly, by removing some of the heavier rosewood and replacing it with a softer, lighter wood such as cypress or Sitka spruce, you end
up with something stiffer and lighter. Laminating offers another advantage, because the
parts are relatively thin and already bent, after the glue cures there is no spring-back; thus,
the sides maintain the shape of your mold exactly. This will give you a very consistent
volume inside your box. It is no doubt a bit more work, but I think there are enough
advantages to justify the effort.

BENDING AND LAMINATING THE SIDES

7-1 Wood options for the sides

The sides will be made by laminating a piece of Indian rosewood, the outer face, to a piece of lighter wood, which can be cypress, Alaskan yellow cedar, Sitka spruce, or something comparable (**7-1**). All the wood used for the sides should be quartersawn. If you have purchased a set of Indian rosewood sides, they are approximately 32 inches long, between 4 and 5 inches wide, and about $\frac{3}{16}$ inches thick. The rosewood may be thicknessed by hand if necessary, but using a drum sander will be faster. It is also sometimes possible to have the sides thicknessed for you by the supplier. When thicknessing wood by hand, especially a rowed-grain wood like rosewood, plane either across the grain or at a 45-degree angle to the grain, and make sure your plane is sharp. By planing across the grain, it is easier to get a consistent thickness. Planing with the grain on the rosewood can lead to some nasty tear-out. Once you have come within approximately 0.005 inch of the

7-2 Planing against the grain

Thicknessing Considerations

The rosewood will be milled to a final thickness of approximately 0.065 inches, and the inside laminate, in this case Sitka spruce, will be milled to about 0.045 inches. The Sitka, being soft and thin, may be difficult to thickness by hand. A drum sander will work best if you have one; if not, it may be possible to rent milling services from a local shop. Milling any wood this thin in a planer can lead to catastrophic results, so I don't recommend it. If you are cutting the stock from a plank, use a well-tuned band saw and cut each part approximately 0.020 inches thicker than the final dimension to ensure a smooth surface after milling. Another alternative is to use a commercially available veneer (0.6 mm, or 0.020 inches, thick) and use two pieces to make up the thickness if necessary.

7-3 Scraping with grain to remove plane marks

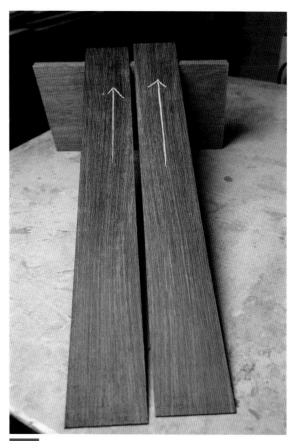

7-4 Chalk mark pointing to the heel

final thickness, use the scraper with the grain to remove all the plane marks (**7-2** and **7-3**). This should bring you to the final thickness.

Once the sides have been thicknessed, lay the two pieces side by side on the bench. The sides need to be oriented for optimal visual effect. The sides should be book-matched, meaning they should be mirror images of each other. Decide which end you would like at the heel, and draw an arrow in chalk on the outer surface pointing toward the heel on each side (**7-4**). This will avoid confusion when bending. Next, take your sides to the bending iron and lightly moisten the surface that will touch the iron. Place the wood on the iron, and move it slowly back and forth to avoid burning (**7-5**). Just slight pressure is needed to bend the wood. You will feel it give as it heats up. Remember, you don't have to get these to the

7-5 Keep the wood moving on bending iron

exact shape, only close. The laminating will take it the rest of the way. A good bend at the waist will eliminate any spring-back after laminating. A little practice on a less expensive wood may ease the anxiety when working with the rosewood.

Sanding and Laminating the Pieces

Once you have all the pieces bent, they must be lightly sanded before laminating. Prepare a space to do the glue-up. Some newspaper may be helpful to keep glue off your bench. We will use the lamination mold prepared in Chapter 3 along with the Masonite cauls. According to the spacing of your blocks on the outer caul, you will need an equal number of clamps. I generally use yellow PVA glue on all laminates. Use a roller to apply the glue to the inside of the rosewood, and remember to strive for the right amount of glue. The right amount will always produce a thin bead around the edges after the clamps are applied. Mate the Sitka to it and place it against the surface of the mold, making sure the two pieces stay lined up and the bottom edges are against the table. Begin applying the clamps at the waist. As you tighten, be sure the pieces remain lined up. Work the clamps from the waist out to the ends. After all the clamps are on, turn over the mold and wipe off the glue that has squeezed out on the bottom. Let the glue cure overnight; then repeat for the other side (**7-6** through **7-12**).

7-6 Side mold and laminations

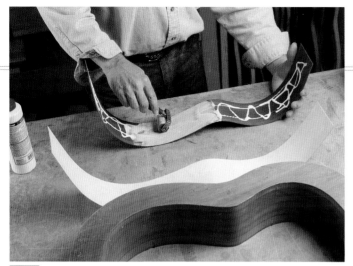

7-7 Applying the glue

7-8 Align laminater

7-9 Position the caul

7-10 Start clamping at the waist

7-11 Clamping

7-12 Allow clamped sides to cure overnight

7-13 Flattening edges with a plane

7-14 Marking centerline with half plantilla in mold

Once the two sides are laminated, decide which surface will be the top, scrape away any dried glue, and flatten the edge with a plane, checking against a flat surface (**7-13**). Once flat, place the half plantilla inside the mold and mark the centerline at both ends (**7-14**). Place the sides back in the mold, mark the ends, cut to the line, and clean up with a plane (**7-15** through **7-17**). Set aside the cut-off piece; it will be used to determine the width of the slots in the neck for the sides.

The sides need to be cut along the edge that supports the back before the linings can be glued on. The back is not flat but rather domed to a radius of 15 feet and tilted forward slightly. The template for this shape is provided in the "Plans and Layout" section of Chapter 5. Make a cardboard template from the drawing, use this to trace the shape onto the wood, and then cut to the line with a handsaw (**7-18** and **7-19**).

7-15 Marking end with side back in mold

7-16 Cutting to the line

7-17 Cleaning up with a plane

7-18 Tracing shape to wood

7-19 Cutting to line with hand saw

7-20 Four pieces resawn for linings

LININGS

The linings are made from four thin pieces of mahogany 32 inches long, ⅝ inches wide, and 0.045 inches thick. These strips can be made from rough stock by cutting a piece 3 inches wide and 32 inches long. This wood does not have to be quartersawn, although quartersawn mahogany has a look that is hard to resist. Resaw four pieces approximately 0.060 inches thick, and mill to 0.045 inches (**7-20**). Again, the mahogany may be difficult to thickness by hand. Using a drum sander may be best.

Once the wood is milled, put the stack of laminates back together the way they were sawn off the plank and cut them all together on the band saw to a width of ⅝ inches (**7-21** and **7-22**). Prepare the lining molds made in Chapter 4 along with the eight clamps necessary for each one and a few pieces of masking tape to hold the laminates while you apply the clamps. Place the outer portion of the mold in the bench vise. Sand each surface prior to gluing with 180-grit sandpaper, and apply the glue with a roller.

7-21 Cutting laminates as sawn off the plank

7-22 Linings cut on the band saw

Placing the Linings in the Mold

Take the stack of laminates and tape them to the lower bout portion of the mold, making sure just a little hangs over the end at the lower bout. Remove this from the vise, and put the inner portion of the mold in place. The first clamp should be the one at the waist. The mold should be the same thickness as the width of the laminates. This will make it easier to get all the laminates to line up on edge. Apply all the clamps, wipe off any excess glue, and set aside (**7-23** through **7-26**). The linings should remain in the mold for at least four hours.

Once you have all four linings out of the molds, lay them out as they will be on the guitar and mark the edge that will be rounded over. There should be two sets of two linings oriented

7-23 Lining laminations and mold

7-24 Applying glue

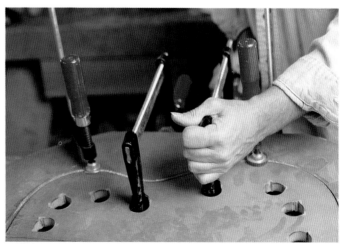

7-25 Clamping

Linings Affect the Sound

The purpose of the linings is to provide a glue surface along the perimeter for gluing the top and the back. Do the linings affect the sound? You bet. In the beginning, I used tantalones, which are individual blocks spaced approximately ⅟₁₆ inches apart, and glued them on with hide glue. Torres' guitars were built this way. The guitars had a big yet unfocused sound. In trying to find a method I was more comfortable with, I laminated some thin strips on a form to make linings. The difference in sound was noticeable. The sound was more focused and sharper. I have been using this method ever since.

7-26 Leave clamped for at least four hours

7-27 Shaping the inner edge

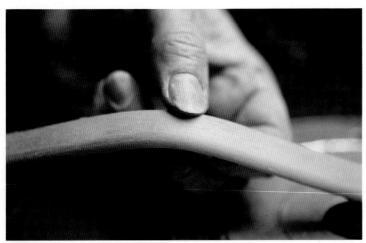

7-28 Lining

opposite to each other. Chisel the excess dried glue off this edge, and plane flat with a small hand plane. In the shaper or router table, insert a ¼-inch round-over bit with a bearing. Raise the bit until the lower edge is just below the surface of the table, so as not to put a bead on the linings. Using push blocks to feed the work to the blade while holding it down on the table, round over the edges on the machine (**7-27** and **7-28**).

Gluing the Linings to the Sides

The linings are now ready to be glued onto the sides. To facilitate the gluing process, I have made a laminated caul to prevent the linings from being dented by the clamps (**7-29**). It is not necessary to have one as fancy as this—an extra laminate will do.

When working alone, holding more than one thing in place while trying to apply clamps can be quite challenging. One way to simplify things is to use double-stick tape to hold the caul to the linings while you are getting the clamps in place. The sides are placed in the side lamination mold when gluing on the linings to facilitate clamping. Apply the glue with a roller and clamp in place. The linings should be slightly proud of the edges of the sides all the way around by approximately ⅟₁₆ inches. Once the clamps are on, set the timer to eight minutes (**7-30** through **7-35**). If the correct amount of glue has been applied, eight minutes is enough time for the squeeze-out to have dried to the point where it will be easy to remove without making a mess. When the time is up, take a chisel and scrape away the excess (**7-36**). The linings should remain in the mold for at least four hours.

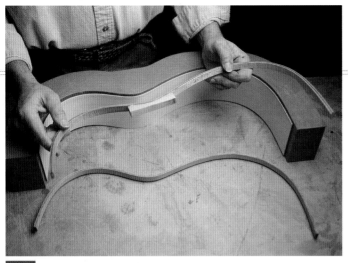

7-29 Laminated caul to prevent denting by clamps

7-30 Applying double-stick tape

7-31 Tape holds the caul to the linings

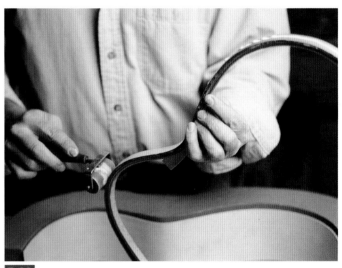

7-32 Applying glue

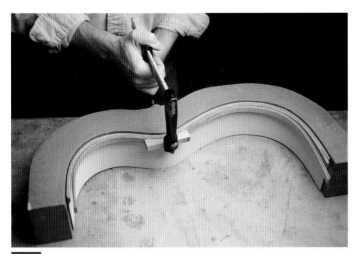

7-33 Clamping caul and lining to mold

7-34 Applying clamps

7-35 Timing eight minutes for squeeze-out

7-36 Chiseling away excess glue

Neck and Side Construction

The traditional Spanish method of construction is where the sides are let into slots in the neck at the heel. From this point on, the neck and sides become one assembly, which may be awkward to work with. This method also determines how certain things are handled, such as the bindings. The last inch or two of the binding channel must be cut by hand, as the router will not cut all the way up to the heel. The alternative method is to make the body and the neck separately, which is becoming more and more popular with builders today. Using this method, the bindings can be cut all the way around, eliminating the need for time-consuming hand tool work, but this is the subject of another book.

ASSEMBLING THE NECK AND SIDES

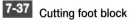
7-37 Cutting foot block

7-38 Planing foot block

The foot block is a piece of mahogany 3 inches wide and 12 mm thick. It is used to hold the sides together at the butt of the instrument. Measure the height needed and cut to length (**7-37**). The surface of the foot block that will be glued to the sides needs to be planed to conform to the shape at the butt of the instrument (**7-38** and **7-39**). Place the sides in the solera with the rims installed, and mark on the linings the edges of the foot block (**7-40**). This portion of the linings must be removed so that the foot block rests firmly against the sides at the butt. Cut along the line on the linings, and remove the lining material inside the cut with a chisel; then scrape the surface clean (**7-41** through **7-43**). The outer edges of the foot block are beveled with a hand plane (**7-44**). Place the sides back in the solera and fit the foot block, making any necessary adjustments (**7-45**).

7-39 Foot block shaped to conform to bottom

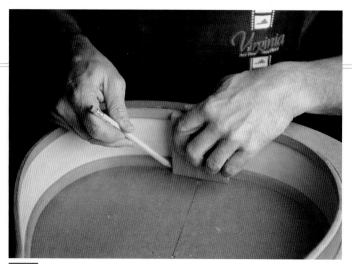

7-40 Marking edges of foot block on linings

7-41 Cutting along the line on the linings

7-42 Removing material inside cut with chisel

7-43 Scraping the surface clean

7-44 Beveling foot block with hand plane

7-45 Fitting the foot block

7-46 Measuring slot in neck

7-47 Setting angle of slot with bevel gauge

7-48 Using bevel gauge to draw angle

The slot in the neck at the top is 18 mm out from the centerline on each side of the top of the heel block (**7-46**). With a bevel gauge, set the angle of the slot on the neck (**7-47**). Make a mark on both top linings 18 mm in from the centerline at the upper bout. Using the bevel gauge, draw this angle from the 18-mm mark on the top lining to the back edge of the bottom lining (**7-48**). Cut down to the inside laminate with a thin-blade handsaw along these lines, and chisel away the linings (**7-49** and **7-50**). Fit the sides into the slots so that they go in without having to be forced (**7-51**). If they are too loose, thin veneer can be glued to the laminate to make up the difference.

7-49 Cutting with thin blade hand saw

7-50 Chiseling away the linings

7-51 Fitting the sides into the slots

7-52 Sanding the inside of the sides

7-53 Sanding the heel block

Finishing the Inside Surfaces

All the parts have now been fitted, and before they are assembled, a finish will be applied to the inside surfaces. Shellac will be applied to the inside of the sides, the heel block, and the foot block before they are glued together. The surfaces should be sanded using up to 320-grit sandpaper (**7-52** through **7-54**). But before the finish is applied, the surfaces that will be glued must be masked off to prevent finish from getting on them (**7-55**). Any finish on the glue surfaces will lessen the effectiveness of the glue.

The method used to apply the shellac to the inside of the guitar is sort of a faux French polishing. The idea is to get enough shellac on as fast as possible and then polish to a nice shine. After sanding the heel block using up to 320-grit sandpaper, apply shellac with a brush, allowing adequate drying time and sanding between coats until there is a sufficient buildup. Sand the final brush application with 600-grit sandpaper, and then polish to a nice shine by French polishing (see Chapter 16). Just a couple of applications will be necessary if enough finish has been brushed on (**7-56** through **7-60**).

7-54 Sanding the foot block

7-55 Masking surfaces that will be glued

7-56 Applying shellac to inside of sides

7-57 Applying shellac to heel block

7-58 Sanding between coats

7-59 Polishing

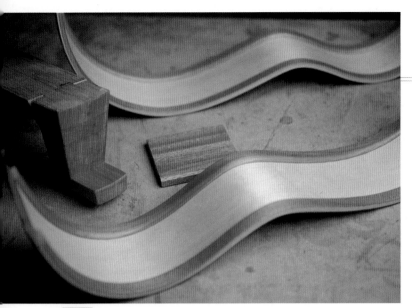

7-60 Finished sides

7-61 Planing linings to level of the sides

7-62 Flattening along the entire length

Preparing the Top Edge of the Sides

The top edge of the sides needs to be flattened at this time in order to have everything lie flat while being glued together. First, with a hand plane, take the linings down to the level of the sides. Then take the side to a flat surface with some 80-grit adhesive sandpaper on it and flatten along the entire length (**7-61** and **7-62**).

Gluing

The foot block and the neck can be glued on at the same time, but if you don't have much experience it may be best to glue them separately. If this is the case, glue the foot block on first. Prepare a caul to protect the sides and provide a rigid support for the clamp. Put some wax paper on the solera, spread the glue on the foot block, and clamp in place (**7-63** and **7-64**).

When the top is glued on, it must be flush with the neck at the heel. In order to make this possible, the sides must be glued on the thickness of the top away from the surface of the neck (**7-65**). To do this, prepare a piece of scrap the thickness of the top with a cutout for the heel block and set it on a flat surface. This will keep the sides at the correct depth when being glued to the neck. Before gluing, fit the sides in the slots as they will be when being glued and coat the sides and heel with wax (**7-66**). This will allow the squeeze-out to be easily removed after it has dried. Apply the glue, fit the sides in the slots, and clamp into place on a flat surface (**7-67** and **7-68**). Set aside and let dry.

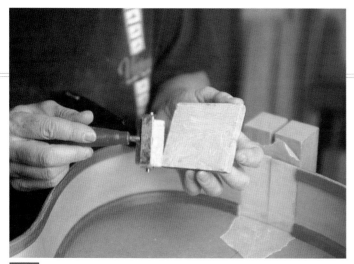

7-63 Spreading glue on foot block

7-64 Clamping foot block in place

7-65 Top edge flush with neck at heel

7-66 Setting up and coating with wax

7-67 Applying the glue

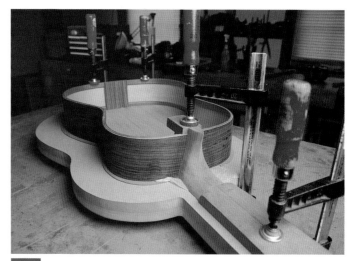

7-68 Clamp and set aside to dry

CHAPTER EIGHT

The Details

Bindings, Purflings, and Back and Butt Strips

The Wheat Motif

Wᴴᴬᵀ ᵂᴵᴸᴸ ᴹᴬᴷᴱ ᴼᴺᴱ ᴳᵁᴵᵀᴬᴿ ꜱᵀᴬᴺᴰ ᴼᵁᵀ ᴬᴳᴬᴵᴺꜱᵀ ᴬᴺᴼᵀᴴᴱᴿ ᴠᴵꜱᵁᴬᴸᴸʏ ᴬᴿᴱ ᵀᴴᴱ ᴰᴱᵀᴬᴵᴸꜱ, ꜱᵁᴄʜ ᴬꜱ ᵀᴴᴱ ᴮᴵᴺᴰᴵᴺᴳꜱ, ᴘᵁᴿꜰᴸᴵᴺᴳꜱ, ᴬᴺᴰ rosette. Traditionally, a wood mosaic had been used almost exclusively in rosette design in one form or another, but recent trends have begun to depart from this. More and more, we are seeing very inventive and highly stylized motifs appearing in the form of a rosette. Guitar builders are using the natural beauty of wood, shell, and even some metals to adorn their rosettes. These materials are sometimes used in combination with a mosaic design. Being particularly fond of the beauty of natural wood, I have always tried to incorporate some in my rosettes.

When creating an identifiable rosette for my guitars, I made choices based on how well the colors of the woods in the rosette went with the color of the top. For instance, opposite and in **8-1**, the wheat motif used on this guitar with a cedar top is black with Alaskan yellow cedar. The cedar darkens considerably after finishing, so the black looks quite striking. The same color scheme used on a guitar with a spruce top would have far too much contrast. The black-and-yellow wheat motif would have made the rosette appear as a black hole against the stark white top. On a guitar with a spruce top, a better choice would be a wheat motif in mahogany and Alaskan yellow cedar. When selecting mahogany for this purpose, only that with the deepest brown color should be considered. The brown goes well with the creamy-white/yellowish color of the spruce.

The same scheme is used again in the purflings and the back and butt strips, to give the design cohesiveness. On a guitar with a cedar top, ebony, Louro Preto, or Indian rosewood are just some of the choices of wood that can be used for the bindings. As long as the wood is hard, it will work well for bindings. On guitars with spruce tops, I have been using Louro Preto for bindings. This wood was selected for its subtle color and its beautiful medullary rays, or silk. It matches up well with both the Indian rosewood and the spruce.

BINDINGS, PURFLINGS, AND BACK AND BUTT STRIPS

8-1 Wheat motif on cedar top

THE PURFLINGS FOR the bindings and the back and butt strips can be made up ahead of time. Two sheets of purflings are necessary, one bent laminated on the side mold and one laminated flat. The flat sheet will be used as purfling, which will be glued to the bottom edge of the bindings before bending, and on each side of the back and butt strips. Both laminations call for a stack as follows:

- 0.015-inch Alaskan yellow cedar
- 0.020-inch mahogany
- 0.015-inch Alaskan yellow cedar
- 0.020-inch black veneer

The black veneer will always go on the inside and form a border with the Indian rosewood (back) or the western red cedar (top). Begin with the bent sheet laminated on the side mold. In order to end up with four pieces of bent

8-2 Four pieces of purfling material

8-3 Applying glue with roller

8-4 Taping purflings

8-5 Clamping

purflings, a sheet just over an inch wide will be needed. Some builders prefer to install the veneers individually without laminating them first. If it is more comfortable this way for you, by all means do it. I find it easier to deal with only one piece rather than four while trying to glue the purflings into the channel. Laminating the purflings is also a time-saver if you are building more than one instrument.

Purflings

Cut four pieces of purfling material approximately 1 inch wide and 32 inches long. These will be glued on the side mold used to laminate the sides. The bent purflings go inside the bindings, so use one of the Masonite cauls, which is approximately equivalent to the thickness of the bindings, up against the face of the mold to compensate for the smaller radius needed in making the purflings. Apply the glue with a roller and tape the purflings to one side of one of the cauls, making sure the black veneer is facing up (**8-2**, **8-3**, and **8-4**). Apply the clamps and set aside until the glue cures (**8-5** and **8-6**).

8-6 Leave clamps overnight

8-7 Applying gluing

8-8 Taping stack to caul

8-9 Applying clamps

Next, cut four more pieces of purfling material approximately 1½ inches wide. These pieces will be glued together between two flat pieces of wood used as cauls. It is advisable to cover the faces of the cauls that will touch the purflings with tape to prevent any squeeze-out from sticking to the cauls. Apply the glue with a roller, and tape the stack in place, to keep it from twisting, while applying clamp pressure (**8-7**, **8-8**, and **8-9**). Set aside and let the glue cure (**8-10**).

Once the purflings are ready, set up the band saw to cut strips 0.085 inches wide off the bent sheet. Cut these purflings carefully and slowly, making sure the edge remains against the fence (**8-11**). The sheet will not rest flat on the table near the waist, so proceed with care here. Four sets of bent purflings are required (**8-12**).

Bindings

Bindings can be purchased as such from a luthier supply house, cut from the side stock before thicknessing, or they can be cut from a piece of stock that is at least 32 inches long. If cutting the bindings from larger stock, cut a piece 0.225 inch high and thickness to 0.200 inches with a hand plane or in a planer. At this point, there is the option of gluing the piece of binding stock to the sheet of purflings and then cutting each binding off or cutting the bindings and purflings off individually and then gluing them.

To prepare the bindings individually, set up the band saw to cut the sheet of straight purflings (**8-13**). The bindings will be approximately

8-10 Allow glue to cure overnight

8-11 Cutting strips with band saw

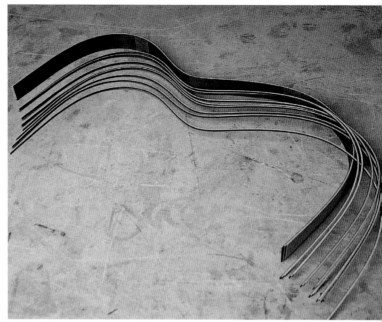

8-12 Four sets of bent purflings

8-13 Cutting bindings with band saw

0.100 inches thick and 0.200 inches high; therefore, it will be necessary to cut strips of purfling about 0.120 inches wide and 32 inches long. Two additional cuts 0.170 inches wide will be enough for the back and butt strip. Also, cut five pieces of wood for the binding back and butt strip approximately 0.115 inches thick and plane smooth to a thickness of about 0.105 inches. Plans for the back and butt strip are shown in **8-14**.

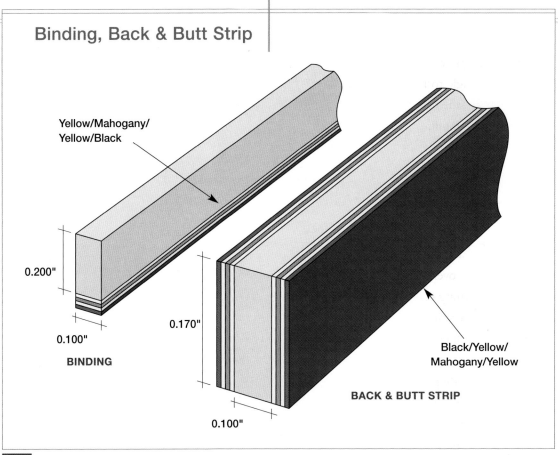

Binding, Back & Butt Strip

Yellow/Mahogany/
Yellow/Black

0.200"

0.100"

BINDING

0.170"

0.100"

Black/Yellow/
Mahogany/Yellow

BACK & BUTT STRIP

8-14

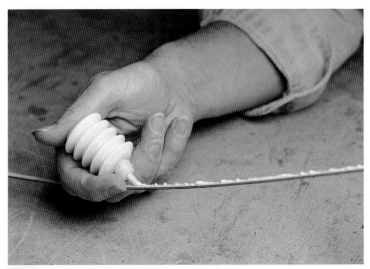

8-15 Applying glue to purfling

The four straight purflings must be glued to the bottom edge of the bindings. First, prepare a piece of wood to be used as a caul approximately ½ inch square and 34 inches long, and get about twelve small hand clamps ready. Apply the glue and mate the purfling to the binding, making sure that some purfling is hanging over each side of the binding (**8-15** and **8-16**). Push one against the other back and forth a little to ensure a good seal with the glue. Apply the hand clamps to the top edge of the binding, starting at the middle with the purfling resting on the caul (**8-17**).

The clamps will work best if put on at a 45-degree angle to the binding. Alternate the clamps from side to side as you go down the length of the binding. After the glue is cured, remove the clamps and clean up the excess purflings on each side of the binding with a hand plane, coming very close to the surface of the binding, and then trim the rest of the way with a scraper. It is a good idea to wait until the glue cures before attempting to bend the bindings; letting it cure overnight is best. Lastly, cut two pieces of purfling 0.170 inches wide for the back and butt strip. Glue these to the faces of the extra binding cut previously the same way as the bindings.

Before bending, the bindings must be brought to final thickness (0.100 inches) with a hand plane, because they are too thin to be put through a planer. The best way to do this is to plane two at a time on the shooting board with the bindings side by side, rough side up, about ½ inch apart (**8-18**). It will be easier to plane them flat this way. Planing them one at a time, it is easier to tilt the plane to one side or the other, which will result in a face that is not parallel to the opposite one. Thickness them to 0.100 inches; the extra thickness can be removed after the bindings are installed. The extra thickness is to make up for any irregularities in the binding channel and to remove any burn marks created by the binding iron.

On the bending iron, bend the purflings beginning at the waist (**8-19**). Using the ½-inch-thick half template of the top as a guide, bend the bindings with the purflings along the bottom edge to shape, making sure that in the end there are two oriented properly for each side (**8-20**).

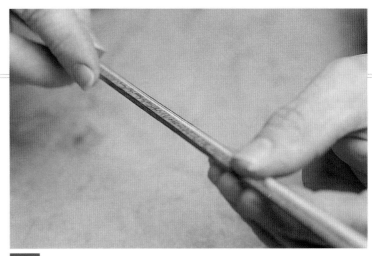
8-16 Mating purfling to binding

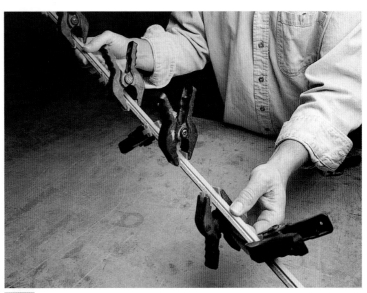
8-17 Clamping purfling to binding

8-18 Planing on shooting board

8-19 Bending the purflings on bending iron

Back Strip and Butt Strip

The back strip and butt strip can be constructed out of the remaining two 0.170-inch pieces of purfling and the fifth binding cut previously that is 0.200 inch × 0.100 inch × 32 inches. Plane the height down to 0.170 inches. The easiest way to do this is to take a piece of scrap material at least 32 inches long and put a kerf in it on the table saw that is 0.170 inches deep and at least 32 inches long. Stand the piece up in the kerf, and hand-plane down to the surface. Once this piece has been sized, glue the two remaining pieces of 0.170-inches-high purfling to each side face. These pieces are easiest to glue up on the gluing fixture shown in **8-21**. This will be used again to make the wheat motif, discussed in the next section.

Apply glue to each surface of the center material, and mate the purflings to each side (**8-22**, **8-23**, and **8-24**). Lay the back strip on the fixture as it will look on the guitar. Cut a piece of wood 0.170 inches high and wide enough to hang over the edge of the fixture to get a clamp on with the back strip and purflings in place. Secure with five or six large hand clamps (**8-25** and **8-26**). The 32-inch-long piece will be enough for a back strip and a butt strip, with a couple of extras if necessary.

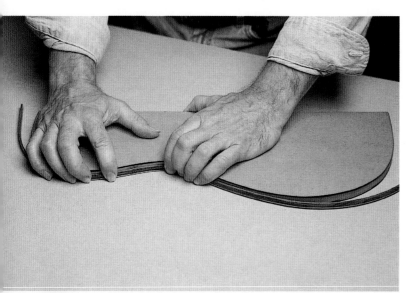

8-20 Bending to shape using half template

Gluing Fixture

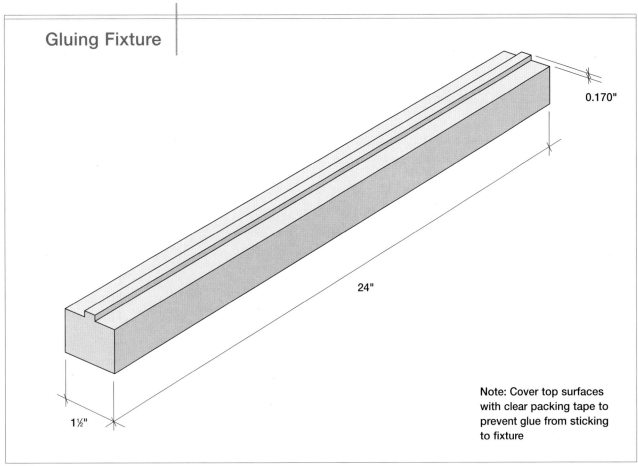

0.170"

24"

1½"

Note: Cover top surfaces with clear packing tape to prevent glue from sticking to fixture

8-21

8-22 Applying glue

8-23 Mating purflings

8-24 Mating purflings to each side

8-25 Clamping

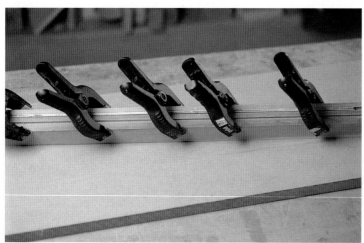

8-26 Clamped purflings

THE WHEAT MOTIF

CREATING THE WHEAT motif will take some time, but the result is well worth the effort. The wheat motif created for this instrument is made of black and maple veneer. The black is 0.020 inches thick and the maple is 0.010 inches thick, and they can be purchased at these dimensions. The same dimensions can be used for a brown-and-yellow motif; just substitute mahogany for the black veneer.

To make the wheat design, 1-inch-wide strips of veneer are glued one on top of the other in a regular pattern of black and maple, creating a stack. The stack is cut into equal pieces on a 12-degree angle. The pieces are then glued back together on the bias. Slicing off the face of this new stick will yield a piece with a herringbone pattern. The pieces are then cut from this piece in sequence and glued together in the form of a chevron with a piece of yellow in between and a piece of black on each outside face, creating the wheat motif (**8-27** and **8-28**).

For one instrument, the initial stack does not have to be very high. The stack shown in the photos is approximately 35 mm high and will be used for multiple instruments, therefore only six pieces are needed to create the necessary length stick. For one instrument, the stack needs to be only about 10 mm high.

Pieces of the Wheat Motif

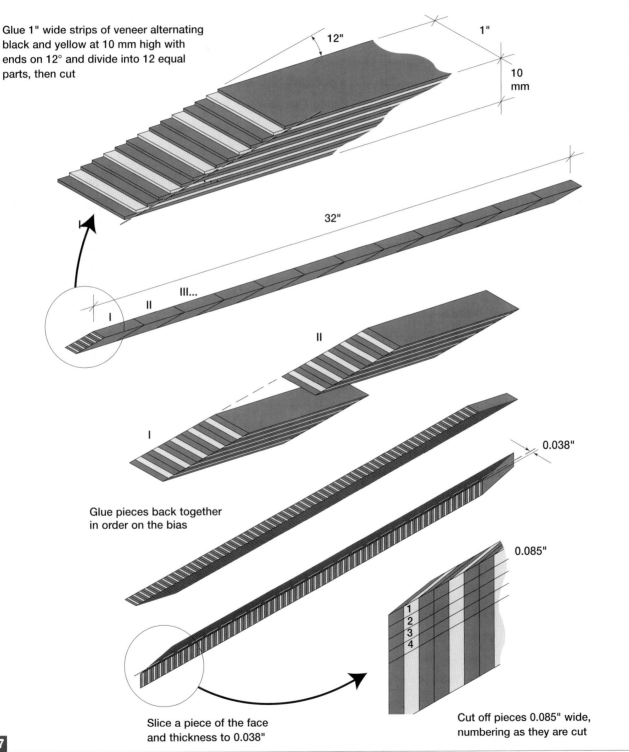

Glue 1" wide strips of veneer alternating black and yellow at 10 mm high with ends on 12° and divide into 12 equal parts, then cut

12"

1"

10 mm

32"

III...

II

I

II

I

Glue pieces back together in order on the bias

0.038"

0.085"

1
2
3
4

Slice a piece of the face and thickness to 0.038"

Cut off pieces 0.085" wide, numbering as they are cut

8-27

Cutting the Back and Sides

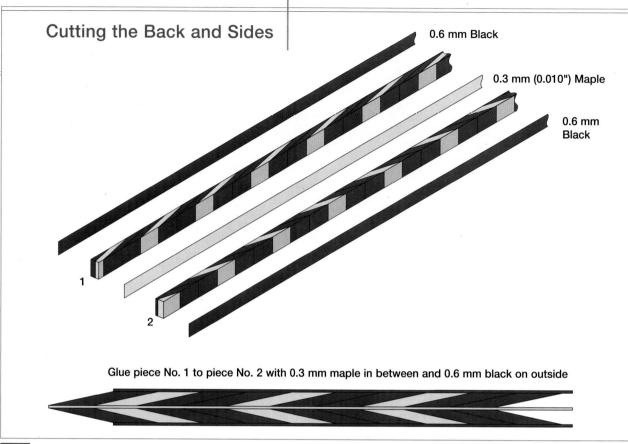

0.6 mm Black

0.3 mm (0.010") Maple

0.6 mm Black

1

2

Glue piece No. 1 to piece No. 2 with 0.3 mm maple in between and 0.6 mm black on outside

8-28

Wheat Stick Gluing Fixture

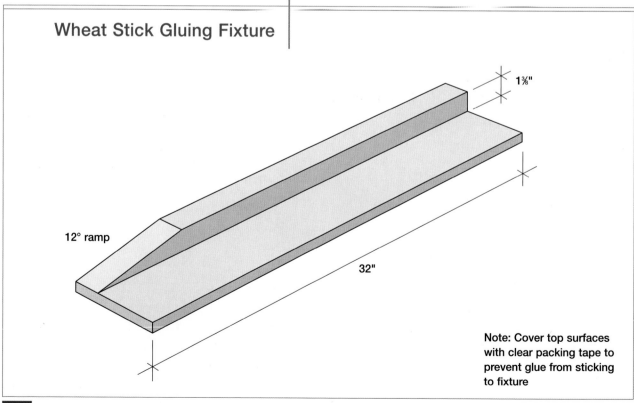

1⅜"

12° ramp

32"

Note: Cover top surfaces with clear packing tape to prevent glue from sticking to fixture

8-29

Strips of veneer

Making the Stack

The stack is formed by gluing two black veneers between each maple veneer, except at the top and the bottom. Since, after cutting the stack, the pieces are glued together at the top and bottom, there should be only one piece of black veneer on the top and bottom surfaces.

Cut enough 1-inch-wide strips of veneer to create a stack approximately 10 mm high. Begin to glue the veneers one on top of the other on the fixture shown in **8-29**, with one black veneer on the bottom, followed by a maple, then two black veneers, then a maple, then two black veneers, and so on, making sure to end up with one black veneer on top. Use yellow PVA glue, and be sure to follow the 12-degree ramp of the fixture with the ends of the stack as you go, and glue only a few strips at once (**8-30** through **8-36**). Do not try to glue the entire stack at one time, because the glue dries too fast and this will lead to problems.

8-31 Applying glue

8-32 Gluing strips of veneer

8-33 Clamping strips of veneer

8-34 Gluing more strips

8-35 Applying glue

8-36 Clamped strips of veneer

Cutting the Stick

The stick will now be divided into equal parts to be cut at a 12-degree angle. The stick in the photos is 35 mm high (**8-37**), so in this case only five pieces are necessary. If the stick is 10 mm high, twelve equal pieces will be required to make a stick long enough to cover the circumference of the rosette. First, divide the stick and number the pieces (**8-38** through **8-40**). The pieces will be cut using a jig (**8-41**). Make the jig out of a piece of plywood or scrap about ¾ inch thick. The ramp of the jig should be approximately 12 degrees. The exact angle is not important; the most important thing is that all the pieces get cut at the same angle and perpendicular to the top surface.

Prepare two pieces of scrap wood about the same cross-sectional size as the stack and approximately 6 to 8 inches long, and cut one end of each with the jig to create the 12-degree ramp (**8-42**, **8-43**, and **8-44**). These will be glued to the

8-37 Glued-up stick

8-38 Dividing stick

8-39 Marking the 12-degree angle

8-40 Numbering the pieces

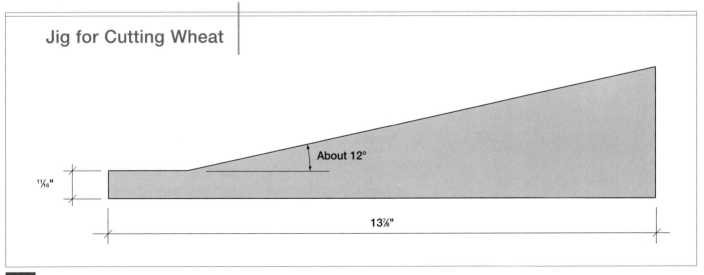

Jig for Cutting Wheat

About 12°

11/16"

137/8"

8-41

8-42 Creating the 12-degree ramp jig

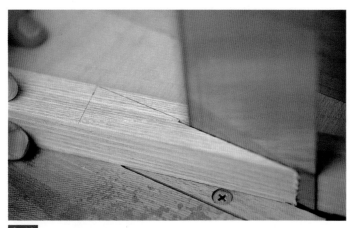

8-43 Using the jig with scrap wood

8-44 The 12-degree ramp on scrap wood

ends of the wheat stick to eliminate wasting any of the length while slicing off thin sheets on the band saw. Then plane the stripped edges of the stack smooth and perpendicular to the top and bottom surfaces. Mill the two end pieces to the same cross-sectional size as the stack.

The stick is then cut on the band saw into equal pieces, using the jig to create the 12-degree ramp on each end (**8-46** through **8-47**). Plane the surface of the bias flat **8-48**. An indication of flatness is when the maple resembles the rungs of a ladder with all the rungs parallel. The top and bottom surfaces should be perpendicular to the stripped faces **8-49**. Plane the stripped faces to achieve this (**8-48** and **8-49**). It may be necessary to plane a bit on the top and bottom surfaces to get everything perpendicular. If so, be sure to remove very little material from these surfaces, as any irregularity in thickness here will show in the final product. Plane the bias surface of the scrap the same way.

8-45 Using the jig

8-46 Number pieces as they are cut

8-47 All the pieces with scrap wood at each end

8-48 Planing the striped faces

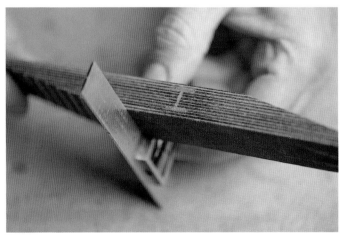

8-49 Surfaces perpendicular to the faces

Fitting the Pieces

Using the same fixture employed to glue the stack, line up all the pieces of the stack, with the stripes facing up and the biased surface against the stop block, in numeric order with a scrap piece at either end. The pieces should line up against the stop block rather flat without gaps using only hand pressure. Once a good fit is established, glue in place (**8-50** through **8-55**).

Once the glue is cured, flatten the surface that was up against the stop block with a hand plane, making sure the stripes remain parallel. Set the band saw fence at approximately 0.060 inches, and slice a piece off the face of the new stick (**8-56**). In order to slice the wheat stick safely and to avoid variations in thickness, use a fingered hold-

8-50 Applying glue to jig piece

8-51 Clamping first piece of stack

down clamped to the surface of the band saw so that the wheat stick is pushed against the fence while being cut. When cutting, make sure the angled stripes are facing up. Plane the surface of the stick flat, and cut another piece to be certain there is enough material for some practice and the actual rosette. Thickness the sheets with a hand plane, making sure to plane in the direction of the angles lying down so that they won't be pulled up as they are planed (**8-57**). Make an identifying mark across the scrap end of each sheet to orient them after they are cut (**8-58**). Cut pieces about 0.085 inch wide, and number each one as it comes off the saw (**8-59** and **8-60**). From two sheets, there should be more than enough for the rosette and a few practice sessions.

Gluing the Wheat

All that is left to do is to glue the pieces together (**8-61**). Taking pieces 1 and 2, orient them so that they form a series of chevrons along their entire length. A piece of maple is glued in between them as a middle stripe, and a piece of black veneer is glued to each outside edge. Glue the remainder of the adjacent pieces together along with the maple and black veneer on the fixture as above to create enough material for the project. The wheat is now ready to be bent for installation in the rosette (**8-62**).

8-52 Applying glue to next piece

8-53 Clamping pieces in order

8-54 Pieces glued and clamped in order

8-55 New stick

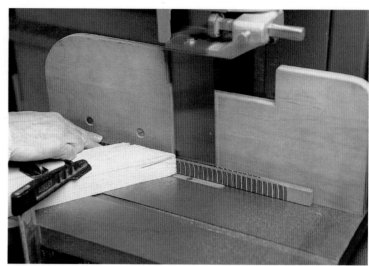

8-56 Slicing piece face of new stick

8-57 Hand planing the sheets

8-58 Marking scrap end of each sheet

8-59 Cutting pieces

8-60 Number each as it comes off the saw

8-61 Gluing pieces together

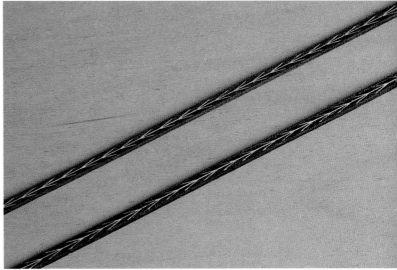

8-62 Finished wheat strips

CHAPTER NINE

The Top

Selecting a Top
Jointing and
  Thicknessing
The Rosette
Bracing and Patches

THE WOOD USED FOR SOUNDBOARDS, OR TOPS, IS MOSTLY OLD-GROWTH TIMBER. AND, AS WITH THE REST OF THE WOODS USED IN guitar making, the wood for good soundboards is becoming harder and harder to find. Sadly, our forests are shrinking at an alarming rate. Substitute woods are being introduced all the time to make up for the lack. Therefore, we must be careful with what little materials we have and use them well.

Without a doubt, the top is the most important element in sound production on the guitar. More myth and mystery surround the soundboard than any other part of the instrument. Every builder has his or her own criteria as to what makes a good-sounding top, and this is as it should be. Sound is subjective to a degree; therefore, everyone will have a slightly different concept of the ideal sound.

It is very important as a builder to find your own sound. You first need to have a good idea of what that sound is. Then you need to strive to attain it by finding a way to convey that sound through the design and materials. If you are sensitive to the materials, and only change them a little bit each time, experience will be your guide in finding and creating your own sound.

When selecting the wood for the soundboard for my first guitar, I was able to find a top-quality piece of cedar with a negligible blemish and for a great price. Experience with furniture making had left me with some strong impressions regarding wood. I always loved the look of quartersawn wood. I preferred it to almost any wildly figured wood. The calming straight-grain lines are enhanced to new levels with the presence of some silk. The piece I had found for the top on my first guitar sounded good when tapped and was covered with silk. I had no prior knowledge upon which to base my decision other than it made a nice musical sound when struck and it looked great, so I bought it. As luck would have it, this cedar made a great-sounding instrument. That first guitar literally changed my life and propelled me into guitar making. I had customers before I knew it. I got lucky the first time out, and it was a while before I would surpass the sound of that first instrument. But that was just the beginning of the journey for me. Every guitar since then has been part of a quest for that ultimate sound. With every guitar, I would try something new, at the same time building on the things that worked and leaving behind the things that didn't. It is still exciting to dip into a new batch of tops for the first time.

Neatness Counts

To make the best guitar possible, it is important to work cleanly. This is especially true when putting together a top; neatness counts here. To create an instrument with a refined sound, you must work in a refined manner. If you have never made a guitar before, be warned: soundboards are made of soft woods that are easily damaged. Care must be taken at all times in order not to mar the surface. A fingernail can easily leave a mark that may be too deep to sand out without making the top too thin, so be careful and enjoy your work.

SELECTING A TOP

THERE ARE TWO MAIN CRITERIA for selecting a top: tone-production potential and visual properties. The visual properties are subjective. Some builders will tolerate more variations in coloration, tightness of grain, and blemishes than others. This is not to say these builders are constructing inferior guitars. The properties necessary for sound-production potential generally have nothing to do with visual properties, except in the case of medullary rays, or silk. The presence of medullary rays indicates that the wood is perfectly quartersawn. This will increase its stability and its

stiffness. Although there is no substitute for experience in selecting tops, it will help to understand a few of the characteristics sought after to maximize sound-production potential.

In order for the top on nylon-string guitars to create enough quality sound, it must be thin. It must also be structurally sound. Stiffness and density are important both structurally and for sound production. All my tops are weighed and given a crude stiffness test so that I can get some relative idea as to where each one is on a continuum. A stiffer and more dense top may be thinned a bit more than one that is less stiff and dense. Stiffness should be checked both laterally and longitudinally; the general rule of thumb is the stiffer the better. There is a limit as far as density goes, but generally I try to avoid tops that are noticeably on the light side. For your first instrument, elaborate measurements will not be needed. It would be a good idea to go to the supply house to select a top; this way, comparisons can be made between one top and another as to stiffness and density. Poking through a pile of tops, it is immediately noticeable how they are all so different. Visually inspect each one, looking for silk and flex in both directions. Make your initial determination using your most valuable measuring device, your senses.

It is debatable as to whether or not the tap tone is any indication of sound potential, but I always look for a clear musical tone that sustains. A dull thud simply won't do. Top wood is usually about ³⁄₁₆ inch thick when purchased. Wood this thick will usually produce some type of tone. As the wood is thinned, the pitch and character of the tap tone will change, usually not for the better. It is important to be aware of this when selecting wood, because the thickness may vary even in the same batch.

Top wood is graded by the seller. Master grade is the best grade. This generally will yield the best-sounding tops, but if you take the time and sensitively inspect the other grades no doubt you may find some bargains. Use the best wood you can afford, even for your first instrument. It is very difficult if not impossible to make an inferior piece of wood sound great.

9-1 Flattening the two halves

Jointing Two Pieces

When jointing two halves by planing on the shooting board, be sure to alternate the faces on each one; plane one face up and the other face-down. This will compensate for the blade being not quite perpendicular. The joint must be a perfect fit all along its length with no pressure. If the plane is tearing out along the edge, it may be necessary to use sandpaper glued to a straight, stable piece of wood.

JOINTING AND THICKNESSING

9-2 Marking a cabinetmaker's triangle

BEFORE JOINTING THE TWO halves of the top, flatten each half, removing as little material as possible; take off just enough to make it flat (**9-1**). The thinner they are, the more difficult it will be to joint them. Flatten with either a hand plane or a drum sander. I don't recommend thicknessing any plate wood in a planer. It is too expensive and rare to risk ruining. Once both halves will lie flat, orient them the way they will go together, and mark with a cabinetmaker's triangle on the top face (**9-2**). This mark will act as a reminder for both the orientation and which face is the top. Straighten the edge to be joined by first scoring a line parallel to the grain and cutting along the line on the band saw (**9-3**).

The book-matched pair can be cut together by folding the two back along the center seam and securing with double-stick tape (**9-4**). Once they are cut, pull them apart, remove the tape, and plane straight the edges on the shooting board (**9-5**). Hold the two together and up to the light to check for any gaps. The joint must be a perfect fit all along its length with no pressure. If the plane is tearing out along the edge, it may be necessary

9-3 Scoring a line parallel to the grain

9-4 Folding back along center seam

to use sandpaper. In this case, first plane one edge of a stable piece of wood perpendicular to the face. The piece will work best if it is as long as the top. Make sure it is straight along this edge with a straight edge held up to the light. Once straight, glue sandpaper to the edge. Use this to joint the edges on the shooting board just as with the plane (**9-6**).

Gluing the Two Halves

If the two halves can be held together up to the light with no light shining through, they are ready to be glued. I use a simple fixture to assist in gluing up plates (**9-7**). It is just a piece of ½-inch plywood with a cleat on one edge. This cleat is secured with screws, and its inner edge is used as a

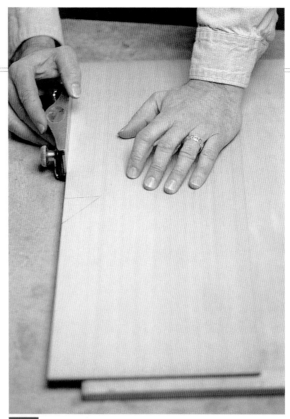

9-5 Planing the edge on the shooting board

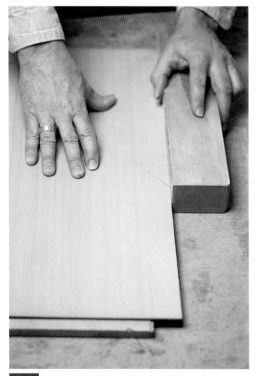

9-6 Jointing with sandpaper

9-7 Fixture used to glue halves

9-8 Spreading glue along entire edge

9-9 With top in fixture, tap wedges gently to tighten seam

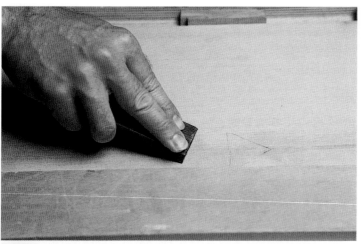

9-10 Drag wood along seam to flatten and remove excess glue

wall to put the wedges against when gluing. For a typical plate, three sets of wedges are used. Another piece of plywood 3 inches wide or so and as long as the fixture is needed to clamp over one of the pieces to be glued. By not securing the second cleat, the fixture can be used for any number of sizes of plates.

Before gluing, cover the fixture with wax paper to prevent the top from being glued to it. Perform a dry run, clamping and wedging everything in place. Leave the clamp and remove the wedges. On the free half, spread glue along the entire edge, making sure the glue is evenly distributed and covers the entire surface of the edge (**9-8**). Put in place on the fixture and tap the wedges in gently (**9-9**). Not much force is needed if the joint has been fitted properly. Using a hard piece of wood with a squared clean edge, press the edge over the joint, and drag it along the seam (**9-10**). This will push each half flush to the fixture while removing any squeeze-out. To prevent the uncovered half from rising up, I usually place something heavy on top of that half (**9-11**).

Set aside to let the glue cure. I may take the top out of the fixture in a couple of hours, but I always wait until the next day to do any further work on it.

Using the Template to Cut the Top

On the top face, draw the centerline on the seam with a sharp pencil. Place the clear template on the top so that the centerline of the template is directly over the centerline of the top and positioned lengthwise as desired. Clamp in place and drill the ³⁄₃₂-inch registration holes, using a backing

9-11 One half is clamped; weight on the other half keeps it flat

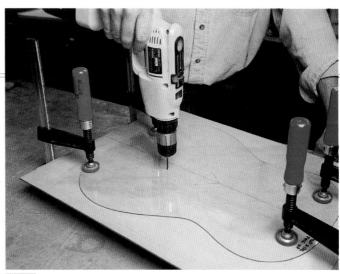

9-12 Using template to trace outline and drill registration holes

9-13 Cutting outline with band saw

9-14 Planing the top

board so as not to tear out the inside face (**9-12**). Without removing the clamps, trace the outline of the top on the wood. Remove the clamps and cut out the outline on the band saw (**9-13**).

Initial Thicknessing of the Top

The top should now be thicknessed to approximately 0.130 inch. This is not the final thickness; after the rosette is installed, the top will be thicknessed to its final dimension. After installing the rosette, flatten the side with the rosette then thickness the other side using either a drum sander or a hand plane. If you are using a hand plane, clamp the top to the gluing fixture, employing the fixed cleat as a stop, and plane either across the grain or diagonally to it (**9-14**). Make sure that the plane blade is sharp. Remove wood from one half and then the other. Flip the piece around and plane the same way on the other side. Stop when within 0.005 inch of the desired thickness, and smooth the surface with a palm sander.

THE ROSETTE

9-15 Measuring center of sound hole

9-16 Drilling hole for dowel

TRADITIONALLY, ROSETTES HAVE been mosaics composed of tiny pieces of end-grained colored wood laid out in repeating patterns around the sound hole. Lately builders have been departing from this model a bit and trying different designs with different techniques with amazing results. The elements used in the rosette for this guitar are nothing new. The wheat motif has been around at least since Torres, and many builders use natural wood in one form or another in their rosettes. The selection and arrangement of the elements are its identifying mark. This rosette combines the wheat motif with a natural-wood center ring. The center ring in this case is from spalted maple, cut into sheets approximately 0.080 inches thick.

The rosette is built a piece at a time into the top, starting at the outer edge and working in toward the sound hole. The channels are cut with a router and the circle-cutting attachment (see Chapter 3). End mill bits work well in this application—when sharp, they will leave a clean edge. These bits are available at some industrial supply companies (refer to the listing on my Web site, given on pages iv and 310) in the small sizes required for this application and are relatively inexpensive.

Using the Router Attachment

The router and attachment rotate on a ¼-inch steel dowel. A ¼-inch hole is drilled in the top at the center of the sound hole. The center of the sound hole is located by measuring 112 mm plus 41.5 mm (the radius of the sound hole) or 153.5 mm down from the top along the center seam (**9-15**). Mark the spot and drill a ¼-inch hole for the dowel with a Forstner bit (**9-16**).

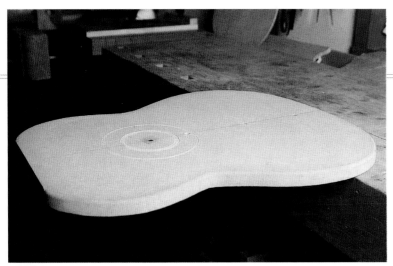

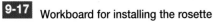
Workboard for installing the rosette

Prebending strips on bending iron

Create a workboard out of a ¾-inch piece of MDF or similar material, with a ¼-inch hole for the shaft and a cleat on the bottom, which is held in the bench vise (**9-17**). The top is mounted on the workboard with two pieces of double-stick tape, one on either side of the rosette area.

Preparing the Veneer

There are two types and sizes of veneer used in making this rosette: 0.6-mm (0.020-inch) black veneer and 0.6-mm or 0.020-inch Alaskan yellow cedar. Cut enough strips of each veneer for the entire rosette. The outer ring will require a length of 17 inches, and the length will decrease as you work in toward the sound hole. Bend all the strips on the bending iron (**9-18**). Bend the strips into an approximate circle; the shape doesn't have to be precise—you just don't want to be fighting the veneer to get it into the channel.

The rosette will be constructed in stages, beginning with the outer ring, which comprises three pieces of black veneer 0.020 inch thick and cut to a height of approximately 0.080 inch. The three pieces of black veneer will fit into a channel cut with a ¹⁄₁₆-inch bit. The depth of the rosette should be about 0.055 inch. See **9-19** for the sequencing of the elements.

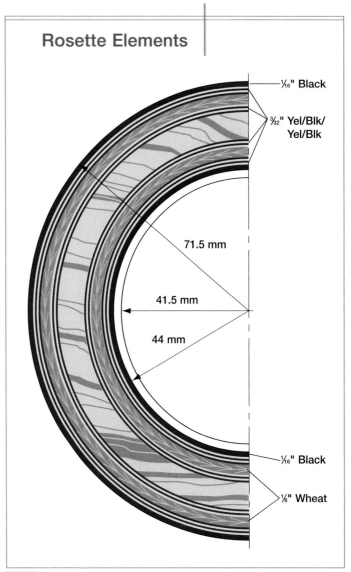

Rosette Elements

¹⁄₁₆" Black

³⁄₃₂" Yel/Blk/ Yel/Blk

71.5 mm

41.5 mm

44 mm

¹⁄₁₆" Black

⅛" Wheat

9-19

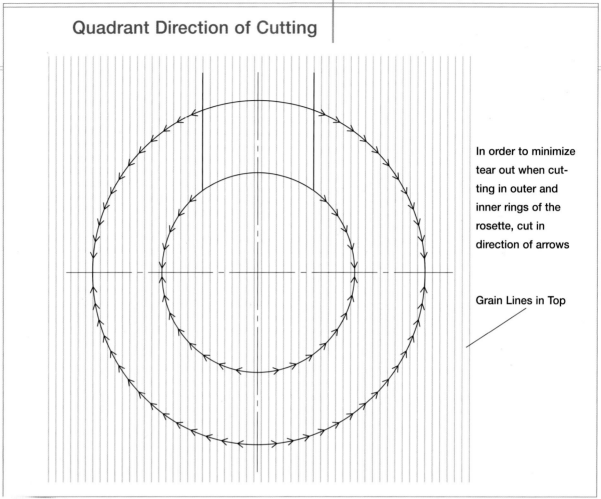

Quadrant Direction of Cutting

In order to minimize tear out when cutting in outer and inner rings of the rosette, cut in direction of arrows

Grain Lines in Top

9-20

Routing Channels and Gluing Veneer Strips

When routing out the channel, refer to **9-20** for the direction of cut to avoid tearing out along the outer edges. Carefully lower the router to the surface of the top near the center seam at the bottom of the rosette to begin the cut. The lower half of the circle can be cut without removing the router. Turn off the router and lower it to the surface again, starting at the uppermost corner under the fingerboard, and cut down to meet the cut on each side. Fit the three veneers in the channel. If the fit is too snug, sand a bit off the face of one or more of the pieces until a good fit is achieved. Remember, when the glue is applied, the veneer will swell a bit, so don't make it too

snug. Once the veneers are glued in the channel, trim flat with a plane, letting them protrude a bit; cover with wax paper; and clamp with a caul (**9-21** through **9-24**).

The glue needs to dry for only about twenty minutes before cutting the next channel, but before routing you will need to trim the outer ring flush with the surface of the top with a hand plane (**9-25**). The next installation will be for the yellow/black/yellow/black combination. Rout out a channel up against the outer black ring with a ³⁄₃₂-inch bit. The four pieces should fit in this channel without much fuss—if they don't, thin as above. Glue in the channel and trim flush after the glue has set up, as done previously (**9-26** through **9-28**).

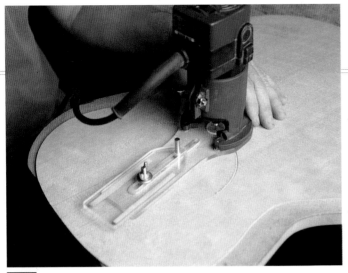

9-21 Cutting channel with router

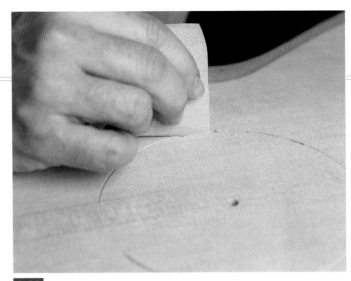

9-22 Clean edges of channel with sandpaper

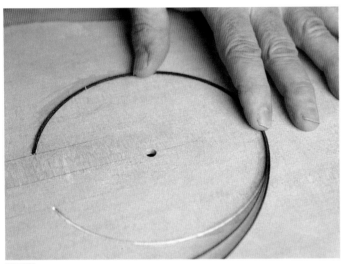

9-23 Gluing the three veneers into channel

9-24 Clamping with a caul

9-25 Trimming outer rim

9-26 Routing the next channel

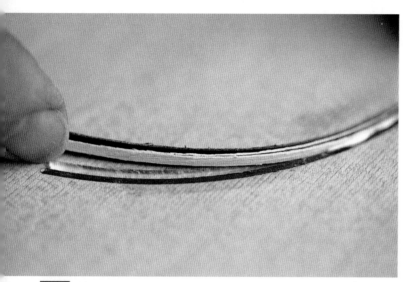

9-27 Gluing four pieces in this channel

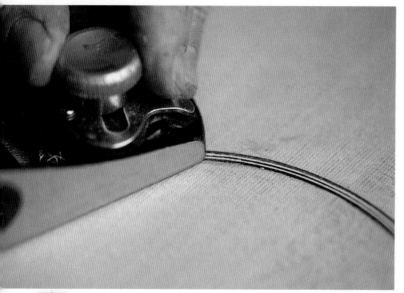

9-28 Trimming flush with hand plane

The First Wheat Strip

The wheat motif is next. The wheat strip has been made to a thickness of 0.125 inch, so the channel can be routed with a ⅛-inch bit. On a scrap piece of MDF or similar material, cut a circular channel with a radius equal to the one you are about to cut for the wheat. Make it a bit wider than ⅛ inches, because the wheat must fit in easily without a struggle. Bend the wheat strip on the bending iron a little at a time, fitting it into the channel in the scrap piece as you go (**9-29** and **9-30**). Fit the entire strip into the channel on the scrap piece. If you intend to have the points of the wheat meet on the centerline, find an appropriate spot to cut the strip and mark (**9-31**). Do not cut right to the point of the arrow; leave some material and trim it away as you fit the two halves together (**9-32**).

Rout the 0.125-inch channel in the top adjacent to the previous installation (**9-33**). The points of the two pieces of wheat meet at the center seam. They must be trimmed so that they fit together nicely. Trimming here should be done with sandpaper glued to a flat piece of stock, because only small amounts of material should be removed at a time without chipping out to create a good fit (**9-34**). Once a good fit has been established, apply the glue and install the first half right up to the centerline (**9-35** and **9-36**). Butt the second piece right up to the first at the center. Plane the pieces flat, leaving them protruding a bit; cover with wax paper; and clamp using a caul. After the glue has set up, plane flush to prepare for the next installation (**9-37**).

The yellow/black/yellow/black combination is installed next to the wheat, as done previously (**9-38** through **9-40**).

9-29 Prebending the wheat strip

9-30 Fitting wheat strip in the scrap piece

9-31 Marking the strip

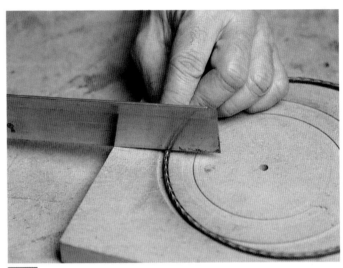

9-32 Allow material to trim off when cutting

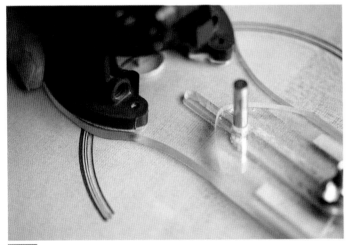

9-33 Routing channel adjacent to previous installation

9-34 Trimming with sandpaper glued to block

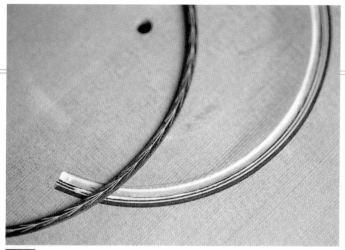

9-35 Applying glue

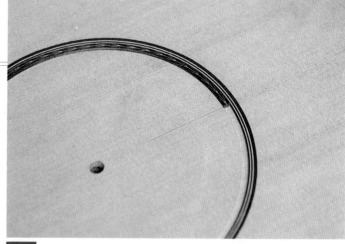

9-36 Installing first half up to center

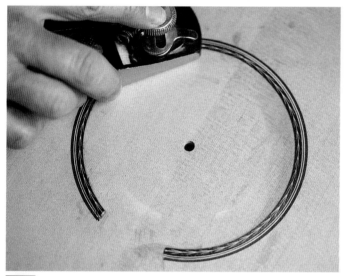

9-37 Planing flush to prepare for next installation

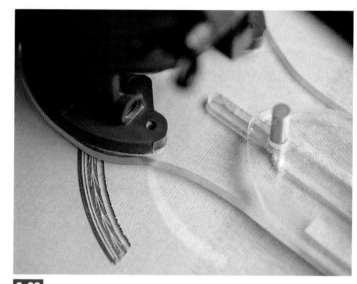

9-38 Routing next channel

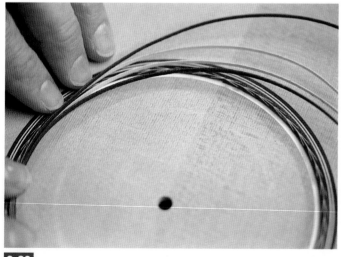

9-39 Gluing yellow/black/yellow/black strips

9-40 Trimming flush with scraper

Creating the Center Ring and Completing the Rosette

There are many ways to create the center ring. This can be done with one piece, as demonstrated here, or it can be composed of any number of pieces. Finding a piece of wood worthy of putting in the center ring may not be easy, and finding a proper color match may make this even harder, but the results are well worth the effort. Whatever wood you choose to use must be sliced into sheets approximately 0.080 inches thick.

If you don't have much experience doing this, try to find a piece that is large enough to cut out the ring in one piece. Using a compass, locate the portion of the piece you intend to use for the center ring and mark it out (**9-41**). Be aware that the ring you cut out initially must be oversized and trimmed to fit. If you have a scroll saw, it could be used to cut out the ring, but a large gouge will also work (**9-42** and **9-43**).

The ring is laid out and cut on a flat board. On a scrap piece of MDF larger than the rosette, mark the centerline and drill a ¼-inch hole in the center (**9-44** through **9-46**). Draw the exact size of the ring on the board, and secure the ring in the correct spot with double-stick tape (**9-47** and **9-48**).

If spalted wood is being used, it is necessary to coat with cyanoacrylate glue to harden the fibers prior to routing (**9-49**). This should be done in a well-ventilated area, because the fumes produced by this glue are harmful and unpleasant. As the router has already been set to the outside diame-

9-41 Marking center ring

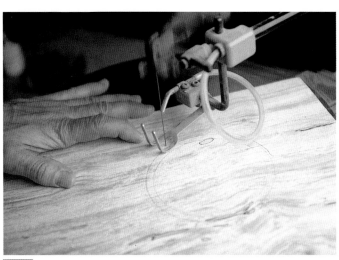
9-42 Cutting out ring oversized

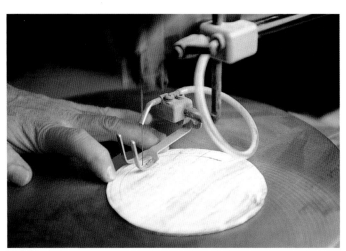
9-43 Cutting out center of ring

9-44 Marking centerlines on scrap MDF

9-45 Marked scrap of MDF

9-46 Drilling the hole for the dowel pin

9-47 Applying double-sided tape

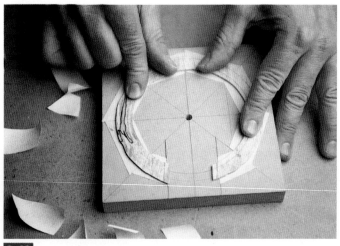

9-48 Securing ring in the correct spot

9-49 Coating with cyanoacrylate glue

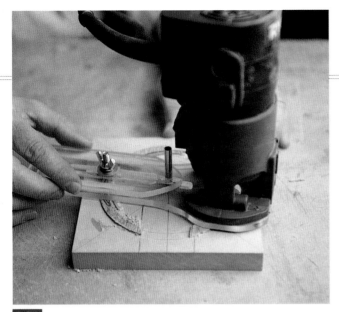

9-50 Trimming outer edge of ring

ter from the previous cut, trim the outer diameter of the ring (**9-50**); then measure the inner diameter and trim with the router (**9-51**). Rout out a channel for the ring in the rosette, being careful not to make it too large—you'll want a snug fit (**9-52**). Glue the ring in place and sand flush (**9-53** and **9-54**).

The remainder of the rosette from the center ring to the inner edge is a repetition of what has already been done (**9-55** through **9-63**).

Cutting the Sound Hole

Once the rosette is completed, and without removing the top from the workboard, measure in approximately 2.5 mm from the inner edge of the rosette and cut out the sound hole with the router (**9-64** and **9-65**). The top can now be removed from the workboard and thicknessed.

9-51 Inner and outer edges trimmed

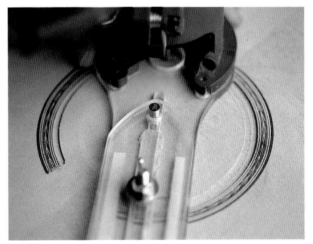

9-52 Routing channel for ring in rosette

9-53 Gluing ring in place

9-54 Sanding ring

9-55 Routing next channel

9-56 Gluing strips

9-57 Planing flush

9-58 Marking next wheat strip

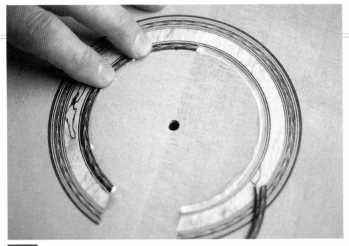

9-59 Gluing wheat strip

9-60 Planing wheat strips flush

9-61 Scraping

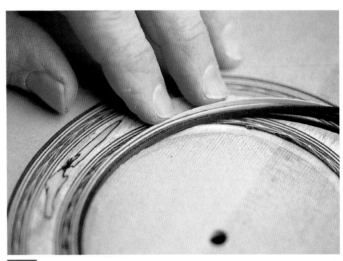

9-62 Installing next strips beside wheat

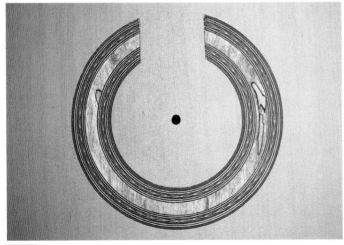

9-63 Completed rosette

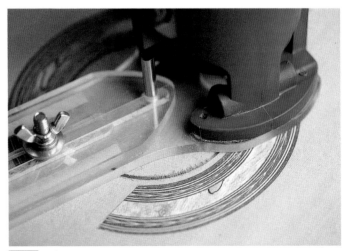

9-64 Cutting sound hole with router

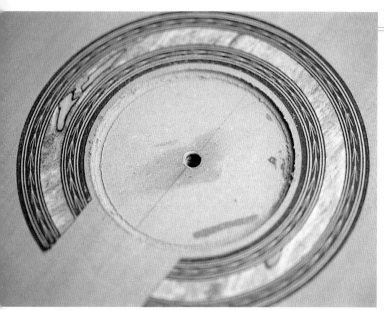

9-65 Cut sound hole

9-66 Planing the top

9-67 Cleaning up plane marks with sander

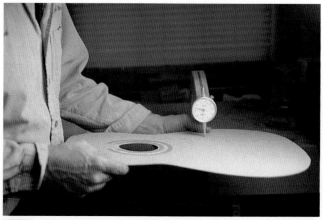

9-68 Checking the thickness of the top

Final Thicknessing of the Top

Take the top to its final thickness with a hand plane, and clean up the plane marks with a sander (**9-66** through **9-68**). The top should be thicknessed to between 0.090 and 0.095 inches, depending on its stiffness and density. It is hard to make this determination without experience, but if you have poked through a pile of tops, you may have some idea of where this stands with regard to stiffness and density. If it is on the stiff and dense side, it can be thinned to 0.090 inches. If you aren't sure, it's best to err on the thick side, especially if you are doing this for the first time.

Some builders, myself included, prefer to leave a little extra material in the area under the bridge, because this area sees most of the stress. This area may be left at 0.100 inches.

BRACING AND PATCHES

THE SOUNDBOARD MUST be able to generate sound by responding to a fairly gentle touch of the player's fingers and nails. The energy from the plucking of the string is transferred to the soundboard through the bridge. The vibration of the string causes the soundboard to respond by flexing. The motion of the soundboard causes the air to move, creating the sound. In order to perform this task and produce enough volume, the soundboard must be thin. It must also be stiff enough to stand up to the tension and stresses the strings exert on it for the entire life of the instrument. Therefore, the soundboard must be braced to add structural integrity.

The bracing system must add enough stiffness while not inhibiting the soundboard from responding. There are almost as many bracing systems as there are luthiers. A successful bracing system walks a fine line between responsiveness and structural integrity. The bracing system used here is a seven-fan asymmetrical bracing system. It is also not new. Many variations of this system have been used with success for years. Still, I encourage you to research the different bracing systems used by various luthiers to find one that appeals most to you.

Grain and Wood

All the braces and patches on this guitar are made of Sitka spruce. European spruce can also be used if preferred. Brace wood is sold in billets (**9-69**) that have been split to eliminate run-out. The split face is planed flat, and all the patches and braces are cut from this surface (**9-70**). The braces and patches always have the grain lines running perpendicular to the surface of the top (**9-71**). One billet of split brace wood should be enough to

9-69 Split brace-wood billet

9-70 Piece for transverse braces cut from billet

make all the parts necessary for this guitar. The braces and patches on the inside surface of the top serve to both aid structural integrity by adding stiffness in key spots and provide a limited way to tune the soundboard. The tuning can be achieved by changing either the length or the height of the braces. This is done by scalloping the ends of the braces after they are installed.

Grain Direction in Braces and Patches

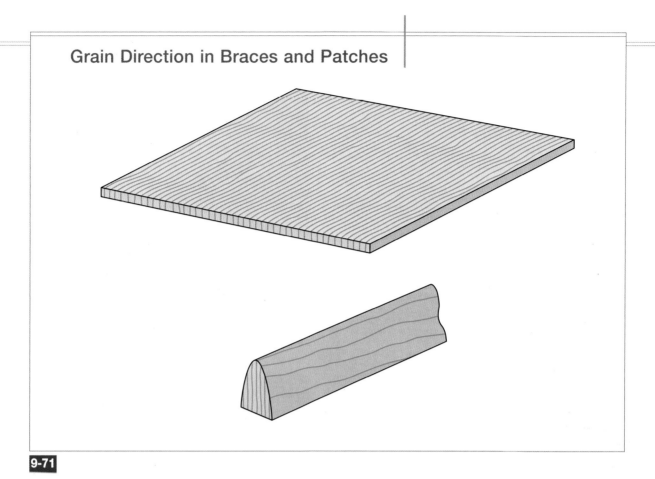

9-71

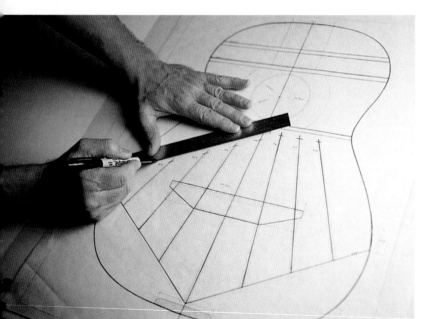

9-72 Laying out the braces on the underside of the top

Laying Out the Braces

The layout of the braces must be lightly penciled onto the underside of the top to locate everything for gluing. Trace the position of the braces from the drawing to a piece of acetate (**9-72**). Place the soundboard on the workboard facedown, and secure with the registration pins. Place the acetate on the back side of the top using the pins to position it, and using a push pin, poke a tiny hole through the acetate at the end of each of the fan braces at their center, making a tiny hole on the top (**9-73**). Make similar marks at the ends of the transverse braces, marking the upper and lower edges. Remove the acetate and connect the dots with a sharp pencil, marking the locations of all the braces on the wood (**9-74**).

There are three patches on this soundboard: the bridge patch, the fingerboard patch, and the donut around the sound hole. In woodworking, the rule is, wherever something is glued to one side, something must be glued to the other, for stability over the long haul. The bridge patch must be installed first, since five of the fan braces fit over it. All patches on this guitar are 0.075 inches thick. Cut enough stock for all the patches, as they are all the same thickness. Make a cardboard template of the bridge plate to shape the patch, and accurately drill the registration holes that are used to position the bridge on the soundboard. Place the template under the acetate in position, and drill the holes in the template. Hand-plane the stock for the patch to the desired thickness; then, using the template as a guide, drill the holes and cut to shape (**9-75** through **9-77**). Save the triangular pieces cut off the ends, because they will be used as depth gauges for cutting the notches in the fan braces (**9-78**).

Cut a caul for gluing out of ¼-inch plywood the same size and shape as the patch, and drill the holes using the template. Apply glue to the patch, and push down over the registration pins, securing it in the correct position. Push the caul down over the patch and clamp in place. Set the timer for eight minutes, and clean the squeeze-out when time is up (**9-79** through **9-81**). Leave the clamps on until the glue cures completely, because the top is domed at this spot and it is necessary for the top to retain this shape.

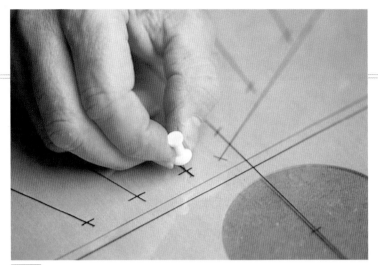

9-73 Using a push pin through the acetate to mark braces

9-74 Connecting the pin marks to locate braces

9-75 Cardboard template of bridge plate

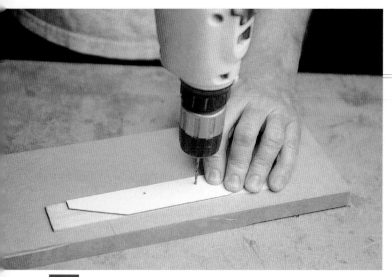

9-76 Drilling holes using template

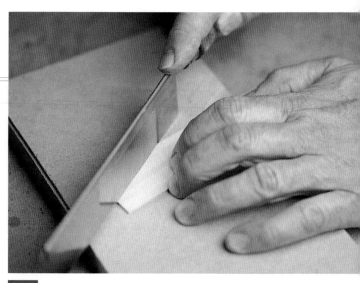

9-77 Hand cutting the stock for the patch

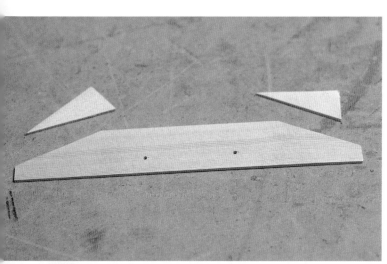

9-78 Triangular pieces cut off the ends

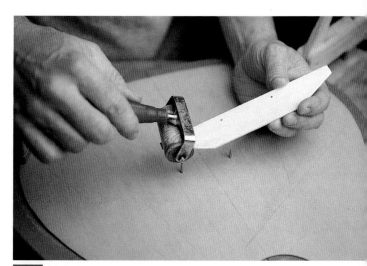

9-79 Applying glue to patch

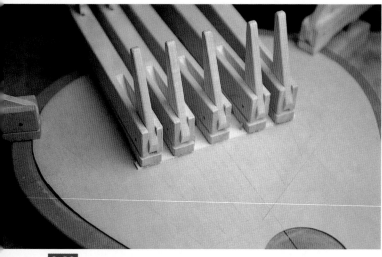

9-80 Caul clamped in place

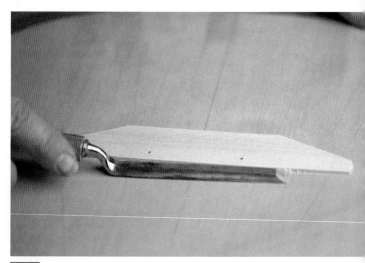

9-81 Cleaning the squeeze-out

Sizing the Braces and Patches

Cut and size enough wood from the billet for all the fan braces (**9-82**). Bring the stock for the braces to final dimensions with a hand plane. Flex the fan braces to separate them in order of stiffness (**9-83**). For the seven fan braces, use the stiffest brace in the middle, the next stiffest on either side of the center, and so on, with the least stiff at the outside.

The triangular cutoffs from the bridge patch will be used to cut the notch in the fan braces that fit over the bridge patch. Place some double-stick tape on one face of the triangular cutoffs from the bridge patch, and cut it into four small pieces (**9-84** through **9-86**). Stick these pieces on the top surface of a small hand vise (**9-87**). The top surface of the vise must be flat. A file can be used to remove any irregularities in the surface.

Take the center brace, hold it in its correct position on the soundboard, and mark its bottom edge where it intersects with the bridge patch using a craft knife (**9-88**). Clamp the brace to a flat piece of stock a bit wider than the brace, and place in the small vise with the flat stock resting on the bridge patch cut-offs (**9-89** and **9-90**). Make cuts down to the surface of the vise inside the notch, remove the material with a chisel, and clean up with a scraper (**9-91** through **9-93**). The depth of the notch should be correct. As the soundboard is domed, the braces should be relieved a bit at their ends to mimic the shape of the soundboard. Take a couple of strokes off the ends with a hand plane, and sand the bottom of the braces to create a curve that will fit the top (**9-94** and **9-95**).

9-82 Enough wood for the fan braces

9-83 Flexing the fan braces

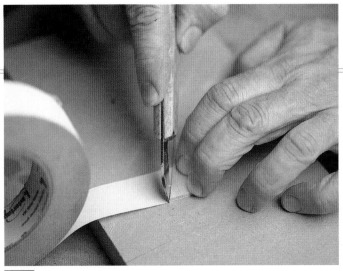

9-84 Applying double-stick tape to face of triangular cut-offs

9-85 Cutting a strip off one triangle

9-86 Cutting strip into four small pieces

9-87 Sticking pieces on top of a small hand vise

9-88 Marking center brace where it intersects bridge patch

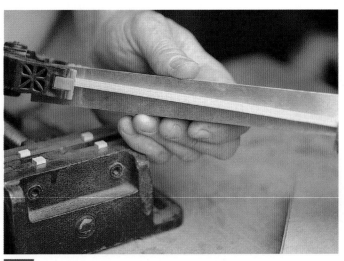

9-89 Clamping brace to a flat piece of stock

9-90 Placing brace in vise with stock resting on cut-offs

9-91 Making cuts to just above the surface of the vise

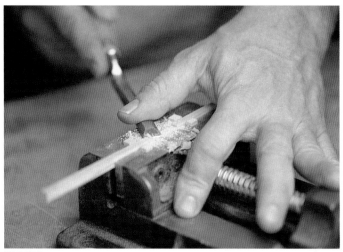

9-92 Removing material with chisel

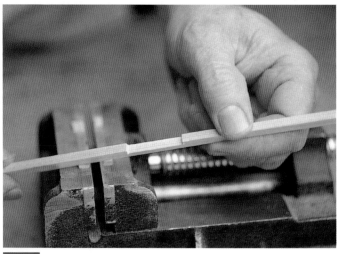

9-93 Brace cleaned up with a scraper

9-94 Hand-planing brace

9-95 Sanding bottom of brace

9-96 Triangulating brace with hand plane

9-97 Bringing to final shape with sandpaper

Shaping and Gluing the Braces

Most builders shape the braces after they have been glued on, but I prefer to shape them before they are glued on because it is easier to get the shape just right and there is less chance of making a mess of the soundboard. Not much clamp pressure is necessary to glue the braces on; therefore, there is little chance of damage from clamping. First, using a hand plane, begin to triangulate the braces, bringing them to final shape with sandpaper (**9-96** and **9-97**). The final shape of the braces should be triangular, as shown in **9-98**. Apply glue and set the timer to clean the glue (**9-99** and **9-100**). Repeat this process for the remainder of the fan braces. The transverse braces are shaped similarly, as shown in **9-101** through **9-104**.

The transverse braces are shaped and glued on the same way as the fan braces, but left flat along the bottom surface. The diagonal brace on the treble side must have its bottom surface accurately shaped to fit the top. This is done on the 25-foot radius sanding disc (**9-105**). Before it is glued on, the upper ends of the fan braces should be scalloped somewhat to allow for room to clean up the squeeze-out (**9-106** and **9-107**).

Sound Hole Donut

To make the donut for around the sound hole, begin with a 5¾-inch-square piece of stock thicknessed to 0.075 inches. Locate its center by drawing diagonals from corner to corner; the center is

9-98 Final shape of braces

9-99 Timer set to clean glue

where these lines intersect. Then draw line through the center, halving the piece in each direction. Drill a ¼-inch hole at the center for the router attachment. Mount this piece to a flat piece of stock with a ¼-inch hole in the middle with double-stick tape (**9-108**). Cut the outer circumference to a diameter of 5⅝ inches with the router; the inner diameter is then cut approximately 4 mm larger than the sound hole (83 mm) (**9-109** through **9-111**).

The top and bottom of the donut must be trimmed to fit in between the two transverse braces. Measure the distance from the inner edge of the lower transverse brace to the center of the sound hole. Mark this distance on the donut, and cut up to the line with a handsaw. Measure and cut the upper half of the donut as above (**9-112** and **9-113**).

9-100 Cleaning glue

9-101 Shaping transverse braces with plane

9-102 Triangulating brace with hand plane

9-103 Bringing to final shape with sandpaper

9-104 Final shape of transverse braces

9-105 Shaping the diagonal brace on the treble side

9-106 Upper ends of fan braces are scalloped to allow for cleanup

9-107 Gluing on diagonal brace

9-108 Stock with donut blank mounted, marked, and drilled

9-109 Cutting circumference with router

9-110 Cutting inner diameter

9-111 Donut for sound hole

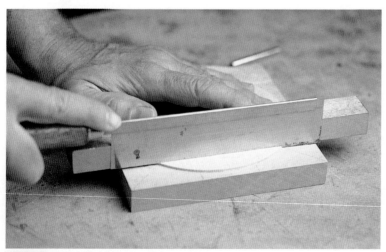

9-112 Trimming donut with hand saw

Fingerboard Patch

The patch under the fingerboard is 75 mm wide. It is installed in two pieces, one above and one below the upper bout cross-patch. Cut a piece of patch stock to the correct width and long enough to reach from the upper transverse brace to the upper edge of the top. Position the patch and mark with a knife (**9-114**); cut and trim to fit between the upper transverse brace and the upper bout cross-patch. The remaining piece is used for the upper part (**9-115**). Glue and clamp in place, setting the timer to remove the squeeze-out.

Scalloping the Braces

Once all the braces and patches are glued on, it is time to scallop the braces. Scallop the transverse braces beginning at approximately 1 to 1¼ inches in from the edge, gradually working inward. Scallop the fan braces similarly. Hold the top with two fingers from the transverse brace at the edge of the upper bout, and tap with your knuckle in the area of the bridge. Continue to scallop and listen for a musical pitch. Use a chromatic tuner and try to stop when the sound produced is right on a note—which note is not important, as this will change when everything is put together (**9-116**).

9-113 Top and bottom of donut trimmed

9-114 Positioning and marking the patch

9-115 Fitting the patch

9-116 The finished underside of the top

JOHN S. BOGDANOVICH
Luthier

A.D. 2005

CHAPTER TEN

*Jointing and
Thicknessing
Bracing*

The Back

ISOLATING THE DIFFERENT PARTS OF THE GUITAR TO OBSERVE HOW THEY AFFECT THE SOUND QUALITY IS VIRTUALLY IMPOSSIBLE. THE guitar is an integrated system and no single part is mutually exclusive. Intuition becomes a large part of making design changes by necessity. The best you can do as a builder is to make an educated guess. Much data has been gathered on the subject, yet there are still surprises and even some mystery remains. This is part of the allure of guitar building, in my estimation. The fact that guitar building is not an exact science has been very much a part of the appeal for me. Fine guitars with incredible sound were built years ago with simple tools, and without scientific information, which would lead one to believe that there is more to it than technology. Starting with a good design is certainly important, as is the technical skill of the builder. But I think the sound is built into the instrument primarily from the intuitive decisions made during the process that come to the builder through experience, touch, and a sensitivity to the materials.

In guitar building, I think it is more important to develop a working mental picture of what is going on rather than getting bogged down in exactness. Of course, if you find that your image of what is happening is proven incorrect empirically, then your vision needs to be revisited.

There is some debate as to the role of the back in sound production. My take is that the back acts as a reflector for the moving air that is producing the sound. Therefore, the back is directly linked to the projection of the sound. A stiffer back closer to the top will help to project better than a thin one farther away. Of course, there are limitations relating to these parameters. Moving too far in any one direction with design parameters will likely have an adverse effect somewhere. Making a back too thick and too close may affect other qualities of the sound in an adverse way. As with any good design, compromises are made. This is how the dimensions for this design were arrived at.

10-1 Planing back across grain

10-2 Using clear template to orient grain

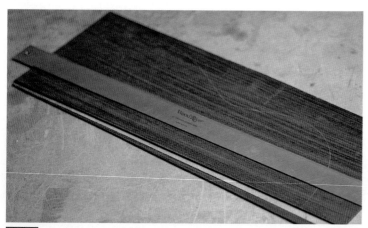

10-3 Marking with straightedge and cutting to line

AT ITS WIDEST POINT, the back is approximately 15 inches wide, making stability ultimately important; therefore, the wood selected for the back should be quartersawn. As there is a lot of surface area, the temptation is to use a highly figured wood. Although this can be striking, it is not recommended for an instrument because of the tendency of this type of wood to develop problems down the road. Highly figured wood is usually quite unstable.

Certainly, the soundboard is mainly responsible for the amount and quality of the sound produced by the guitar, but all the parts contribute something in their own way. The back also contributes to sound production, as speculated above. The stiffer it is, the better a reflector it will be. As with everything, there are trade-offs for excesses. Increasing the thickness of the back unchecked will add weight to the instrument and change the resonance pitch of the cavity. Making the back too thin will cause it to absorb energy rather than reflect it, and may jeopardize its structural integrity. As with all the design factors, a balance has to be reached. It has been my experience that a back with a final thickness between 0.085 and 0.095 inches will satisfy both sound projection and structural integrity requirements.

Since the back strip is the same thickness as the back and sandwiched between the two halves, it will be easiest to thickness each half to around

0.130 to 0.150 inches before jointing them, and then thickness to the final dimension after jointing. This way, it will be easier to get the back flat and have a clean back strip along the entire length. When thicknessing the back with a hand plane, plane across the grain or at a 45-degree angle to the long edge, because rosewood has a tendency to tear out if planed along the grain (**10-1**). It is actually easier to maintain an even thickness this way.

Using the Template to Orient the Halves

Determine how the book-matched pair will be oriented. The clear template will come in handy to orient the grain for maximum effect (**10-2**). If the grain is angled unpleasantly along the center seam, straighten by first marking with a straightedge and then cutting to the line (**10-3**). Do this to both sides equally.

The center seam edges must be planed straight. Plane the inside edge of each half of the back flat on a shooting board, and check against a straightedge until there is no light visible between the straightedge and the inside edge of the board along the entire length (**10-4** and **10-5**).

10-4 Planing center seam edges

10-5 Checking against straightedge

10-6 Gluing back strip

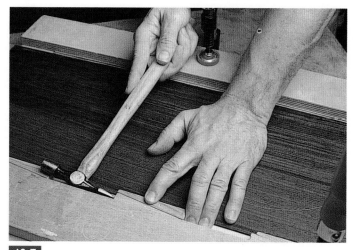

10-7   Using wedges on outside edge

10-8   Making adjustments by planing

10-9   Applying glue

Gluing

The back strip will be glued to one side and then the other. It is easier to get a tight-fitting joint this way rather than trying to do both sides at once. When ready, glue the back strip to the planed edge of the back half on the plate-gluing fixture. Use the wedges on the outside edge of the rosewood and not the back strip, because this could cause dents along the strip that would hinder a good fit with the second half (**10-6** and **10-7**).

After the glue is dry, check for fit with the other half and make adjustments as necessary by planing the rosewood (**10-8**); then glue the second half in the plate-gluing fixture (**10-9** through **10-12**).

Cutting the Back to Shape

Trace the shape onto the back using the template and cut on the band saw. Save the cut-offs, because they can be used for headpiece veneers (**10-13** and **10-14**). Once the back is cut, it can be taken down to final thickness. Again, when thicknessing by hand with a plane, make sure the plane is sharp and always plane across the grain or at a 45-degree angle to it. This will eliminate any deep tearout. Check the thickness with the thickness gauge, stop when within 0.005 inches of the final thickness, and sand smooth (**10-15** through **10-20**).

10-10 Placing second half in gluing fixture

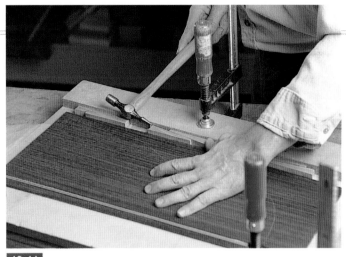

10-11 Adjusting wedges

10-12 Clamped and weighted gluing fixture

10-13 Cutting shape on the band saw

10-14 Shape cut out

10-15 Hand planing across the grain

10-16 Planing the back

10-17 Checking thickness with thickness gauge

10-18 Removing plane marks with scraper

10-19 Using power sander to sand initially

10-20 Hand sand finest grit

10-21 Center patch

BRACING

THE CENTER PATCH is where the bracing of the back begins. The center patch is a piece of cross-grain wood, either mahogany or Spanish cedar, that is 0.100 inches high and ⅞ inches wide and runs the length of the back, covering the back strip on the inside. It is important to orient the grain in the right direction and to use quartersawn wood. This adds strength and stability to the center seam of the back. The patch is made by first cutting some stock to approximately 0.120 inches in thickness. It is unlikely that an 18-inch-wide piece will be available; therefore, it will be necessary to glue up enough pieces to get the length needed. If you started with a piece 6 inches wide, it would be necessary to glue three pieces together to end up with the length needed. The patch does not go under the inside heel or foot block; therefore, 18 inches of length is enough.

Fitting and Gluing the Center Patch

Once you have a piece long enough, thickness with a hand plane to 0.100 inches and cut a piece ⅞ inches wide (**10-21**, **10-22**). Tape the back in position on the back workboard (**10-23**). Make a glue caul out of any ¼-inch material that may be easily bent to make up for the dome of the back. Apply glue to the center patch with a roller and

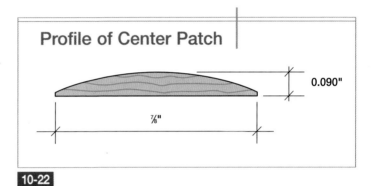

Profile of Center Patch

0.090"

⅞"

10-22

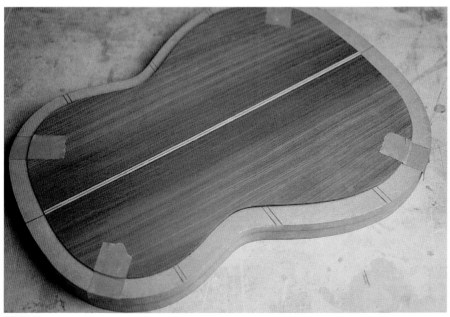

10-23 Back taped on back workboard

10-24 Applying glue to center patch

10-25 Placing center patch

10-26 Taping center patch in place

10-27 Applying clamps

tape in place (**10-24**, **10-25**, **10-26**). Apply the clamps and set the timer for eight minutes (**10-27**, **10-28**); after the time is up, remove the clamps and scrape away the excess glue (**10-29**). Put the clamps back on and let cure on the workboard.

After the glue is dry, the center patch is rounded. Use a wide flat gouge to remove most of the waste, and then shape the rest of the way using a sanding block with the profile carved into the bottom (**10-30** through **10-33**).

Preparing the Braces

There are three back braces, and for this guitar, they will be mahogany, although Spanish cedar can also be used. The wood used for back braces must be quartersawn with the grain lines running perpendicular to the surface of the back (**10-34**). Three pieces approximately ¾ inches high and 15 inches long will be required. I usually cut these from rough stock and thickness them all to 8 mm in the planer. They are then thicknessed the rest of

10-28 Timing for cleaning excess

10-29 Cleaning away excess glue

10-30 Using flat gouge to remove waste

10-31 Sanding block with carved profile

10-32 Rounding center patch with sanding block

10-33 Rounded center patch

Grain Orientation of Braces

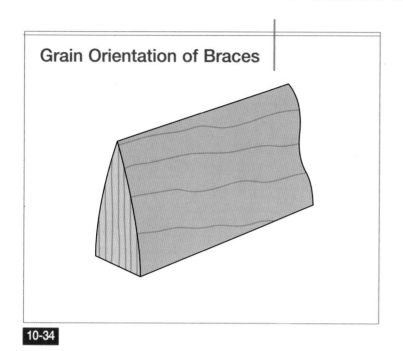

10-34

the way with a hand plane. Trace the shape of the dome onto the bottom edge of the braces using the 15-foot radius stick. The braces should end up being approximately ⅜ inches high in the middle. Cut the shape on the band saw, clean up to the line with a hand plane, and make final adjustments with the 15-foot radius sanding disc. Place the brace in the middle of the disc, and rub back and forth on the sandpaper until the brace conforms to the shape of the disc exactly (**10-35** through **10-38**).

Shaping the Braces

The brace can now be shaped. As with the transverse and fan braces on the top, these braces need to be triangulated. Many builders will glue the braces on first and then shape them. I prefer to shape them first, because this way it is easier to get them shaped properly without damaging the back. Choose whichever way is more comfortable to you. Begin shaping with a hand plane and finish with sandpaper (**10-39** through **10-42**).

10-35 Hand planing brace to final thickness

10-36 Tracing dome shape with 15-foot radius stick

10-37   Radiusing the bottom edge with hand plane

10-38   Sanding so brace conforms to 15-foot radius disc

10-39   Final shaping with hand plane

10-40   Finishing with sandpaper

10-41 Using sanding block

Fitting and Gluing the Braces

Once the brace is shaped, it can be positioned on the back using the lines drawn on the workboard from the acetate (see Chapter 4). Hold the brace in place with two clamps, and mark the intersection on the center strip with a marking knife (**10-43**). The center strip is cut away where it intersects with the braces, to allow the bottom of the braces to ride on the inside surface of the back the entire width of the back. With a chisel, cut away the center patch (**10-44** and **10-45**). The brace should fit nicely with no gaps. Apply glue to the bottom of the brace and clamp in place. Set the timer for eight minutes, and clean the excess glue with a bent chisel and a scraper when the time is up (**10-46** through **10-50**).

10-42 Finished brace

10-43 Marking intersection on center strip

10-44 Cutting center patch with chisel

10-45 Removing waste with chisel

10-46 Applying glue to bottom of brace

10-47 Placing brace in slot cut in center patch

10-48 Clamping brace in place

Scalloping the Braces

After all the braces are on, scallop the ends with a sharp chisel (**10-51**). Scallop the braces so that three distinct tones can be made by tapping on the back just above each one. By scalloping farther in from the edge, you are effectively reducing the length of the brace, which will raise its pitch. Taking some height off the brace will lower its pitch.

Applying Finish

To create a nice look inside the instrument, I like to shellac the center patch and back braces. Using a scraper to keep the shellac off the surface of the back, apply finish to the center patch and polish to a shine (**10-52**). Mask off the braces with masking tape and finish the braces the same way (**10-53**). Once the label is on, the back is completed (**10-54**).

10-49 Timing for cleaning excess

10-50 Cleaning excess glue

10-51 Scalloping ends of braces

10-52 Using scraper to keep shellac off back

10-53 Shellacing braces

10-54 Completed back with label

CHAPTER ELEVEN

Assembling the Body

Before Gluing on
* the Top*
Gluing the Top
Preparing to Glue
* on the Back*
Bindings and Purflings
Heel Cap and Butt Strip

A T THIS STAGE IN THE CONSTRUCTION, THE PACE SLOWS DOWN A BIT SINCE WITH EVERY OPERATION THERE IS A LOT AT RISK. A mistake at this point can be costly in terms of the time it will take to rework completed parts. If this is your first attempt, read over the material carefully until you can visualize what it is you are about to do and then proceed slowly. If all the previous elements have been constructed correctly, they should be able to be put together without any problems. The assembly is not very difficult to do, but care must be taken to ensure that everything ends up being where it should be.

The most difficult aspect of assembling the box is installing the bindings. This operation is much easier if done with a binding cutting machine. The machine can either be purchased or you can build it yourself. The plans for this machine are available at some luthier supply houses. For one guitar, this might not be feasible, but don't worry; there are alternatives. Chapter 3 includes plans for a router attachment that I used to cut the binding channels for more than fifty guitars. I have also cut the channels entirely with hand tools, yet I don't recommend this for anyone without a lot of woodworking experience. As this guitar is constructed using the traditional Spanish method, there will be some hand tool work in cutting the channels in the places that the router will not be able to reach.

This is where the guitar begins to take shape. It is also where the builder may become anxious to see the finished product. This is normal—I have experienced this myself early on. But you must fight the urge to rush things at this point.

Marking position of butt strip

11-2 Cutting along the lines with hand saw

BEFORE THE TOP is glued on, the top edge of the rim must be flattened and the dado for the butt strip cut. Flatten the top rim with a hand plane; then, using the flattened top rim as a reference, position the butt strip in the center over the seam in the lower bout. Use a T square to set the strip perpendicular to the top, mark along the edges with a marking knife, and then cut along the lines with a handsaw (**11-1** and **11-2**). Chisel out the waste at the bottom of the channel down to the foot block, and fit the strip in the channel (**11-3** and **11-4**). The butt strip will not be glued in until later, but it is much easier to mark while the top rim is flat. It is also easier to cut the channel before the top is glued on.

The lower bout must be lowered by 2 mm at the position of the bridge, domed to a 25-foot radius, and tilted toward the butt end. With a silver pencil, mark down 4 mm from the top edge at the butt and 2 mm at each side adjacent to the position of the bridge (**11-5** and **11-6**). Remove

11-3 Chiseling out waste

11-4 Fitting strip in the channel

11-5 Marking down 2 mm at bridge position

the material down to just above the marks with a small hand plane (**11-7** and **11-8**). Do not try to connect these spots just yet, because it is equally as important not to remove too much material. The rims will be brought down to the line slowly with a 25-foot radius sanding disc (**11-9**). Position the disc over the lower bout up to the waist, and rub in a clockwise and counterclockwise motion over the lower bout. Marks left by the sandpaper will reveal the high spots; plane a little off these spots to speed up the process. The rim is domed properly when there are sandpaper marks along the entire lower bout. Sand the top of the rim with 180-grit sandpaper to remove the coarser sandpaper marks left by the disc, being careful not to change the angle or the shape of the edge.

11-6 Marking down 4 mm at the butt

11-7 Hand planing just about to the mark at the butt

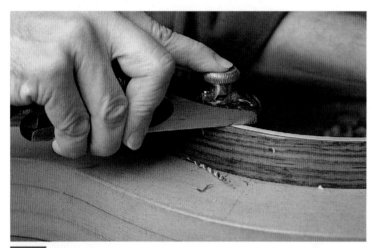

11-8 Hand planing to the side marks

11-9 Sanding rims with 25-foot radius disc

Registration Holes

The registration holes must be drilled in the heel block to position the rim properly. Position the clear template on the rim so that the twelfth fret is exactly at the spot where the neck meets the body. Line the center seam of the top to the center of the foot block. Then drill the registration holes in the heel block through the holes in the top.

Secure the top to the solera with the registration pins. Hold the sides in position with the neck loosely clamped to the centerline of the ramp and the center of the foot block at the center of the solera at the butt. Using a cutoff from the sides, mark the length of the transverse braces so that they will not extend beyond the linings (**11-10**). Mark the locations of two transverse braces on the rims with a marking knife, as these will be notched into the linings (**11-11**). Also, mark any remaining fan braces that extend beyond the inside border of the lining, and trim them so that they will fit inside without touching the lining (**11-12**). Trim the ends of the transverse braces, and remove the remaining brace wood from the top with a chisel and a scraper (**11-13** and **11-14**). Cut and clean up the rest of the braces to fit inside the linings (**11-15**).

11-10 Marking length of transverse braces

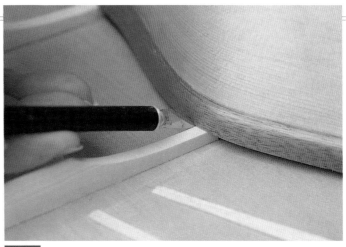

11-11 Marking locations of transverse braces on lining

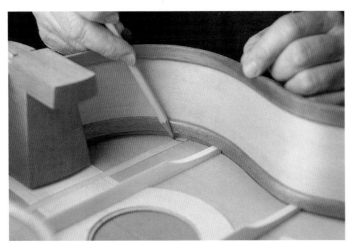

11-12 Marking remaining fan braces

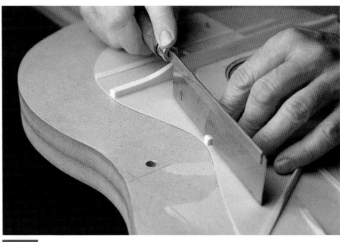

11-13 Trimming ends of transverse braces

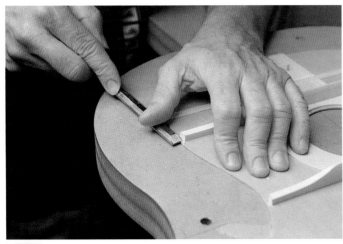

11-14 Removing remaining brace wood from top

11-15 Cutting the braces to fit inside the lining

Before Gluing on the Top | 215

11-16 Marking notches for the transverse braces

11-17 Marking depth and size of notches

11-18 Cutting from top of linings to depth of notch

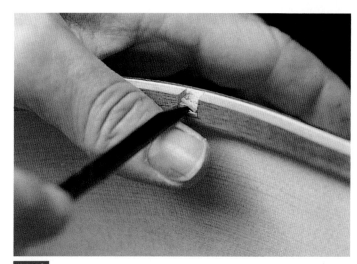

11-19 Removing waste with a chisel

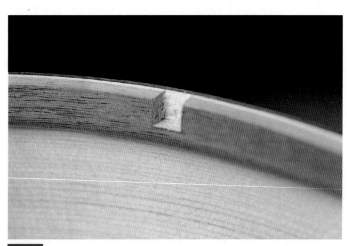

11-20 Notch pared down to the line

Mark the notches for the transverse braces in the linings. With a straightedge, connect the marks made by the marking knife to position the braces on the sides (**11-16**). Using a small square, mark the depth and size of the notch for the transverse braces on the face of the linings (**11-17**). The small square is especially useful in setting the depth of the notch by first setting it to the height of the end of the brace and transferring this to the linings. Repeat this for all the notches.

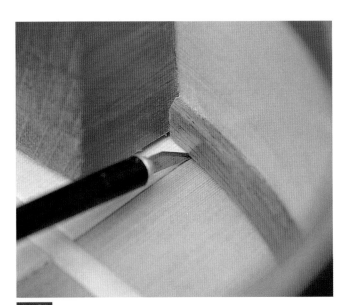

11-21 Marking the linings with a knife

11-22 Removing waste to where neck meets body

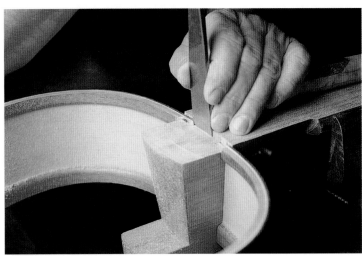

11-23 Cleaning up to the lines with chisel

11-24 Cleaned-up heel block

Begin to remove the waste by first cutting a diagonal with a thin-blade Zona saw from the top of the linings down to the depth of the notch (**11-18**). Remove the rest of the waste with a sharp ⅛-inch chisel and pare down to the line (**11-19** and **11-20**).

As the fingerboard patch is 0.070 inches above the back side of the top, the heel block that sits above it has to be relieved by this amount plus the thickness of the top. The width of this patch also extends beyond the heel block; therefore, the linings must be relieved a bit on either side of the heel block. Mark the linings with a knife (**11-21**). Using a small laminate trimming router with a mortising bit or any flat-topped straight bit, set the height of the blade to match the height of the patch. Then remove the waste up to where the neck meets the body and to the knife marks for the fingerboard patch (**11-22**). Clean up to the lines with a chisel (**11-23** and **11-24**).

11-25 Applying glue to rim

11-26 Clamping rim to the top

11-27 Coating inside of top with shellac

GLUING THE TOP

WITH ONLY SOME fine adjustments, the top should fit in place. If the notches over the transverse braces are tight, or the top does not sit flush on the rim, pare the inside walls of the notch until the fit doesn't have to be forced. Check all around to make sure the linings are making contact with the underside of the top and there are no obstructions. Perform a dry run with the clamps before applying the glue, to become familiar with the process. Clamps should be placed all the way around, but there are a few spots where it is especially important to put at least one clamp; they are the heel block, the foot block, and directly over the notches for the transverse braces.

Applying the Glue

When ready, apply the glue to the rim quickly, being careful to use just the right amount (**11-25**). First, position the rim with the pins in the heel block; next, clamp the neck on the centerline of the ramp; then clamp the center of the foot block over the center seam of the top. Apply the rest of the clamps all around, and set the timer for eight minutes (**11-26**). When the time is up, scrape away the excess glue with a chisel. Then set aside until the glue is dry. When dry, remove the clamps and give the inside of the top a coat of shellac (**11-27**). This will help reduce moisture exchange with the environment and add stability.

PREPARING TO GLUE ON THE BACK

HE RIM IS now attached to the top, and the assembly is still on the solera, being held in place with the registration pins and a couple of clamps on the neck to secure it to the ramp.

Notice that the bottom of the heel block is considerably higher than the top edge of the rim. Using a hand plane, begin to plane down the bottom of the heel (**11-28**). Plane the heel, approximating the tilt and dome shape and being careful not to plane off too much. Check the height periodically with the sanding disc.

Creating a Perfect Fit

When the sides were cut from the template provided, they were already shaped to the tilted 15-foot radius. Since the linings have been glued on the sides a bit proud of the edge, the fit should occur as the top of the side is approached. Plane the linings down, and switch to the 15-foot radius sanding disc as the top edge of the sides is approached (**11-29** and **11-30**). Spin the disc back and forth a few times, and sandpaper marks

11-28 Planing bottom of the heel

will reveal the high spots. Plane the high spots to speed up the process, and continue to sand until there are sanding marks along the entire rim. The sides should fit perfectly under the domed dish. Once a perfect fit has been established, sand the rim edge, the heel block, and the foot block with 180-grit sandpaper, once again being careful not

11-29 Planing the linings flush to sides

11-30 Doming rims for back by sanding with 15-foot radius disc

11-31 Setting depth of the side and foot block

11-32 Transferring depth to inside surface of back center patch

11-33 Trimming center patch to fit inside foot block

to change the shape or contour of any of these parts. All we are trying to do is remove the coarse sandpaper marks to get a better glue surface.

As the back has been cut right to the line at the lower bout in the area of the butt strip, set the depth of the side and the foot block at the butt strip using a small T square. Then transfer this depth to the inside surface of the back at the center strip (**11-31** and **11-32**). Remove the center strip up to this spot (**11-33** and **11-34**). The back can now be set in place with the center strip up against the foot block.

11-34 Removing waste with a chisel

11-35 Marking intersection of braces on rim

11-36 Marking length of the braces at each end

Positioning the Back

Center the back on the rims, making sure the center of the back strip lines up with the channel for the butt strip and with the center of the heel. Clamp in place with a cam clamp on each side and just above the front and rear brace. With a marking knife, mark the intersection of the braces on the rim. And with a pencil, mark the length of the braces at each end so that they will fit just inside the Indian rosewood of the sides (**11-35** and **11-36**).

Remove the back and cut the ends off the braces at the line; remove the waste with a chisel down to the rosewood (**11-37**). Then mark the notches on the linings. With the small T square, draw the outline of each of the notches on the face of the linings. Using the small T square again, set the depth of the ends of each of the braces, and transfer this depth to each notch on the linings (**11-38** and **11-39**). Cut along the lines for the notches with the Zona saw, cutting down to

11-37 Cutting the ends off the braces at the line

11-38 Using a small T square

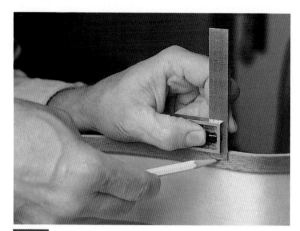

11-39 Transferring depth of brace for notch

the bottom of the notch, and chisel the waste from each notch (**11-40** and **11-41**). Fit the back, one side at a time, widening and deepening the notches if necessary.

Once both sides are fitted, the center patch must be removed under the heel block. Make a mark on the heel where the back ends, and measure from this line to the inside edge of the heel block (**11-42** and **11-43**). Mark this distance on the center patch, and remove material up to this line (**11-44** through **11-47**).

11-40 Cutting along the lines for the notches

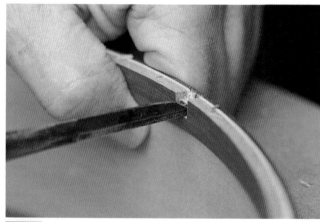

11-41 Cleaning waste from the notch

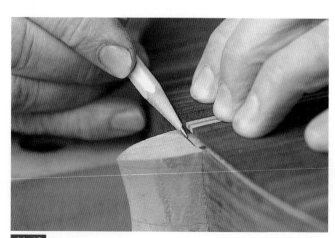

11-42 Marking on heel

11-43 Measuring to inside edge of heel block

If you have a label for your guitar, now is the time to put it in. The label shows pride in a job well done.

11-44 Marking distance on center strip

11-45 Cutting line on center patch

11-46 Removing material up to line

11-47 Cleaned up to line on center patch

Using a Handheld Router

Cutting the binding channels with a handheld router may seem intimidating at first, especially if you don't have much woodworking experience, but it really isn't all that difficult. The channels can be cut using the router attachment shown in Chapter 3 or one of your own design if you prefer. Either way, with a handheld router, the router and attachment touch the guitar in three places. These are: once on either side of the blade; and at the outer edges of the base to keep the router steady as it slides along the top and back as the channels are cut, and the arm which hangs below and behind the blade sliding along the sides of the instrument keeping the router perpendicular to the sides. A ¼-inch down-spiral bit is recommended to minimize tearout along the top edge.

Applying the Glue

The back is now ready to be glued. Spread the glue quickly, being careful not to use too much, as there is no way to clean the excess squeeze-out (**11-48**). Make sure the neck is clamped to the ramp and the centerlines are aligned, because the back will lock in the neck angle. Clamp the back in place all the way around on the solera, and set aside for a few hours to dry (**11-49**). After the glue has dried, trim any overhang on the top and back with a laminate trimmer (**11-50**).

11-48 Applying glue for back

11-49 Clamping back in place all around solera

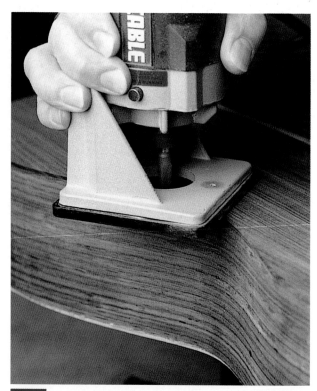

11-50 Using laminate trimmer on top and back overhang

BINDINGS AND PURFLINGS

BEFORE CUTTING THE channels, clean up the sides with a scraper to remove bumps from the surface. The channels will be cut in a series of passes rather than cutting away all the material in one pass. Cutting will be easier this way and will actually minimize the chance of error. Set the router to cut only part of the depth and width of the channel for the bindings.

Cutting the Channels

Check for height and depth on a test piece (**11-51** and **11-52**). Turn on the router and lower it to the work with the arm pressed firmly to the sides. Pay attention to the grain of the wood on the top and back as you cut. Try to avoid cutting in a direction that will pull the fibers away from the surface; always cut in a direction that lays the fibers down. Cutting in the direction opposite to normal use is possible if done carefully and not too much material is being removed in one pass. Cut both the top and back channels at the same setting, reset, and cut again (**11-53** and **11-54**). The final depth is 0.090 inches, and the height is 0.270 inch. The router will be unable to cut right up to the neck, so go only as far as is allowed—the remainder will be cut by hand.

11-51 Testing the routing of channels

11-52 Checking for height and depth

11-53 Routing top and back channels at the same setting

11-54 Resetting and cutting again

11-55 Resetting to cut the purfling channel

11-56 Cutting the purfling channel in the top

11-57 Using template to extend purfling border

11-58 Scoring close to the line with knife

Next, reset the router to cut the channel for the purfling. Because this is small, it can be cut in one pass (**11-55** and **11-56**). When cutting the purfling channels on the back, make sure to stop approximately ⅛ inches before the center strip. The purflings are mitered to the purflings on the back strip here, and this last bit of material is removed by hand.

Begin with the top, and using the clear template, draw the remainder of the inner-purfling border from where it stopped to ¾ inches inside the neck (**11-57**). Score close to this line with a very sharp knife, and begin to remove the material with a chisel (**11-58** and **11-59**). Once the material has been removed to the desired depth, trim the edge to the line with either a sharp chisel or a file with a safe edge. Carefully clean up the edge of the purfling channel with the safe file or sandpaper, and fit the purflings. If necessary, make small adjustments to the depth of

11-59 Removing material with a chisel

11-60 Marking length of the purfling at butt

11-61 Marking length of the purfling at neck

11-62 Cutting purfling to length

the channel so that the purflings fit up to, but do not exceed, the upper edge of the binding channel. The two halves of the purflings on the top will butt up against each other at the centerline just over the butt strip. Mark the lengths at both ends, and cut to length (**11-60** through **11-62**). Before gluing, give the top around the edges a coat of shellac to keep the tape from pulling up wood fibers when it is removed (**11-63**).

Gluing Bindings and Purflings

For gluing purflings and bindings, white wood glue is used because it provides a bit more setup time. When you are satisfied with the fit, spread the glue in the channel, and using masking tape, secure the purflings in place beginning at the seam at the lower bout (**11-64** through **11-66**).

11-63 Coating around the edges with shellac

Safe Edge

To create a safe edge on a file, grind off the teeth on one edge. This edge can now be rubbed safely against a surface without cutting.

Continuing with the Back

The same process is repeated on the back. The only difference is that the purflings must be mitered at both ends where they meet the center strip. This means that the fit along the length will have to be very accurate.

Using the clear template, draw the rest of the purfling-channel border up to the center strip at both ends (**11-67**). Score with a knife and chisel to the depth of the channel up to the purflings on the center strip (**11-68** through **11-70**). Using a very sharp ⅛-inch chisel, cut the purflings at both ends of the center strip from the outer edge of Alaskan yellow cedar diagonally to the outer edge of black veneer, making approximately a

11-64 Gluing purfling in the channel

11-65 Securing purflings with blue tape

11-66 Purflings secured with tape

45-degree cut (**11-71** and **11-72**). Clean out the channel as done on the top, making sure there is a good fit all the way around. Clean up the channel if necessary. Secure the purflings in place at the waist with masking tape, and carefully measure; then cut the purflings, mitering each end to fit the already mitered center-strip purflings (**11-73**). Secure at the waist with masking tape. Trim the rest of the way with sandpaper, making small adjustments and testing the fit as you go.

Repeat the procedure for the other end. Once both sets of purflings have been fitted, apply white glue to the channel and secure the purflings in place with masking tape (**11-74** and **11-75**).

Finishing the Top Purflings and Bindings

When the purflings have had sufficient time to dry, the tape can be removed. Then plane the purflings close to the surface of the top (**11-76**).

The binding channel must first be continued to ¾ inches inside the neck as the purflings were. Chisel out this portion of the channel, and clean up the channel with a chisel (**11-77**). Check that the bindings fit flush against the purflings all the way around, and make adjustments with a file until a good fit has been achieved. Tape into place and mark both ends (**11-78** and **11-79**). Cut the bindings to length (**11-80**). Check for fit before spreading the glue. Spread white glue in the channel, and beginning at the lower bout, secure

11-68 Scoring with a knife

11-67 Using template to draw rest of purfling channel

11-69 Taking channel to depth up to center strip

11-70 Cutting purfling channel to the center strip

11-71 Mitering purflings at neck end of center strip

11-72 Mitering purflings at butt end of center strip

11-73 Mitering each end to match center strip purflings

11-74 Securing with blue tape

11-75 Glued purflings secured with blue tape

11-76 Planing purflings close to surface of top

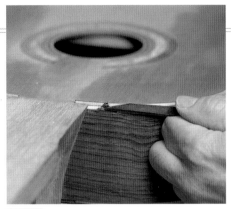

11-77 Cleaning up channel with chisel

11-78 Marking bindings at neck

11-79 Marking ends at butt strip

11-80 Cutting top bindings to length

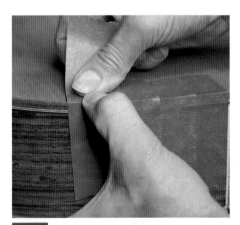

11-81 Securing bindings in place

the bindings in place with masking tape (**11-81** and **11-82**). It may be necessary to fashion a caul for the waist area to hold the bindings up against the purflings using a clamp.

Finishing the Back Bindings

For the back, the bindings must meet behind the heel. Chisel the channel up to the center behind the heel (**11-83**). Cut behind the heel down to the bottom of the binding channel with a saw (**11-84**). Remove the waste with a chisel (**11-85**). Tape the binding in place at the waist, and mark the length at both ends (**11-86** and **11-87**). Cut and check the fit (**11-88**). Spread the glue and tape in place (**11-89** and **11-90**).

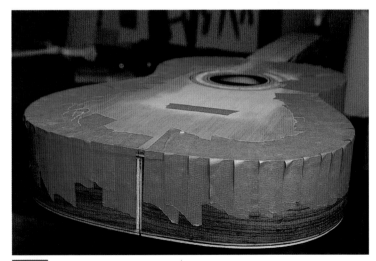

11-82 Glued top bindings secured with blue tape

11-83 Chiseling channel up to center behind heel

11-84 Cutting behind heel to bottom of binding channel

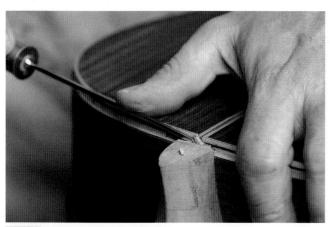

11-85 Removing waste with chisel

11-86 Marking the length

11-87 Marking length of binding at butt end

Once the glue is dry, remove the tape and begin cleaning up the sides, top, and back edges. Clean up the sides with the scraper and sandpaper (**11-91**). Use a plane with a sharp blade to trim the height of the bindings and purflings to just above the surface of the top and back, and sand flush with the random orbit sander using 180-grit sandpaper (**11-92** and **11-93**).

11-88 Checking the fit

11-89 Taping glued binding

11-90 Bindings taped in place

11-91 Cleaning sides with scraper

11-92 Planing height of bindings and purflings on back face

11-93 Planing height of bindings and purflings on top face

11-94 Tracing shape of heel

11-95 Applying glue

11-96 Heel clamped in place

THE HEEL CAP is usually made of the same wood as the bindings. In this case, the bindings are Louro Preto. Simply dimension a piece slightly thicker than necessary, set it in place, and trace the shape of the heel onto it (**11-94**). Cut this out on the band saw, leaving it slightly larger than the heel, fit to the bindings, and glue in place (**11-95** and **11-96**). When the glue is dry, trim the excess flush to the heel with a chisel.

Fitting and Gluing the Butt Strip

The butt strip is the cutoff from the center strip on the back. The channel for it has already been cut after the sides were assembled to the neck. Clean any excess glue squeeze-out from the bindings out of the channel. The butt strip is inlayed into the channel cut for it back in Chapter 6. The purflings at the ends of the strip are mitered to the purflings on the bottom of the bindings. The

11-97 Mitering purflings on the bindings

11-98 Using sandpaper to trim miters on end of strip

11-99 Spreading the glue in the channel

11-100 Planing the strip close to the surface

11-101 Cleaned-up strip

purflings on the bindings are mitered first with a
sharp chisel. Cut on a diagonal from the outside
edge of the Alaskan yellow cedar to the inside
edge of the black veneer (**11-97**). Next, measure
and cut the miters on one end of the strip and
mark the orientation of the strips to avoid confusion. Use sandpaper to achieve a good fit (**11-98**).

Position the strip into the channel, and mark
the length of the strip. Cut to length and miter

the purflings at this end of the strip. The strip
should fit well without being forced. Once a
good fit is achieved, spread glue in the channel
and tap in the strip (**11-99**). The strip can be
cleaned up right away. First, plane the strip close
to the surface, and then sand it flush with the
random orbit sander (**11-100** and **11-101**).

CHAPTER TWELVE

*Making and Installing
 the Fingerboard
Before Fretting
Fretting
Shaping the Neck*

The Fingerboard

THE SCALE LENGTH AND NECK DIMENSIONS USED IN THIS DESIGN ARE WHAT I WOULD CONSIDER STANDARD DIMENSIONS. They are typically used for instruments made for dealers when the player is unknown at the time of construction. Even with custom-made instruments, approximately 90 percent are built to these dimensions. The width at the nut is 53 mm and 63 mm at the twelfth fret. If you are certain that these or any other dimensions in this design will not work for you and you need to change them, make sure to redraw the entire instrument with the new dimensions before attempting to build it. Paper is cheaper than wood and easier to come by.

The distance from the nut to the saddle is known as the scale, or string, length. It is simply the fixed length of the suspended string. This distance is determined when the instrument is designed. As this distance increases, so do the spaces between the frets. The most common scale length in use today is 650 mm. This length seems to work for most hand sizes. The range of scale lengths in use today is typically between 640 and 660 mm. Although the difference between them seems small, your hand is capable of sensing the tiniest of differences.

My guitar teacher back in the seventies had a Ramirez 1A that I found very difficult to play. The main reason was that it had a scale length of 663 mm. At the time, I didn't know what scale length was, but I could tell there was a big difference between my instrument and my teacher's. Although for some a longer scale length may be more difficult to play, there are benefits to a longer scale length. The longer the scale length, the more tension is necessary to bring the strings up to pitch, which translates into more force being applied to the soundboard each time a note is plucked. Also, different scale lengths create different harmonic series (see Chapter 1). Therefore, a different scale length may change the character of the sound slightly.

Preslotted Fingerboard

If this is your first instrument, my advice is to stick to a scale length of 650 mm and to purchase a fingerboard that has the slots for the frets already cut into it. Cutting the slots with a handsaw is certainly possible, but accuracy is likely to suffer. A fretting system for table saw will surely provide the necessary accuracy, but it can be costly unless you plan to build many instruments. Most suppliers that sell fingerboards will also slot the board to any scale length for a fee. This seems to make the most sense if you are building an instrument for yourself.

12-1 Slotted fingerboard

THE 650-MM SLOTTED fingerboard will have a zero fret at the nut end. The distance from the nut end of the fingerboard to the center of the twelfth fret must be 325 mm. The material above the zero fret must be cut off and squared on the bench hook. Trim with a hand plane until the exact length is achieved (**12-1** through **12-4**).

Making a Fingerboard Template

A template of the fingerboard must be made in order to get its taper and shape correct. The template can be fashioned out of any stable material. It is a good general practice to avoid using solid wood for templates because wood changes in dimensions with changes in humidity. If MDF is used, be sure to finish with shellac to seal against moisture. Begin with a piece of ½-inch-thick stock that is approximately 3 inches wide and 20 inches long, and square one end using a hand plane on the bench hook. Check with a small T square for accuracy—this will be the nut end of the fingerboard. Measure down to the half-scale point, or the twelfth fret, in this case 325 mm. Draw a centerline perpendicular to the nut and the twelfth-fret line down the entire length of the piece. On either side of this centerline, mark the width at the nut and the twelfth fret to designate the taper. Draw lines connecting these points and

12-2 Cutting off and squaring at the nut end

12-3 Trimming square with a hand plane

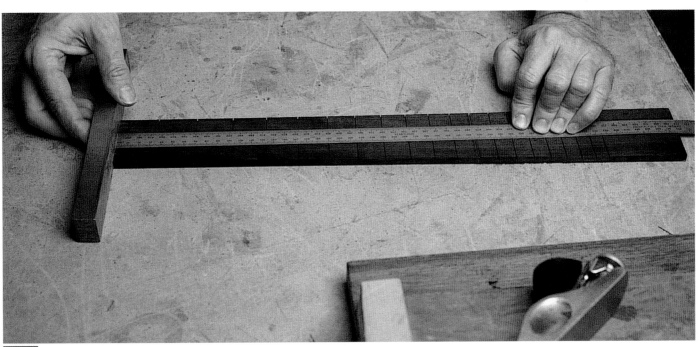

12-4 Determining exact length to the twefth fret

Making and Installing the Fingerboard

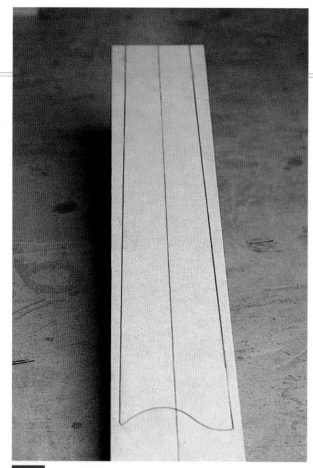

12-5 Lines drawn on template

12-6 Planing sides of template

continue them to the end of the piece (**12-5**). Drill one ⅛-inch registration hole near the nut in the center of the neck and two on either side of the centerline down by the twelfth fret. Their exact position is not important—just remember that shallow holes will be drilled in the neck, so they shouldn't be too deep or out near the edge.

Measure to the top of the sound hole and mark this on the template; then freehand in the shape at the sound hole. Cut out this shape on the band saw, and clean up to the line using a drum sander on the drill press. Cut off the sides just to the waste side of the lines on the band saw, and clean up to the line with a hand plane (**12-6**).

Thicknessing the Fingerboard

The fingerboard should be thicknessed to 0.275 inches. Thickness the fingerboard on the shooting board with a hand plane to 0.280 inches, leaving 0.005 inches to be removed later in smoothing (**12-7**). Center the template on the bottom of the slotted fingerboard, making sure to orient it correctly, and drill the registration holes in the underside (**12-8**). Be careful to drill only shallow

12-7 Hand planing fingerboard to thickness

holes. Trace the outline of the template onto the fingerboard (**12-9**), and cut to within ¹⁄₁₆ inch of the line on the band saw to remove most of the waste.

Attach the template to the fingerboard, orienting with registration pins and securing with double-stick tape (**12-10** and **12-11**). Trim on the router table/shaper with a ⅜-inch trim bit with a bearing (**12-12**). Proceed carefully around the area of the sound hole.

The underside of the fingerboard should be flat. Check with a straightedge and make any adjustments with a scraper (**12-13**).

12-8 Drilling registration holes in the underside

12-9 Tracing template outline on fingerboard

12-10 Applying double-stick tape to template

12-11 Securing template with registration pins and tape

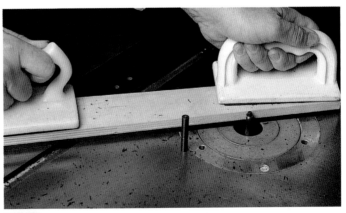
12-12 Trimming with router/shaper

12-13 Using scraper to make underside flat

12-14 Checking flatness of neck

12-15 Planing neck across the grain keeping it flat

12-16 Using template to drill registration holes

Creating a Slight Bow for the Neck

Take a straightedge and check the flatness of the neck (**12-14**). To compensate for the surface tension created by the frets, there should be a slight bow from about the fourth fret to the twelfth. At its center, it should only be approximately ¹⁄₆₄ inch. If necessary, plane the neck across the grain to add this bow (**12-15**).

Placing and Fitting the Fingerboard

Place the fingerboard template on the neck in position, and drill the registration holes, being careful not to drill too deeply—only about ⅛ inch is necessary (**12-16**). Lay the fingerboard in place. It should not be necessary to press down at the twelfth fret to get it to touch the neck. The underside of the fingerboard over the upper bout must be ramped to fit flat against the neck here

12-17 Planing underside at the upper bout

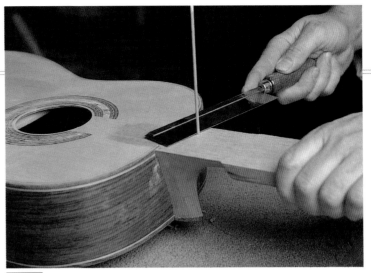

12-18 Cutting dowels

without pushing it down. Using a hand plane with a sharp blade, relieve the underside until a good fit is achieved (**12-17**).

Gluing the Fingerboard

Cut three pieces of ⅛-inch dowel, and glue them into the holes in the neck (**12-18**). Put the fingerboard in place with the dowels in the registration holes. If the dowels are too high for the fingerboard to lie flat, file down the dowels until it does.

Sand the top of the guitar using up to 320-grit sandpaper (**12-19**). With the fingerboard in place, wax the area where the top and fingerboard meet—any paste wax will do (**12-20**). This will make removing any squeeze-out easy after the glue has dried without damage to the cedar. Apply the glue with a roller, and using the template as a caul, clamp in place (**12-21** and **12-22**).

12-19 Sanding top of guitar

12-20 Waxing area where top and fingerboard meet

Making and Installing the Fingerboard | **243**

12-21 Applying glue

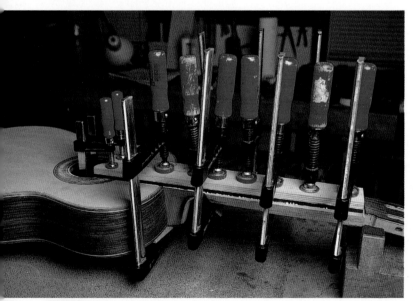

12-22 Clamped fingerboard

Finishing the Fingerboard

When the glue is dry, remove the clamps and trim the neck protruding from under the fingerboard. This material must be removed before fretting. Either plane or cut on the band saw close the edge of the fingerboard; then using a router with a ⅜-inch trim bit with the bearing on top of the blade, trim right up to the fingerboard (**12-23**).

The edges of the fingerboard can be relieved a bit, but only a bit. The fingerboard on a classical guitar should not be rounded, because this may lead to joint problems in the left hand, especially in applying a hinge bar. The edges of the finger-board should only be relieved approximately 0.010 inches to compensate for any tendency of the edges to curl up slightly.

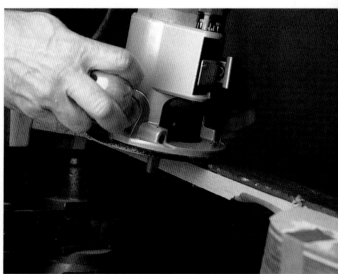

12-23 Trimming neck right up to fingerboard

BEFORE FRETTING

BEFORE FRETTING, THE fingerboard must be checked for flatness. As mentioned above, there must be a slight bow to compensate for the surface tension caused by the frets (**12-24**). The fingerboard must be relieved slightly on the bass side from about the fifth fret to the sound hole, to provide additional clearance for the bass strings that travel considerably more than the treble strings when plucked (**12-25**). The total relief at the twefth fret should be approximately 0.020 inches. The saddle will be higher on the bass side than on the treble side; therefore, it is not necessary to bevel the fingerboard very much. Remove material with a hand plane, checking with a straightedge as you go. Flatten with some sandpaper glued to a flat piece of stock. The fingerboard can be relieved a little more if the player is known to have a heavy stroke.

12-24 Checking fingerboard for flatness

12-25 Relieving fingerboard slightly on the bass side

Width of Tang

0.080"

0.037"

0.094"

0.019"

0.031"

12-26

12-27 Using small triangular file to prepare edges of slots

12-28 Hammering frets into place

THE FRET WIRE used on my instruments is an 18 percent nickel/silver alloy. Suppliers usually designate what type of guitar a particular wire is commonly used for. Wire used for classical guitars is generally softer than that used for steel-string or electric guitars, but I have found that this wire works well with the nylon strings.

The fret wire is held in the slot by the little barbs along the tang. The width of the tang, including the barbs of the wire used here, is 0.031 inches (**12-26**). The width of the slots cut into the fingerboard should be 0.025 inches. This size slot works well with this wire. If the slot is too small, it really takes some force to get the frets in, and more importantly, more surface tension is created on the fingerboard, which may cause it to bow upward in the middle.

Prepare the slots for fretting by using a small triangular file to knock the edges off the tops of the slots (**12-27**). This will make them seat better and will also prevent pulling up wood when removing them. Cut the frets slightly longer than the slot, put some glue on the tang, and using a fret hammer (nonmetallic head), hammer the fret into place, making sure it sits flush along its entire length (**12-28**). Clear any squeeze-out with a small scraper (**12-29**).

Checking the Seating of Frets

As you progress down the fingerboard, check for high spots or improperly seated frets with a short metal straightedge and reseat with the fret hammer, making it as level as possible. Nip the ends of the fret protruding from the fingerboard with a pair of end-cutting pliers (**12-30**). The remaining bit of fret sticking out will be trimmed at the end.

12-29 Clearing any squeeze-out with small scraper

12-30 Nipping ends of fret protruding from fingerboard

12-31 Relieving barbs on frets used near sound hole

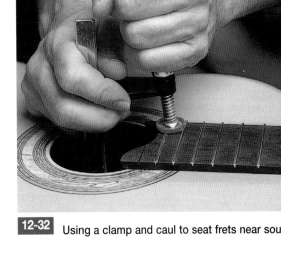

12-32 Using a clamp and caul to seat frets near sound hole

It may be necessary to relieve a little of the barbs with a file for the frets that are installed over the soundboard (**12-31**). It is not a good idea to hammer away in this area. Use a clamp and caul with a cutout for the upper transverse brace through the sound hole to seat these frets (**12-32**).

12-33 Filing frets flush to edge of fingerboard

12-34 Using cardboard and sheet metal to protect top

12-35 Fret beveling file

12-36 Filing edges to a slight bevel on ebony

Finishing the Frets

After all the frets have been installed, file the ends of the frets flush to the fingerboard with a smoothing file (**12-33**). Cover the top with cardboard, and use a piece of sheet metal to protect the top when filing over the upper bout of the guitar (**12-34**).

The frets at the edges of the fingerboard must be beveled to an angle of about 35 degrees and then sanded to provide a smooth edge for the fingers as they move up and down the fingerboard. A fret beveling file (**12-35**) can be either purchased or easily made from a block of wood and a flat file. File the edges until a slight bevel has been achieved on the ebony (**12-36**). After beveling with the file, go over with 320-grit sandpaper to remove any burrs (**12-37**). It should be smooth to the touch as you run your fingers along the edge of the fingerboard.

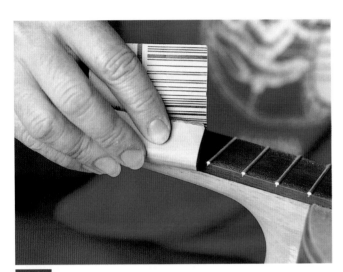

12-37　Sanding to eliminate burrs

12-38　Running flat smoothing file along frets

12-39　Wood with ⅛" bead for sanding frets round

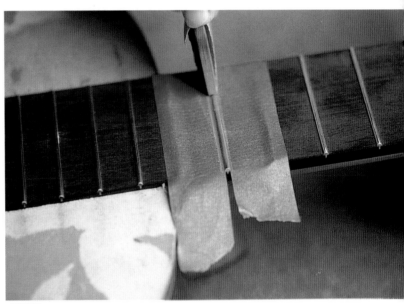

12-40　Rounding frets as tape protects fingerboard

The frets must be leveled to ensure the proper clearance from fret to fret down the fingerboard. Rub a flat smoothing file along the tops of the frets until all the frets show scratch marks from the file (**12-38**). Starting at the twentieth fret and working down toward the first fret, tape off the fingerboard and round the frets using sandpaper and a piece of wood with a ⅛-inch bead along its edge (**12-39** and **12-40**). Use 180-grit sandpaper first, and then 320-grit, and polish to shine with

0000# steel wool (**12-41**). Check the frets for flatness with a straight piece of metal as you progress down the fingerboard by setting the metal across three frets (**12-42**). If the metal rocks back and forth even a tiny bit, it will make a clicking sound, indicating that the middle fret is high. Use sandpaper and steel wool until flat.

12-41 Shining frets with steel wool

12-42 Checking for high frets with small straightedge

12-43 Applying boiled linseed oil to fingerboard

12-44 Rubbing entire fingerboard with steel wool

Oiling the Fingerboard

After flattening, give the fingerboard a coat of boiled linseed oil. Brush on the oil and let it sit for a few minutes; then wipe off the excess. Let it dry overnight, and then rub the entire fingerboard with 000# steel wool, bringing it to a dull sheen (**12-43** and **12-44**). Repeat the process once more time.

Adding a Seventh-Fret Indicator

All my guitars get a seventh-fret indicator. I have been playing for more than thirty-five years and still hesitate for a fraction of a second when jumping up the fingerboard if there is no indicator. In between the sixth and seventh fret, drill a small hole and epoxy in some galvanized wire (**12-45** and **12-46**). When the epoxy is dry, file the wire flush (**12-47**).

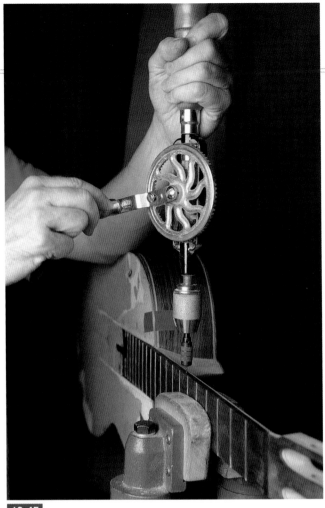

12-45 Drilling hole for seventh fret indicator

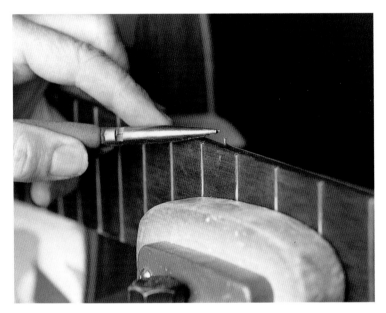

12-46 Galvanized wire set in hole with epoxy

12-47 Filing the wire flush

12-48 Trimming excess at the heel

12-49 Trimming excess at the nut slot

What Neck Shape Do You Prefer?

Neck shape is a matter of personal preference. Some players prefer a round neck shape, while others prefer one that is flatter in the middle. Some like a combination of both. The templates provided in Chapter 5 are on the round side. If you prefer a different shape, make a couple of templates with the shape you like and shape the neck with these.

SHAPING THE NECK

THE EXCESS MATERIAL at the heel just under the fingerboard is trimmed flush to the fingerboard with a chisel (**12-48**). Also, the excess material on the neck at the nut slot and lower headpiece must be trimmed with a chisel (**12-49**). The top part of the heel and the neck at the headpiece will need to be shaped a bit, but we will wait until the neck is rough-shaped to do this. When the heel was carved back in Chapter 7, the neck was rounded at the base of the heel and used as a guide in carving the heel to avoid taking off too much material. Roughly reshape this area to the fingerboard (**12-50**).

Similarly, the neck is rounded at about the first fret, to be used as a guide in shaping the slope from the back headpiece veneer (**12-51**). Trim the neck at the base of the rear head plate veneer so that the level of the neck is almost at the bottom of the veneer (**12-52**). Then using the Zona saw, cut the veneer on a diagonal from the center at the bottom to the top of the cleft on both sides (**12-53**). The veneer is removed just down to the neck wood, and the headpiece back veneer should come to a point in the middle (**12-54** and **12-55**). At this time, all these areas should be only rough-shaped. Leave a bit of material to be removed in the final shaping. The point is not to remove too much material at this time.

Begin shaping the neck by removing material with a spokeshave. When close to the shape, switch to a No. 50 pattern maker's rasp and rough in the rest of the way (**12-56** and **12-57**).

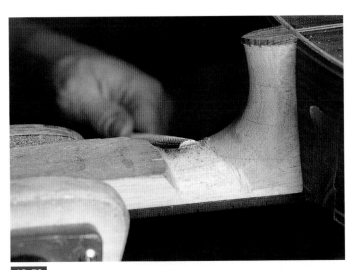

12-50   Roughly reshaping heel area

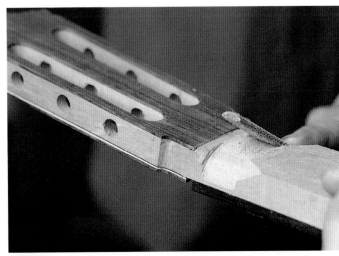

12-51   Rounding neck at about the first fret

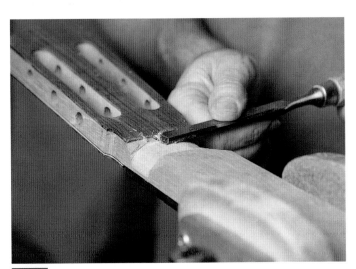

12-52   Trimming at base of back head plate veneer

12-53   Cutting veneer on a diagonal on both sides

12-54 Veneer removed just down to neck wood

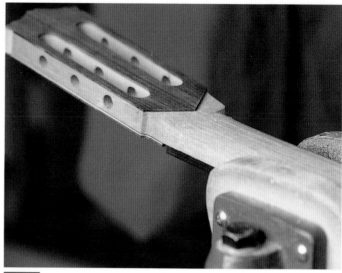

12-55 Headpiece back veneer comes to a point

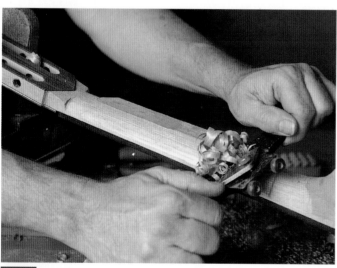

12-56 Shaping the neck with a spokeshave

12-57 Neck shaped with spokeshave and roughed in with rasp

Nut End Detail

The detail at the nut end of the neck is now shaped. Carefully carve each side to the same gentle curve. The neck material is carved in a sweeping curve from the new edge of the veneer down to meet the neck just below the nut (**12-58**). At the same time, bring the edges in to round the neck, until a continuous, symmetrical shape has been reached, and sand smooth (**12-59** and **12-60**). After shaping, the neck should come to the bottom of the rear head plate veneer. I don't use a template to carve any of the neck—this is done by eye. Your eye can be trained to see the slightest imperfection in a three-dimensional surface of almost any shape with a little practice.

If you are not comfortable with this, make a template out of cardboard and check the shape with it as you go.

The neck on this instrument should be 22 mm deep at the first fret and 24 mm deep at the eighth fret. Continue to pare down the neck, using finer cutting tools the closer you get to these dimensions.

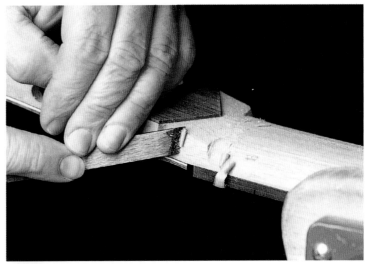

12-59 Rounding the edge of neck

12-58 Carving side to a gentle curve

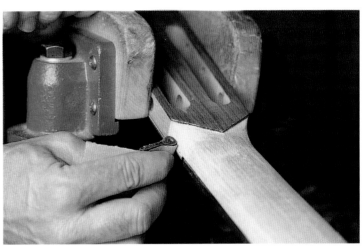

12-60 Sand the neck smooth

12-61 Shaping heel cap area

Shaping the Heel

Shape the heel cap and heel area with a chisel or gouge (**12-61** through **12-63**). Again, I do not use templates to shape the heel, but if you are not comfortable doing it by eye, a template can be made from the drawings in Chapter 5.

Adjusting the Final Neck Shape

Once the final shape has been reached, sand the entire neck smooth (**12-64** and **12-65**). At this point, I usually grip the neck as I would when playing and move around the fingerboard looking for any spots that feel irregular and adjust the shape accordingly (**12-66**).

Filling Holes Under Frets

The final touch in preparing the fingerboard is to fill in any holes along the edges under the frets. This is done with stick shellac. Stick shellac is available in black and is applied by heating up a metal applicator (a propane torch works well) and melting the shellac onto it (**12-67**). The shellac is then immediately applied to the hole (**12-68**). After the shellac cools, it can be either filed or sanded flush.

12-62 Shaping where heel meets the side

12-63 Final shape of heel

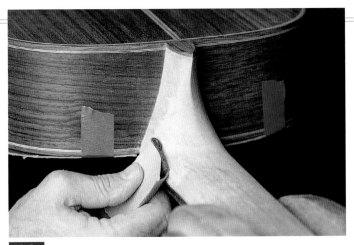

12-64 Sanding neck near heel

12-65 Sanding entire neck smooth

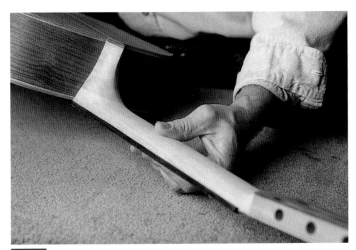

12-66 Checking for any irregularities

12-67 Filling holes under edges of frets with stick shellac

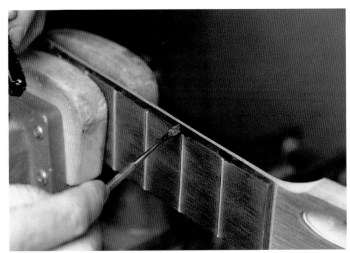

12-68 Applying shellac to holes

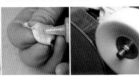

CHAPTER THIRTEEN

Finishing

Understanding Finish
Final Touches and Prepping
  for Finishing
French Polishing
Lacquering

B ELIEVE IT OR NOT, AN UNFINISHED INSTRUMENT WILL NOT SOUND AS GOOD AS ONE WITH A PROPER FINISH ON IT. THIS IS because the finish when cured will further stiffen the top. Early on I actually made an instrument and did not put a finish on it, at least not right away. The unfinished instrument sounded raw and unrefined. Needless to say, it was much more difficult to finish after the bridge had been glued on.

Besides acoustics, there are other reasons to have a nice finish on the instrument. The most obvious is looks. An often-forgotten characteristic of some finishes is their ability to limit moisture exchange between the wood and the environment. Every instrument built in my shop gets a coat of shellac on the outside and the inside of the top and sides.

There are also practical considerations when selecting a finish. First and foremost, the guitar is a musical instrument meant to be played. There are parts of the instrument that come in contact with the player and are prone to scratching, denting, and discoloration due to sweat, and certain finishes will be degraded faster than others because of this.

The finish of choice acoustically is French polish. This is a hand-rubbed shellac finish, which will be described later in this chapter in more detail. This finish is also an excellent moisture-barrier. However, it is very soft, offering almost no protection against scratching and denting, and in fact one must be very diligent to keep the finish looking good.

I have played instruments that have been French-polished, and after some time they begin to resemble Willie Nelson's guitar—the neck becomes full of nail marks, the back gets scratches from belt buckles and buttons, and it becomes discolored wherever it comes in contact with sweat. With this in mind, I have reached a compromise for finishing my instruments. The tops are French-polished and the rest of the instrument is lacquered. In this way, the finish is hard where it needs to be and acoustically optimized.

Type of Finish

The philosophy in applying a finish is the same regardless of the type of finish used. Since all my instruments are lacquered and French-polished, that is what will be discussed here, but feel free to investigate other finishes and methods of application. There are references in the bibliography for further information on finishing and the different types of finish. Lacquer is a highly toxic finish and should be applied either outside or in an adequate spray booth. Also, not everyone has spray equipment. Not to worry; there are alternatives, such as varnishes and polyurethanes that can be brushed on.

THE APPEARANCE OF the final finish can vary quite a bit depending on the desired look. Most instruments on the market these days have a mirror-smooth high-gloss finish. This look can be achieved with a number of different finishes that can be buffed to a high shine, such as lacquer, shellac, varnish, and polyurethane. On the other hand, almost any finish can be rubbed with steel wool or a similar abrasive that will result in a dull shine, or patina, which can be very attractive if a high-gloss shine is not to your taste.

The Finishing Material

The finish material itself is typically in solid form and dissolved in a solvent. For instance, shellac is actually made from the excrement of the lac bug and is dissolved in alcohol. The solvent, in this case alcohol, is used not only to dissolve the finish material but also to transport and spread it to the

13-1 Ingredients for preparing shellac

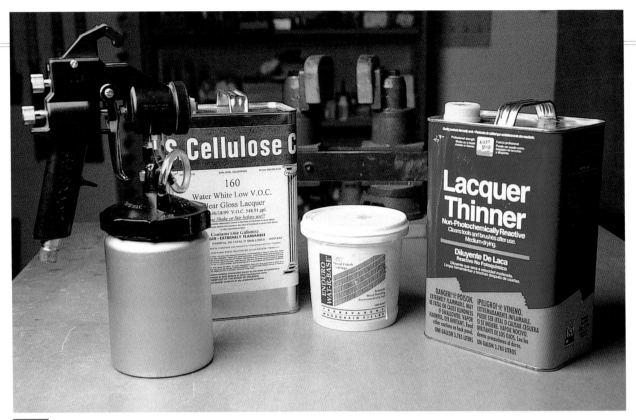

Spray gun, lacquer, water-based filler, thinner

surface. After the finish is applied, the solvent evaporates, leaving only the finish. In French polishing, mineral oil is used to lubricate the applicator as the finish is rubbed over the surface. All the ingredients for preparing shellac are shown in **13-1**. Every finish material has its own solvent. In the case of lacquer, it is lacquer thinner. Lacquer thinner is highly toxic, so care must be taken in handling and spraying it. If you are uncertain as to what solvent will dissolve a particular finish, consult the manufacturer or check out the references in the bibliography on finishing. A spray gun, lacquer, water-based filler, and thinner are shown in **13-2**.

The Three Basic Steps in Finishing

Regardless of the type of finish used, there are three basic steps in finishing: preparing the surface, applying the finish, and finishing the finish. An inferior job at any one step will create more work in the next and may be evident in the final product.

The surface of the wood is prepared by making it as flat, free of voids of any type, and smooth as possible. The next step is to apply the finish. The point here is to get as much finish on as necessary to achieve the desired look, and to get it on as flat as possible. The last step is the most important, and that is to finish the finish. Once there is enough buildup of finish on the surface, it is time to flatten and buff up to the desired shine. If all the previous steps have been performed correctly, this will solely determine the final look of the surface.

FINAL TOUCHES AND PREPPING FOR FINISHING

13-3 Rounding edges with smooth rattail file

13-4 Binding edges sanded smooth

AFTER COMPLETING CONSTRUCTION, you will need to go over the instrument thoroughly, looking for any gaps or voids that should be filled in accordingly with stick shellac, epoxy, or cyanoacrylate glue. Cyanoacrylate glue is sold in a few different viscosities and works well to fill small gaps and surface imperfections because it dries hard and clear, which allows it to be finished over virtually without detection.

The edges of the bindings should be rounded over to create both a finished look and a soft surface for the arm to rest on while playing. Round the edges over with a smooth rattail file, being careful not to mar either the top or back surface, and sand smooth (**13-3** and **13-4**).

Sanding the Surface

The entire surface should be sanded up to 320- or 400-grit sandpaper. When sanding a surface for finishing, begin with 150 or 180 grit and let the coarser-grit paper do most of the work. The higher grits should be used to remove the scratch marks left by the coarser-grit papers. When prepping for finishing, always sand with the grain. Cross-grain scratches will be visible through the finish and are difficult to remove (**13-5** and **13-6**).

Shades of Shellac

There are a number of different shades of shellac available such as Blonde, Kusmi, Amber, and Garnet, but since the top on this guitar is cedar, Super Blonde will be used, because this shellac alters the true color of the wood the least. All the other colors will tend to darken the original color of the wood. As this guitar has plenty of natural color, there is no need to enhance anything; therefore, Super Blonde shellac will work the best, providing the most natural-looking color. The shellac will be used for the sealing wash coat here, and later to French-polish the top, is prepared by mixing 21 grams of shellac flakes in 150 ml of alcohol. Let the flakes dissolve overnight, occasionally stirring to assist the process.

13-5   Sanding the surface

13-6   Sanding the headpiece

The Need for Filler

For a smooth finish on woods like Indian rosewood, mahogany, or Spanish cedar, which are porous, the pores must be filled. If the pores are left unfilled, the surface will have the appearance of being covered with pinholes, because the finish will not likely fill the pores. To avoid this pock-marked look, filler must be rubbed into the pores before the finish is applied, to create as smooth a surface as possible.

13-7 Applying shellac to the purflings

Applying Shellac

Apply the shellac carefully on the purflings with a brush, because the rosewood resin will have a tendency to run or bleed into the lighter-colored woods (**13-7**). It may be best to apply a coat or two to these areas. The rest of the rosewood and the neck may be given a wash coat of shellac to improve the efficiency of the filler. Either apply the shellac with a brush, as shown here, or wipe it on with a rag (**13-8** through **13-10**). Depending on the thickness of the coat, shellac dries fairly quickly. Allow about a half an hour, and lightly sand back the raised grain with 400-grit sandpaper. It will be obvious right away if the shellac is not yet dry; if tacky, allow more drying time. The top is not done at this time, because the next step is to fill the pores, which can be sloppy. Therefore, waiting may save an extra clean-up job.

Using Filler

There are many types of filler and they all work about the same way. I prefer clear fillers, which tend to be water-based. Pumice rubbed in with shellac will also do a nice job. Just sprinkle a bit of

13-8 Applying shellac to the lower bout sides

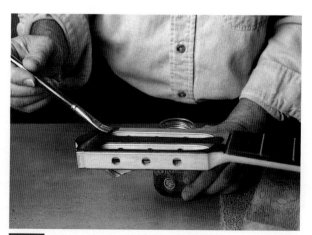

13-9 Applying shellac to the headpiece

pumice on the surface, and rub it in with a pad like the one used to French-polish (see the section on French polishing below). Avoid tinted fillers because they will discolor the purflings and anything else with which they come in contact. As we have gone to the trouble of selecting all this beautiful wood based on color and so on, it would be a shame to stain it at this point. The fillers labeled "Natural" usually appear gray and will be visible through the finish.

If using water-based clear filler, wipe it on with a rag in all directions, making sure to get it into the pores; let it sit for a few seconds; and before it dries completely, scrape it off (**13-11** and **13-12**). It is advisable to apply the filler only to a small area at a time because it dries quickly. A small cabinet scraper will remove the excess filler by actually cutting it at the surface, leaving the pores filled.

A couple of applications may be necessary to achieve the desired results. The surface will not likely be perfectly smooth, but there shouldn't be any empty pores. Sand after each application, and be sure to remove all excess filler from the surface without leaving any lumps on the surface (**13-13**). The filled surface should be let to stand at least overnight, since the filler tends to shrink a bit and another application may be needed.

As shellac is such a good moisture-barrier, I like to give the entire instrument a couple of coats of shellac after filling the pores (**13-14**). Almost any finish will adhere to shellac, so this will not create any problems when lacquering or varnishing over it.

13-10 Applying shellac to the neck

13-11 Wiping on water-based clear filler

13-12 Scraping filler off before it dries

13-13 Sanding after each application

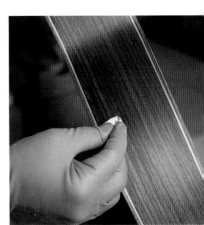

13-14 Applying coats of shellac after filling

FRENCH POLISHING

13-15 Ingredients for French polish

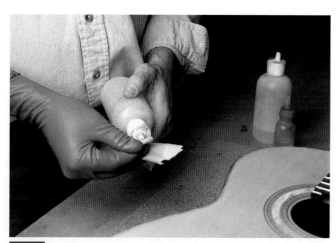

13-16 Thoroughly sanding top

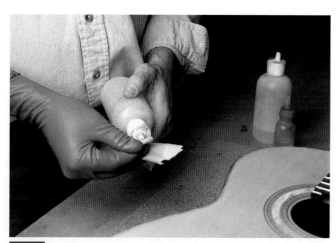

13-17 Preparing to apply wash coat of shellac

Everyone seems to have his or her own way to French-polish, although everyone virtually follows the same basic two-step process, which is to first apply a finish and then to spirit off the finish, or finish the finish.

French polishing is a technique of applying shellac that has been in use for centuries. The shellac flakes are dissolved in alcohol, as described previously (21 grams of shellac flakes to 150 ml of alcohol), and applied to the cloth along with a bit of alcohol and a drop of mineral oil (**13-15**). The shellac used should be fresh, because old shellac will not dry properly. A good test for shellac is to rub some between your fingers. It should feel dry in less than thirty seconds. If it doesn't, throw it away as it will not cure properly.

The top can now be sanded thoroughly using up to 320-grit sandpaper (**13-16**). Before polishing, apply a wash coat of shellac to the top with a clean rag, wiping in one direction to avoid pulling any color from the bindings or rosette onto the cedar (**13-17** through **13-19**).

To French-polish, the shellac and alcohol are applied to a cloth, which is wadded up inside another piece of cloth, preferably fine linen. Then a drop of mineral oil is added to the outside of the pad to lubricate it as it is wiped on the surface (**13-20** through **13-22**). Tap the pad on the palm of your hand to disperse the shellac, and then rub the pad on the surface in a circular or figure-eight pattern (**13-23**). The shape of the rubbing pattern is not important, as long as there is no stopping to change direction.

13-18 Applying shellac in one direction

13-19 Avoiding pulling color from rosette or bindings

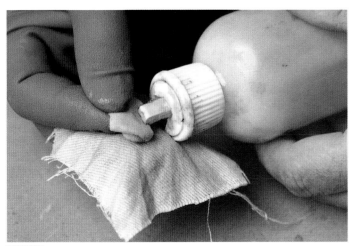

13-20 Preparation of French polish

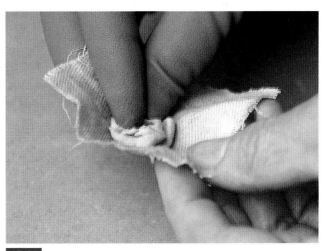

13-21 Cloth with shellac and alcohol wadded in fine linen

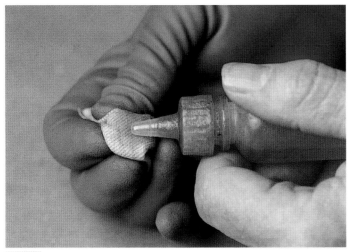

13-22 Drop of mineral oil to lubricate

13-23 Rubbing in circular or figure-eight pattern

The idea is to get on as much finish as flat and even as possible. Move the pad fairly slowly, and as the pad dries, gradually increase the pressure until the pad is completely dry.

Reload the pad as before and resume the pattern. Each application must be fused to the previous one, so don't be afraid to use some pressure when rubbing. Store the pad in an airtight jar in between sessions. The outer cloth can be changed as it wears out. Apply a couple coats and let it dry for a couple of hours.

Each new coat softens the finish; therefore, if you keep applying many coats in one session, you will not achieve the buildup you are looking for, because you will just be pushing around the shellac on the surface without adding any new shellac. When applying the finish, spend more time on the edges, since it is important to get a good buildup on the edges as they are usually handled more.

Once there is enough buildup on the surface, gradually decrease the amount of shellac loaded into the pad to the point where just alcohol is being used. Using only alcohol in the pad will remove the oil on the surface and polish it to a clear shine. This is known as spiriting off. Only use a small amount of alcohol at this point, being careful not to make the pad wet. The pad should be fairly dry or cool to the touch. Once the surface is clear, the finish is done.

Further Polishing

To polish it further, the finish must be hard; therefore, it must cure for about a week. Once it has hardened, buff it to a mirror shine with a fine plastic polishing compound such as Novex or Maquiar's Mirror Glaze No. 17. Apply with a piece of cotton, rubbing vigorously. Let it sit for a few minutes and wipe it clean with a fresh piece of cotton.

LACQUERING

THE SAME PRINCIPLES apply in creating a lacquer finish as with the French polish. The only difference is how the finish is applied. Most lacquers dry too fast to be brushed on and therefore must be sprayed on. Any type of spray system will work, but the HVLP systems get more finish on the surface with less overspray wasting less lacquer. Lacquer thinner is highly toxic and should not be allowed to touch the skin, nor should the fumes be breathed in. Always wear rubber gloves and a proper respirator designed specifically for solvent fumes when spraying. Spray either outside or in a properly ventilated spray booth.

This guitar was sprayed outside in the summer in North Carolina, so the humidity level was high. In **13-24**, the white milky haze from moisture being trapped is evident. This haze dissipated after a bit, because retarder had been added to the lacquer, slowing down the drying time and allowing the moisture to escape. If this happens and retarder is not available, just spray again in drier conditions to release the moisture.

What Is Lacquer?

Nitrocellulose lacquer is made from cotton. Only part of the finish is nitrocellulose; most of it is a resin, which is usually alkyd or mastic. The nitrocellulose part gives lacquer its fast-drying property. The resins are added to improve the flexibility and building ability. Generally, the more elastic, colorless, and resistant the lacquer is, the more it costs. The lacquer used in my shop is Water White Low VOC Clear Gloss Lacquer.

It takes just as long to create a quality finish using lacquer as it does with any other finish. The principles are the same: get as much finish on as flat and even as possible, and then finish the finish. With practice, it may be easier to get a flat, even buildup with spraying lacquer. Even the surface of a sprayed finish will require a lot of work to get to a mirror shine.

13-24 Spraying on lacquer

Spraying Lacquer Is Not Easy

The common belief is that spraying lacquer is an easy finish to use; this is just not true. There are as many things that can go wrong with a lacquer finish as with any other finish, if not more. For instance, if you are spraying lacquer outside, you will be subject to the humidity level. Since the lacquer dries very quickly, if there is a lot of moisture in the air, it may become trapped in the finish, which will cause the finish to appear milky-white. This is easily avoided by adding a lacquer retarder, which will cause the lacquer to dry more slowly and allow the moisture to escape.

13-25 Freshly sprayed wet surface

Positioning for Spraying

Half the battle with spraying is holding the instrument while it is being sprayed and repositioning it without touching the wet finish. To facilitate this, first mask off the top surface of the fingerboard with masking tape. Then clamp a block of wood with cork or other soft material glued to its face to the fingerboard just above the sound hole, and be sure to use a caul inside the instrument to protect the inside of the top. This block can then be clamped in a vise mounted on a stand for easy access all the way around. In spraying a guitar, it is necessary to change the orientation only twice. The first position is laying flat on its back to spray the front of the headpiece. Then the block is secured in the vise with the top facing down; the entire remainder of the instrument can be sprayed in this position.

Preparing the Lacquer for Spraying

To make the lacquer more suitable for spraying, it is first thinned with lacquer thinner. Thin until the stream of liquid that runs off the stirring stick breaks into drops. The correct viscosity will yield the best results. Also, if the humidity is too high, add retarder in the quantity as directed by the manufacturer.

Spray on a test surface first, and adjust the spray gun to provide the best flow of the finish once you start working on the surface of the instrument. Consult the manufacturers' manual for adjusting the airflow and the width of the fan pattern. I use an upright oval fan pattern, which is about as wide as half the back at the lower bout. Adjust the airflow and finish flow so that the surface is wet and flat. A freshly sprayed wet surface is shown in **13-25**. If the surface resembles that of an orange peel, there might have been too much finish and not enough air coming out of the gun, the finish may not have been thinned adequately, or the gun might have been held too close to the surface. For more information on spraying, see some of the finishing references in the bibliography.

Applying the Lacquer

When spraying, the gun should be held approximately 6 to 8 inches away from the surface and as perpendicular as possible to it for the best results. Each pass should generously overlap the previous one and conclude several inches beyond the edge, with the trigger being released at the end of each stroke (**13-26** through **13-28**).

Spray on the first coat and let it dry overnight. When dry, sand smooth using 320-grit sandpaper. The subsequent coats can be sprayed within a couple of hours of each other. Sand with 400-grit sandpaper after the second coat; it will not be necessary to sand the finish again until it is done. For a quality finish on a guitar, five or six coats will be necessary. Before spraying the last coat, sand the finish flat with 600-grit sandpaper. Spray each coat heavy and wet, just short of running. Once you are satisfied that enough finish has been applied, let it cure for a minimum of three days, but preferably up to a week.

13-26 Hold sprayer 6" to 8" away

13-27 Keep sprayer perpendicular to surface

13-28 Generously overlap previous pass

13-29   Sanding the cured finish

13-30   Be careful around the edges

13-31   Clean sheets when clogged

Finishing the Finish

After the finish has cured hard, it is time to finish the finish. Begin by sanding flat with 3600-grit Micro Mesh, being careful around the edges; it is easy to sand through the finish here (**13-29** and **13-30**). Micro Mesh should be used with a lubricant. Water will work best if a bit of soap is added to slow down the cutting action. The sheets can be cleaned as they begin to clog up (**13-31**) and may be reused again and again. When the surface is flat, remove the marks left by the 3600-grit Micro Mesh with progressively finer grits up to 6000 or 8000. The surface is then buffed to a shine with a buffing wheel and polishing compounds (**13-32** and **13-33**), or if a buffing wheel is not available, it can be rubbed out by hand.

A high-gloss surface is usually achieved using a combination of both methods. To rub the surface out by hand, there are a couple of choices. One is to rub it out with fine rottenstone on a felt pad with a little water as a lubricant. The other is to rub out the surface first with white polishing compound No. 7, which is used on automobiles. The compound is applied sparingly to some cotton and rubbed on the surface (**13-34**). The residue is removed with a clean piece of cotton. The finish is then brought to a high gloss with a fine polish used for plastics such as Meguiar's Mirror Glaze No. 10 clear plastic polish. Apply with cotton, rubbing vigorously, and remove the residue with a clean piece (**13-35**).

By following the instructions and being careful, it is possible to achieve a high-gloss mirror-smooth finish. Finishing is an art and can be enjoyed by anyone. The most common mistake when finishing is to rush the job. A fine finish takes time. Relax and enjoy the process.

13-32 Buffing surface with buffing wheel

13-33 Buffing surface to a shine

13-34 Rubbing surface out by hand

13-35 Applying clear polish

CHAPTER FOURTEEN

The Bridge

Bridge Design
Building the Bridge
Installing the Bridge

THE BRIDGE PERFORMS A FEW VERY IMPORTANT FUNCTIONS. IT ACTS AS A TERMINUS FOR THE STRINGS, DETERMINES THE string spacing, and sets the string length. Its purpose is to transfer the force of the player's stroke on the strings to bring about movement in the top, or soundboard, which will create the sound that we hear. The angle the strings make as they leave the tie block and rise over the saddle determines the attack, or crispness of the strings' tone.

The selection of the material, along with the design of the bridge, is critical to the bridge's performance. Factors to consider with material selection are strength, flexibility, and density. For optimal sound, the string height above the surface of the soundboard should be between 10 and 12 mm. The bridge is designed to provide this string height with only about 3 mm of saddle sticking out.

The position of the bridge is also critical in producing a playable instrument. The point where the strings leave the saddle sets the string length in conjunction with the spot where the strings leave the nut. Since by this time the fingerboard and neck are firmly in place, the string length can be set only by the location of the bridge. Another important factor in positioning the bridge is its role in providing adequate clearance between the first and sixth strings and the edge of the fingerboard. The bridge must be positioned so that the outer strings provide a symmetrical 5-mm porch on each side.

In my early years as a player, I had a guitar that gave me fits as I played above the seventh fret on the first string. I would continually "fall off the porch." If you have ever experienced this, you know what an awful sound that can make. At the time, I assumed it was my poor technique. After I began building instruments myself, I noticed that the bridge had shifted slightly to the treble side, causing the porch to gradually narrow the entire length of the fingerboard, becoming too close to the edge at around the seventh fret. This could have happened either when gluing it on or it was never in the right spot in the first place.

Building a Successful Bridge

The importance of the bridge in producing a fine instrument cannot be stressed enough. The design of the bridge has evolved to the point where it is today. Slight variations still exist, but by and large the basic design remains. With the information gained from experience, we can build a successful bridge for our instrument without having to go through a lot of trial and error.

14-1   Drawing line on grain lines to straighten

14-2   Cutting along the line with band saw

One of the functions of the bridge is to set the height of the strings above the fingerboard. The ideal range of height for the strings is between 10 and 12 mm. The amount of saddle sticking out of the slot on the bridge should be the same as the amount in the slot—between 3 and 3.5 mm seems best. In order to put us right in the middle of the height range, the bridge should be approximately 8.5 mm high in the center (see the drawings in Chapter 5).

For this bridge, we will use Indian rosewood. A finished bridge this size out of Indian rosewood should have a weight of approximately 20 grams (weighed with tie block inlays but without the saddle). The range of weight for a bridge should be between 15 and 25 grams. Being on the light side will produce a more crisp sound, where the notes will seem to pop to the touch. The heavier the bridge is, the more sluggish the response will be to the player.

Tilt of the Tie Block

Notice that the tie block tilts forward slightly. The angle the strings make as they rise to meet the saddle is important. This tilt, combined with the distance from the tie block to the saddle, has a direct effect on this angle, and this angle has a direct effect on the sound and the responsiveness of the instrument. A shallow angle will produce a muddier tone, and a steeper angle will produce a crisper sound. The lower the angle is, the less energy transference there is to the soundboard. The optimal practical angle is about 45 degrees.

As in almost all aspects of the guitar, no two things are mutually exclusive. The bridge is no exception. All the design elements must be in balance with one another for optimal results.

BUILDING THE BRIDGE

To start, select a bridge blank that is quarter-sawn with as straight a grain as possible and free of defects of any kind such as knots, wind shakes, and so forth. Ideally, the grain lines in the blank should run perfectly parallel to the longer sides. The blank chosen here has grain running at a slight angle to the long sides, so the first order of business is to make the grain lines parallel to the long side. Draw a line directly on the grain lines, from end to end, and cut along this line with a band saw (**14-1** and **14-2**).

Sizing the Bridge Blank

You now have a bridge blank that is a rhombus of sorts. Clean up the cut edge on a shooting board with a hand plane, and cut on the band saw to a width of approximately 30.5 mm (**14-3** and **14-4**). Plane the rough edge on the shooting board until you have a final width of 30 mm. Square one edge on the shooting board, and crosscut to a final length of 188 mm (**14-5** and **14-6**). Crosscut the blank a touch long, and trim to final length on the shooting board.

14-3 Cutting to width

14-4 Planing the edge

14-5 Squaring one end

14-6 Crosscutting to length

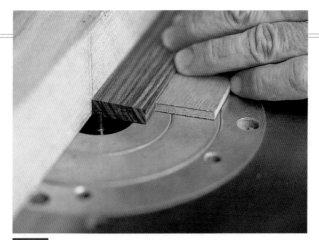

14-7 Cutting slot for the saddle

Cutting Slots for the Saddle and Tie Block

Once the blank is sized, the slots for the saddle and tie block inlays are cut. To cut the slot for the saddle, set up the shaper or router table to cut a 3.5-mm-deep channel that is ⅛ inch wide and 3 mm in from the front edge of the bridge. Cut this channel along the entire length of the bridge (**14-7**). Avoid cutting the saddle slot on a table saw, because the ⅛-inch-wide blade may wobble a bit, causing the slot to be too wide.

The channels for the tie block inlays can be cut either on the shaper/router table or on the table saw. The setup for these cuts is easier and faster on a table saw equipped with a flat-topped blade, so if you have one, I recommend it. The back-edge rabbet is cut first. Size the channel to fit the bone inlay, and cut the entire length of the blank (**14-8** and **14-9**). The inside channel is cut so that the inside edge of the channel is 11 mm from the back edge of the bridge and the depth is increased by 1 mm. Bone inlay is usually 2 mm square, so the inside channel is set to a depth of 3 mm. This channel is also cut the entire length of the blank (**14-10**).

14-8 Cutting back-edge rabbet

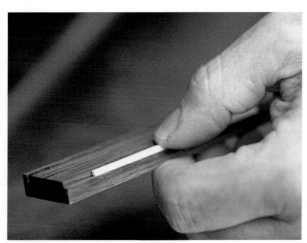

14-9 Rabbet sized to fit bone inlay

14-10 Cutting inside channel for bone inlay

Drilling Holes for Strings

The tie block is marked 54 mm in from each end of the bridge, which gives a tie block that is 80 mm long directly in the center of the blank. The string spacing I use is 60 mm. Measure in 10 mm on each side of the tic block and two outer holes for the strings. Mark the remaining four holes 12 mm apart from each other and ⅛ inch up from the bottom edge of the bridge. Using a 0.078-inch bit, drill the holes on the drill press to a depth of 13 or 14 mm (**14-11**).

Cutting Channel in a Series of Passes

A channel now needs to be cut between the tie block and the saddle slot. As this channel deepens, the string holes will be revealed. Cut this channel only deep enough to remove all the string holes from the bottom surface. The bottom of the front edge of this channel will also be the bottom of the ramp up to the saddle. This channel is cut on the shaper/router table fence by making a series of stop cuts using a ⅛-inch bit. The depth will be reached with a series of passes, because this channel is too deep for a ⅛-inch bit to cut all at once.

Mark the edges of the bit on the fence to give the stopping points (**14-12**). Set the fence so that the inside edge of the channel is just beyond the inside tie block inlay, or approximately 13.5 mm in from the back edge. Mark the stop points on the bottom of the bridge blank. These points should be just inside the outer reaches of the tie block on each end.

Carefully lower the blank to the spinning bit, while pushing up against the fence (**14-13**). Try to get it right up to the mark on the far edge,

14-11 Drilling string holes

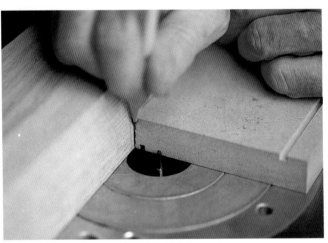

14-12 Marking stopping points on fence from edges of the bit

14-13 Pushing blank against fence while lowering on spinning bit

14-14 Exposed string holes

14-15 Crosscutting wings

14-16 Sawing to the crosscut

14-17 Rough-cut wings

because when cutting in the direction opposite to normal (the normal direction to feed stock into a spinning blade is to have the cutters coming toward the direction of the feed), there is a tendency to grab. Push the blank up to the second stop line, and carefully lift up the back edge of the blank while keeping it against the fence. Do not turn or twist the blank as you lift. Raise the blade and repeat until you have exposed the string holes and there are no remnants of the holes on the floor of the cut. It is important to raise the bit only slightly each time after the holes are visible, since no more material should be removed than necessary (**14-14**).

Cutting the Wings

The wings can now be marked and cut. Using a handsaw, cut down to the depth of the saddle channel (3 to 3.5 mm) along the line for the ends of the tie block, which is 54 mm in from the ends of the blank (**14-15**). On the band saw, resaw the wings to a thickness of 4 mm up to the crosscut at the tie block ends (**14-16** and **14-17**).

Gluing the Inlays

The blank is now ready to have the tie block inlays glued in. The outside tie block inlay is glued in first, using tape as a clamp (**14-18**). After sufficient setup time, remove the tape, and with a chisel remove enough material from the ramp to get a few small hand clamps on the inside tie block inlay, and glue it in (**14-19**).

Beginning Final Shaping

After the glue has dried, final shaping can begin. Starting with the wings, take a No. 50 pattern maker's rasp and quickly round over the wings, leaving the center height about what it is (**14-20**). Do not round all the way to the bottom; leave a little less than a ⅟₁₆-inch lip around the bottom of the wings.

The top surface of the tie block should be tilted forward, being approximately 1 mm taller in the back. The inside tie block inlay should be sitting 1 mm lower than the top surface. Using a shoulder plane set to take a fine cut, plane the top of the tie block, creating a flat surface with the

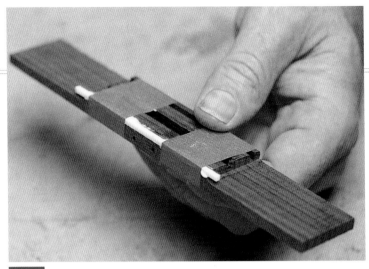

14-18 Outside tie block inlay "clamped" with tape

14-19 Small hand clamps on the inside tie block inlay

14-20 Rounding the wings

14-21 Planing top of tie block

14-22 Rounding top edge in front of the saddle

correct slope (**14-21**). Remove the sharp edges of the tie block with some 320-grit sandpaper.

The angle of the ramp itself is not important, but there must be enough clearance to get the strings through the holes and up to the saddle. Shape the ramp by cutting with a sharp chisel (**14-22**), and clean up with a small scraper and sandpaper. Round over the top edge in front of the saddle with a file, and clean up with sandpaper (**14-23**). The ends of the bridge are beveled to about 45 degrees with a hand plane (**14-24**).

Fitting to the Domed Top and Applying Finish

The final shaping of the bridge is to make the bottom to fit the dome of the top. Clamp the handle of the convex 25-foot radius sanding block in the bench vise, and pass the bottom of the bridge over it until it fits the top of the guitar without having to use any pressure to get the ends down (**14-25**). Prepare the bridge for finishing by sanding, using up to 400-grit sandpaper, and give it a coat of shellac. Lightly sand back the shellac, and give it at least two coats of finishing oil. I prefer the bridge not to shine and give it a dull sheen, as with the fingerboard (**14-26**). After the final coat of oil, rub it with 0000# steel wool. Try to make sure that no oil has gotten on the bottom glue surface area. If it has, take some fine sandpaper and clean it off. The bridge is now ready to be glued on.

14-23 Rounding over the front edge

14-24 Beveling ends of bridge with hand plane

14-25 Passing bottom of bridge over 25' radius sanding block

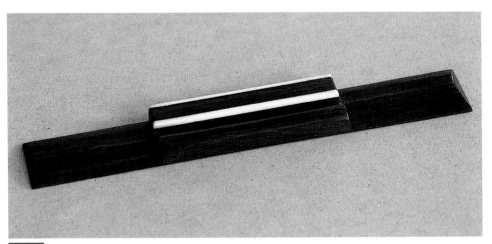
14-26 Finished bridge

Using a Marked Stick to Measure

One thing that was impressed upon us in the Fine Woodworking Program at the College of the Redwoods is to get away from using numbers as a means of measurement as much as possible. This is something that I learned the hard way. Wherever possible, use a stick with a mark on it that is labeled and carefully measured with a ruler, so that while you are working it is not necessary to remember number measurements and details, and you can concentrate on what you are doing. There could not be a more appropriate place to introduce this practice than here.

INSTALLING A BRIDGE is not as difficult a task as it is nerve-racking. The bridge is installed after the instrument has been finished, which puts everything at risk. This is not meant to scare you, but to make you conscious that concentration and care are necessary to install a bridge correctly.

Bridge Measuring Stick

Before doing any work installing the bridge, build a bridge measuring stick (**14-27**). Start with a piece of ¼-inch plywood or similarly stable material approximately 3 inches wide by 24 inches long and square one end. The end just squared will be the nut end. Now measure from the nut edge down 650 mm plus 1 mm. This extra millimeter is for compensation due to string tension and other factors that make the system imperfect. Mark a centerline down the middle of the stick, and draw in the taper of the fingerboard, which is 53 mm wide at the nut and 63 mm wide at the twelfth fret, and continue this taper all the way to the end of the stick. This stick will be used to position the bridge.

Fitting the Nut Blank

Cut and file or sand the nut blank to fit in the slot. It is all right if it is too wide and too high at this point; it just has to fit in the slot. Sand a saddle blank to fit in the saddle slot on the bridge. The slot is ⅛ inch wide; therefore, using a ⅛-inch saddle blank will require only a little sanding. Sand with no less than 320-grit sandpaper, and be sure to sand both sides to remove any marks.

Bridge Measuring Stick

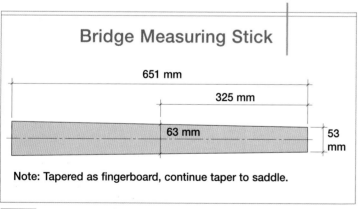

651 mm

325 mm

63 mm

53 mm

Note: Tapered as fingerboard, continue taper to saddle.

14-27

Positioning the Bridge

Once both the nut and the saddle fit their respective slots, place the bridge stick on the fingerboard up against the nut and clamp in place. The stick should fit perfectly over the fingerboard without hanging over on either side. Take the bridge and place it on the lower bout, up against the saddle (**14-28**). It is important that the middle of the bridge be lined up with the centerline of the stick. The middle of the bridge should also be lined up with the center seam in the top. If this is your first guitar and it is not lined up with the center seam, it's okay. You'll get it the next time. It is much more important that the stick be placed properly on the fingerboard and the center of the bridge be lined up to the center of the stick.

Masking the Bridge Area and Protecting the Top

Once the bridge is positioned correctly, take a piece of low-adhesive masking tape and place it on the top, up against the back edge of the bridge. Place another piece up against the edge of each wing. Remove the stick and place a piece along the front edge of the bridge. Continue to mask off the bridge until there are about three layers of tape on each edge. Make a cardboard template of the top with a cutout for the fingerboard and the bridge area. Tape this down to protect the finish from damage while you are working, and remove the bridge (**14-29**).

14-28 Positioning bridge with bridge stick clamped to fingerboard

14-29 Bridge postion masked, cardboard to protect the top

14-30 Scraping off finish

Preparing the Bridge Area for Gluing

Using a chisel you feel comfortable with, begin to scrape off finish in the masked-off area (**14-30**). Scrape right up to the tape without forcing it beyond, and scrape all the way down to the wood. Once the finish has been removed, sand lightly with 320-grit sandpaper.

Going through the sound hole, tape a caul to the underside of the top directly under the bridge with regular adhesive masking tape (**14-31** and **14-32**). The caul should have notches for the fan braces, enabling it to fit over the braces without crushing them. Place the bridge in the masked-off space, and perform a dry run with the bridge clamp to make sure there are no problems. Small cauls will be necessary to protect the bridge from the metal and screws of the clamp. These should be fashioned out of thin material and covered with a thin gasket cork to prevent damage to the bridge.

14-31 Caul for under the bridge

14-32 Taping caul to the underside of the top

14-33 Applying glue to bridge

14-34 Placing cauls in position on the bridge

Gluing the Bridge

Apply glue evenly to the bottom surface of the bridge, and let it sit for a few minutes (**14-33**). This allows the glue to get a little tacky, which will prevent the bridge from sliding around as you apply pressure to the clamps. Place the glued bridge in position, and rock it back and forth slightly as you apply hand pressure to get a good seal. Place the cauls on top of the bridge, and apply the bridge clamp (**14-34** and **14-35**). The stacked tape will serve to keep the bridge in place as you tighten the clamps. Set the timer for eight minutes, and when time is up, clean any excess glue off the surface of the top with a damp cloth; make sure to dry the surface when finished, leaving a clean surface (**14-36**). I usually let the glue cure overnight with the bridge clamp on.

14-35 Applying bridge clamp

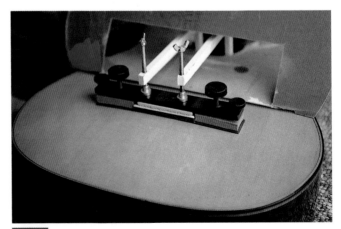

14-36 Clamped bridge

CHAPTER FIFTEEN

The Setup

The Nut, Saddle, and
Tuning Machines
Strings and Final Setup
Care of Your Guitar

A GUITAR'S SETUP IS VITAL TO ITS LIFE AS AN INSTRUMENT. A GOOD SETUP CAN MAKE A GREAT-SOUNDING GUITAR A JOY TO play. A bad setup may render an otherwise wonderful instrument useless. One benefit of a good design is that very little will need to be done at setup to create a playable instrument. The features necessary for an instrument to be player-friendly have already been designed into the instrument, and major adjustments and tinkering should not be necessary. All that is needed to be done is for the strings to be put on and the nut and saddle heights set.

In setting up a guitar, there is a certain amount of personal preference regarding action. Some players with a particularly light touch may like a low action, finding it easier to play, while players who exercise a full range of dynamics, from fortissimo to piano, require a little higher action to avoid string buzz. There are limits to both extremes. Too low an action produces unwanted effects like string slap, where, if the string is plucked hard, it will actually slap against the fingerboard. Also, pull-offs are more difficult to perform and require more exertion with too low an action. In addition, as the action is lowered, so is the string angle. Too low a string angle will result in an unresponsive, muddy-sounding instrument. On the other hand, if the action is high, the instrument will undoubtedly be more difficult to play. As always, there are trade-offs at the extremes and a good balance is desired most of the time.

Besides setting the action, the instrument will need to be intonated. The instrument's intonation is simply how well in tune it is all over the fingerboard. It must be realized that the guitar is not a well-tempered instrument. A well-tempered instrument is one that has a string for every note. On a guitar, one string must play nineteen or even twenty notes. To do this perfectly with fixed frets and a fixed string length is impossible. There have been efforts to improve the approximation of the tuning, but it will always be an approximation and never be perfect.

THE NUT, SADDLE, AND TUNING MACHINES

THE TYPICAL NUT and saddle on a classical guitar are made of cow bone owing to the scarcity of ivory. The bone is very hard but easily cut with a saw or hand planed. The bone can be further whitened by soaking it in hydrogen peroxide. Leave it in a jar of hydrogen peroxide for a few days, and then let it dry for a few more days before using it, as the liquid will swell it slightly.

Shaping the Nut and Saddle

The nut and saddle have already been fitted into the slots; now they must be cut to the correct height and shaped. Starting with the nut, first cut it and then file or sand it to a height approximately 0.090 inches above the fingerboard. With a file, ramp the back edge of the nut at about 35 degrees, stopping just before the front edge and leaving approximately 0.070 inches flat (**15-1**). Measure the length in the slot (**15-2**), and cut the nut just slightly longer than necessary (**15-3**); sand to the final size to remove the tool marks without making it too small.

15-1 Filing nut to correct height and shape

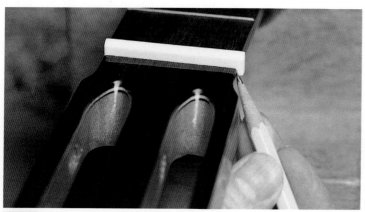

15-2 Measuring length of slot

15-3 Cutting nut slightly longer than necessary

15-4 Marking positions of first and sixth strings

15-5 Cutting slots for the strings with a shallow kerf

Preparing the Slots for the Strings

Mark the positions of the first and sixth strings 5 mm in from the edges (**15-4**). There should be 43 mm of space in between, which allows a string spacing of 8.6 mm. Mark the positions of the rest of the strings, and begin to cut the slots for the strings with the Zona saw by making a shallow kerf (**15-5**). The thin kerf left by the saw is then widened with a triangular file (**15-6**).

The slots are then filed so that the strings fit about halfway down in the slot without being pinched on the sides. Nut files are available that have the dimensions printed on them, making it easier to size the slots for the strings being used. With the appropriate file, round and slope the slots for the strings, making sure the highest point is right at the front edge of the nut (**15-7**). The strings must break over the front edge of the nut for proper intonation. Knock the visible edges off the nut with 400-grit sandpaper, and buff the nut on the buffing wheel or with polishing compound. Any additional adjustments in height will be made by removing material from the bottom edge after the instrument is strung up.

15-6 Widening kerf with a triangular file

15-7 The highest point should remain at the front

15-8 Measuring distance from top of twelfth fret using straightedge from bass side of nut to saddle

15-9 Saddle marked to cut slant

15-10 Marking length of saddle

Adjusting the Saddle

A good range for the height of the strings above the surface of the top at the bridge is between 10 and 12 mm. This height will work best with this particular bridge design with about 3 mm or so of saddle sticking above the slot. This will provide a good string angle (as discussed in Chapter 14), which will not only help balance the trebles and the basses a bit but also create an instrument responsive to the touch.

The saddle should fit in the slot well enough not to fall out if the guitar is turned upside down but should not have to be forced into the slot. Sand the saddle with fine sandpaper to achieve this type of fit. Once the saddle is in its slot, find a rigid straightedge that will make the span from the nut to the saddle. Place the straightedge in one of the nut slots on the bass side and rest it on the saddle. Measure the distance from the top of the twelfth fret at about the fifth string to the bottom of the straightedge, and add 0.010 inches to compensate for the difference in height with the strings tensioned (**15-8**). This distance needs to be approximately 0.140 inches. Subtract 0.140 inches from the measurement taken and divide by two. This is approximately the amount needed to be removed from the height of the saddle at the bass side. Slightly more can be removed from the treble side. Mark the saddle accordingly (**15-9**) and cut on this slant. This is an approximate amount and some final trimming will be necessary; therefore, cut just to the waste side of the line. The string height on the treble side can be less than that on the bass side. Measure the length of the saddle in the slot (**15-10**) and cut to length. Trim the back edge off the saddle before intonating so that the string will lie flat on a narrow portion of the top (**15-11**).

Installing the Tuning Machines

The tuning machines can be any brand for this guitar as long as the rollers are on 35-mm centers. Before putting the machines in the holes, first clean out any finish that may have accumulated by twisting a 0.390-inch drill bit into the holes by hand (**15-12**). Seat the machines, making sure the gears are facing the body of the guitar, and using an awl, create small pilot holes for the screws, and screw the machines in place (**15-13** and **15-14**).

15-11 Trimming the back edge off the saddle

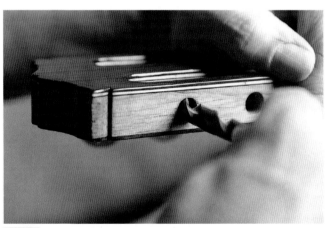
15-12 Cleaning out any finish in holes

15-13 Creating pilot holes with an awl

15-14 Screwing the tuning machines in place

String Tension

Strings come in different tensions. Be aware that using a different brand and tension than that used to intonate the instrument may require it to be intonated again. In the equation used to determine pitch, string tension is a variable. If you change that variable, you change the pitch. In general, high-tension strings need more tension to be brought up to pitch. This additional tension may translate to slightly more sound, but it will definitely put more strain on the top and neck. For this design, strings with normal tension should be fine. High-tension strings are sometimes used to boost a particular response if lacking in the instrument itself. For instance, if the trebles are not bright enough, they can be improved slightly with a higher-tension string. A lower-tension string will have the opposite effect. Compensating in this way, however, will have a limited effect. The object is to design and build into the instrument things like balance across the range of notes, because it will be very difficult if not impossible to adjust it after the fact. Strings with normal tension are adequate in most cases.

STRINGS ARE OF course a matter of personal preference. With classical guitar strings, almost every different brand will make the instrument sound slightly different. Experiment with various strings until you find the strings for you.

Before winding the strings around the tie block, take a match and burn a little ball on the end of the three treble strings. This will prevent them from slipping through the tie holes in the tie block as they are brought up to tension and may also prevent a ding in the finish behind the bridge (**15-15**). A hand crank for winding the knobs on the machines will help to speed up the process of stringing up the instrument. Once all the strings are on, bring them up to pitch. An electronic tuner of some kind may be necessary. Bend a thin piece of metal wire such as an electric guitar string into a U shape, and beginning with the first string place it under the string on the saddle so that this is the only spot where the string touches the saddle.

15-15 Treble strings have a ball on the ends to prevent slippage

With the string up to pitch, compare the fretted note at the twelfth fret to the harmonic created by plucking the string while touching it over the twelfth fret. Move the wire back and forth until they are the same. If the fretted note is flat, move the wire forward toward the nut; if sharp, move it back. Mark the spot where they are the same on the top of the saddle with a pencil (**15-16**). Do this for all six strings. The marks on the saddle designate where the string must break over the saddle in order to be in tune. Generally, these peaks will be closer to the front edge on the treble side and progress slightly toward the back edge as you move toward the bass side with a slight jump at the third string. Shape the top edge of the saddle so that the peaks are in the places marked (**15-17**). Take care to round these peaks to eliminate sharp edges that may cut into the strings.

15-16 Marking the spot where string pitch and harmonic are the same

15-17 Shaping top edge of saddle so peaks are in places marked

Author enjoying the guitar

Fine Adjustments

Now that the instrument is intonated, some fine adjustments in the height of the nut and saddle may be necessary. First, check the nut end. The height at the bass side over the first fret should be about 1 mm. It may be a little less than half that on the treble side. This is a matter of personal preference. The only precaution is not to make it so low that an open string buzzes when played hard. Next, set the final height of the saddle. A typical string height for the sixth string over the twelfth fret is 0.140 to 0.145 inches. The height of the first string at the twelfth fret is typically 0.125 to 0.135 inches. However, there may be slight variations in these numbers from player to player.

The guitar is now finished. The strings will take a while to stretch out and will have to be retuned constantly until they do, but the life of your new instrument has begun. This guitar should bring with it years of enjoyment and pride in a job well done (**15-18**).

CARE OF YOUR GUITAR

THE FIRST STEP in caring for your new hand-crafted instrument is to purchase a good-quality hard-shell case for it. This will make it easier to transport, provide a controlled environment for storage, and limit the amount of UV light that can potentially change the color of the wood after prolonged exposure. If you intend to travel a lot with the instrument, a quality travel case will be a good investment.

Being Aware of Temperature and Humidity

Temperature and humidity are the biggest concerns for your guitar. The ideal environment is one where the temperature is between 65 and 80 degrees Fahrenheit and the humidity is between 45 and 55 percent. As the humidity goes up, the wood will swell; as it goes down, the wood will shrink. Drastic changes in humidity put the guitar at the risk of having its wood either buckling or developing cracks. Heating and air conditioning can lower humidity levels below the acceptable range for your instrument.

Measures should be taken to control the humidity levels in the room where the guitar is stored, and the guitar should be placed in its case when not in use. An accurate hygrometer will enable you to see what the humidity levels are in the room in question. A Dampit or some other humidifying device for guitars can be used when your guitar is temporarily exposed to dry conditions. Avoid humidifiers that cover the sound hole.

Protecting Against Damage

The back and sides of your guitar have been lacquered and the top has been French-polished. The lacquer affords more durability, while the French polish is the finish of choice acoustically. Shellac is soft and flexible and it is easily marred. Extra care is needed to keep the top free from marks. The finish is also easily damaged if it comes in contact with moisture, alcohol, or heat. It is not unusual for a French-polished finish to dull from use and need some touching up with time.

Keeping Your Guitar Clean

Wax should not be used on the top. To clean the top, use Meguiar's Mirror Glaze No. 18, or Novex; these are plastic cleaners. Follow the instructions on the product for use. The back, sides, and neck of your guitar are covered with lacquer. Avoid contact with moisture or lacquer thinner. To clean the lacquered parts, any type of furniture wax will do or you may use the plastic cleaners above. The care of your instrument depends more on how you handle it than anything you put on it, so just be careful and enjoy the instrument.

The Gallery

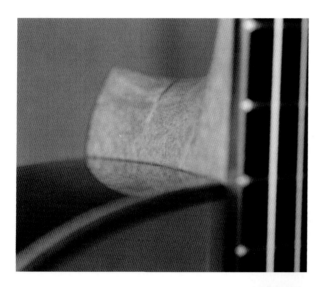

Spruce guitar: Indian rosewood back
and sides, European spruce top with
spalted maple rosette with wheat
motif, and Louro preto bindings.

These details are of the guitar made in the book. The configuration comprises Indian rosewood back and sides, western red cedar top with spalted maple rosette with wheat motif, and Louro preto bindings.

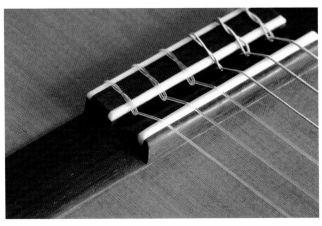

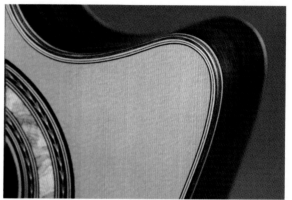

Brazilian cutaway classical guitar: Brazilian rosewood back and sides, western red cedar top with
spalted maple rosette with wheat motif, and
Louro preto bindings. There is an output for the
electronic pickup system for amplification.

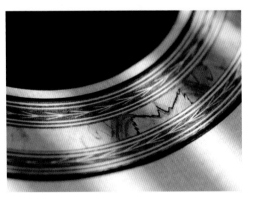

Maple guitar: European maple back and sides,
Engelmann spruce top with spalted maple headpiece
and rosette with wheat motif, and chechen bindings
and bridge.

comfort level determining use, 2, 34

filing, 35, 228

fretting, 36

hand saws, 34, 35

hand tools, 34–36

jointers, 29

making your own, 34

measuring/marking, 34–35

miscellaneous, 36

planers (electric), 29, 30

planing/scraping (hand), 35

power hand tools, 30

radius sticks, 41–42

router table, 29–30

sanders, 29

sanding discs, 41–42

sanding pads/sandpaper, 35, 41–42

setup, 36

specialty items, 40–42

standing drill press, 29

table saws, 29

using hand vs. power, 29, 30

vises/clamps, 26, 27, 37, 42, 43

Top. *See* Soundboard (top)

Torres, Antonio, 7

Transparent top/back template, 48–49

Trim bit sizing, 49

Trimmers, laminate, 30

Tuning

fine adjustments, 296

imperfection of, 289, 290

installing strings and, 294–295

matching pitch/harmonic, 295

string tension and, 294

Tuning machines

drilling jig for, 70–71

headpiece template for, 67–70

illustrated, 9, 10

installing, 293

location of, 10

size, 84

U

Universal binding machine, 33

V

Veneers

applying/trimming, 96–100

bending strips, 169, 172, 173

gluing, 96–98, 150, 151–152

gluing strips into rosette channels, 171–177

headpiece, 81–82, 96–100

purflings, 82

rosette, 82, 169, 170–177

selecting, 96

stripping, 82

wheat motif, 82, 148, 149, 150, 151–153

Vises/clamps, 26, 27, 37, 42, 43

W

Wheat motif, 148–159

bending strips, 169, 172, 173

color/style of, 139, 140

construction overview, 148

cutting jig (12-degree ramp), 152, 153–155

cutting stick into equal parts, 152–155

finished strips, 157, 159

fitting pieces together, 156–159

gluing fixture for, 150, 151

gluing pieces, 157, 159

gluing veneers, 150, 151–152

making stack, 151–153

numbering parts of, 152, 153, 154, 155

pieces, illustrated, 149

placing/gluing in rosette, 172–174

planing in rosette, 172

planing sheers, 157, 158

veneers, 148, 149, 150, 151–153

Wood, 17–23. *See also specific guitar components*

for back/sides, 18–19

burl figure, 23

checking out, 17–18

color scheme, 76, 77–78

connecting desired results with, 18

crotch figure, 23

cuts/grain, 21–23

dimensional stability of, 22–23

drying processes, 20

dyed vs. natural, 20, 77–78, 79

flat-sawn (plain), 22, 23

grades, 163

importance of, 17, 18

intuition in selecting, 18

moisture content, 20–21

pre-purchase tasks, 20

purchasing, 79–84

quartersawn, 21, 22

rift-sawn, 21, 22

selecting, 18, 20, 23, 76–84

spalted, hardening, 175

stickering, 20

types of, 18–20

Workbenches

bench hook for, 38

shooting board for, 38–39

types/features of, 26–27

About the Author

JOHN S. BOGDANOVICH IS A LUTHIER/GUITARIST building mostly concert classical guitars. John brings a unique combination of skills to his craft having been a performer, a builder of studio furniture, and a hardware design engineer. He has lectured around the country and holds classes on guitar making in his shop three times a year. Bogdanovich guitars are sought after by performers and players internationally. Typically there is a waiting list of a year and a half for an instrument. John lives in Asheville, NC with his partner Leila and her son Otis.

http://www.jsbguitars.com